Magnificently MADE

The stories that connect us and common threads that weave us together.

Jennifer Tuma-Young
and
Jessica Varian Carroll

featuring
33 Extraordinary Women

Magnificently Made

an Inspired Girl Anthology

Published by Inspired Girl, an imprint of Inspired Girl Publishing Group,
a division of Inspired Girl Enterprises

inspiredgirlbooks.com

Inspired Girl Publishing Group is honored to bring forth books with heart and stories that matter. We are proud to offer this book to our readers; the story, the experiences, and the words are from each of the contributors. The stories portrayed within *Magnificently Made* are based on actual events. In some incidents, characteristics, names, and timelines have been changed, compressed, or combined to protect the privacy and to preserve the anonymity of people involved. Any conversations in the book all come from the contributor's recollections, though they are not written to represent word-for-word transcripts. Rather, the author has retold them in a way that evokes the feeling and meaning of what was said. In all instances, the essence of the dialogue is accurate.

This book is written as a source of information only. The information contained in this book should by no means be considered a substitute for the advice of a qualified medical professional. In addition, the publisher and the contributing authors assume no responsibility for errors, inaccuracies, omissions, or any other inconsistencies herein. The use of this book implies your acceptance of this disclaimer.

Products, books, trademarks, and trademark names are used throughout this book to describe and inform the reader about various proprietary products that are owned by third parties. No endorsement of the information contained in this book is given by the owners of such products and trademarks, and no endorsement is implied by the inclusion of products, books, or trademarks in this book.

© 2023 All rights reserved.

No portion of this book may be reproduced in any form without permission from the publisher, except as permitted by U.S. copyright law. For permissions: help@inspiredgirlbooks.com

ISBN: 979-8-9878794-6-7

Editorial & Creative Director: Jenn Tuma-Young

Content Editor: Laura B. Ginsberg

Copy Editor: Natalie Papailiou

Cover and Interior Design: KUHN Design Group | kuhndesigngroup.com

Library of Congress Control Number: 2023945730

COME AS YOU ARE, ALL ARE WELCOME

Stories connect us. Common threads bring us together. Even when we have not walked the same walk as another, when we hear another human being's story, we cannot help but feel closer to that person.

This book is a judgment-free zone. When you open it, it is my hope that you release all judgment toward yourself and others. We so often judge our lives, our situations, our experiences, our physical bodies, and our emotional states. We can judge ourselves so much, we forget the magnificence we are made for. We unknowingly shrink or dim our lights in fear that others are judging us. Please let this book be the permission you need to SHINE, because the world needs your beautiful light.

It is also my hope you open your heart to the contributors who so vulnerably and freely opened their hearts for you to read. This book was written for you, the reader, to see yourself on the page and feel less alone or to see someone who is not at all like you, someone whose story you can't possibly relate to through your own human experience but after reading it, you feel a deeper human connection. The stories vary in topic, tone, and style. Opinions, beliefs, and experiences differ chapter to chapter.

Life is full of highs and lows, tragedies and triumphs, mountaintops and valleys, and everything in between. In our humanness, sometimes we need to know we are not alone in our feelings or experiences. Sometimes we just need to feel seen. Sometimes we need to see others. Sometimes we just need to get another perspective. Sometimes we need to know ours is ok. Sometimes we just need to know it doesn't all wrap up in a pretty bow. Sometimes we need to know it does.

In this messy, beautiful human experience, one thing I know to be true: at our core, we are all one.

HOW THIS BOOK CAME TO BE ...

Magnificently Made. To think, two words that were dropped in my heart over sixteen years ago have now become the title of a book with 33 contributors!

I wrote about the origins of this phrase in my books and on my Inspired Girl blog, but if you haven't read them yet or you are just meeting me, I'll share a little summary here.

After some financial issues during the very early years of my marriage, we sold our first home, turned in our vehicle, auctioned off our wedding china, sold my engagement ring and our wedding bands ... many of the "things" that typically define a person, we shed.

I remember crying, sobbing one day while my baby girl napped. I prayed for an answer, and God told me to write. Writing is something I've done practically since birth. And, for some reason, I didn't even feel worthy of picking up my pen at that time.

Grabbing whatever scrap piece of paper I could find, I started jotting down my thoughts. In that moment, I realized it would be alright, to carry on. And, a whole new chapter emerged, a peace came over me, that no material thing could ever deliver. I can only compare it to the intense love I feel when I hug my children, kiss my husband, spend time with my parents, or witness a person truly and fully plugged into the present moment. A peace enveloped me and stayed with me and I let this love guide me back ... I remembered that faith was my anchor. I remembered that I am worthy (no strings attached).

Within months of that day, I was sharing my writing with the world in so many ways, eventually even becoming a published author, even creating a career around it!! Today, I am the founder and CEO of Inspired Girl Publishing Group where we work with writers to publish their words in print.

And the phrase that I heard in my heart has been with me ever since that day all those years ago:

You are magnificently made, born for a purpose, and capable of more than you know.

While my life at times has felt like a rollercoaster ride, exhilarating and beautiful and messy, through all the ups and downs, the anchor of this phrase has kept me centered and fueled me.

In 2020, as Inspired Girl grew in this iteration of publishing books, I felt called to share this phrase so if anyone was feeling lost, they could remember that they too are magnificently made.

Purpose is woven into every breath we take. No need to search, no need to try to find it.

Fast forward to the end of 2021, and this idea for an anthology swirled around my heart. And what would it be about? I had no idea. I just knew it had to be called Magnificently Made. Denise Cesare was the first to sign on as a contributor—she's always jumping in heart first and shortly thereafter Jessica Varian Carroll became a partner in Inspired Girl and a contributor in this book—she trusted my vision and was there rallying the troops with me!! Within a few months, in March of 2022 with 33 contributors signed on, the writing began!!!

I gave the contributors the space to write about anything they felt compelled to share—kind of broad I know! But the stories that emerged and the range of topics, tone, opinions... I call it "a work of heart"!! As I read and read, a poem flew out of my pen onto paper - 11 lines creating 11 sections with 3 chapters each. I can't believe how it all came together. But I guess I can. Always amazing, never surprising.

Wow.

33 chapters written by 33 magnificently made humans designed to remind YOU that you, in all your glorious humanness, through joys and pains, through judgement and empathy toward yourself and others, through moments where you

How this Book Came to Be...

are elated to moments where you feel deflated, through it all ... YOU are magnificently made, born for a purpose, and capable of more than you know.

When this idea for an anthology came to me, I wasn't sure exactly exactly how it would come together, but 33 extraordinary humans jumped on board with me trusting that it would. They broke open onto the page and poured out words and stories that made me laugh out loud, stories that made me stream tears for days, stories that made me rest easy in the present moment. It is my hope that it does the same for you, so you connect with your heart, you connect with others, and never forget the awesomeness that is YOU.

Warmly from My Heart to Yours,

Jenn

WE ARE

We are dreamers.
We are torch bearing believers.
We are joy seekers.
We are keepers of light.

We are the epitome of love and Grace personified.

We are bold and courageous.
We are wise and powerful.
We are ready to soar.

We are deeply poetic.
We are healers on our own journeys of healing.
We are compassionate, caring, and kind.

We are Magnificently Made.

A COLLECTION OF STORIES BY:

Denise Cesare	Nichole M. Palmer	Stacey Anne Wade
Emily Yablonski	Maureen Spataro	Danni Heuer
Patty Lennon	Laura B. Ginsberg	Veronica Yankowski
Kerry Bray	Joy M. England	Jenn Garcia Mawson
Terisa Taylor	Frankie Winrow	Risa Baghdadi
Brianna McCabe	Jessica Varian Carroll	Krista Lynn
Reilly Carroll	Dr. Veera Gupta	Wendy Laffey
Tracey Hall	Kara Burke Manna	Jessica Baguchinsky
Trisha Kilgour	Kayla Harris	Chrisie Canny
Jessica Rojas	Alicia Marie Geczi	Jazimin Garrett
Susan Giacchi	Brenda Karinja	Veronica Woods

"I WISH I COULD SHOW YOU WHEN YOU ARE LONELY OR IN DARKNESS THE ASTONISHING LIGHT OF YOUR OWN BEING."

HAFIZ

CONTENTS

WE ARE DREAMERS
1. *Journey to Dreams* by Susan Giacchi ...29
2. *Making Moves* by Jenn Garcia Mawson ...45
3. *Turning Over a New Leaf* by Jessica Rojas ...59

WE ARE TORCH-BEARING BELIEVERS
4. *Let it Be* by Denise Cesare ...73
5. *Wearing Your Crown of Greatness* by Veronica Woods ...85
6. *The Boldness of the In-Between* by Joy M. England ...97

WE ARE JOY SEEKERS
7. *Finding Our Superpower* by Chrisie Canny ...109
8. *Flipping Off Fear and Doubt* by Danni Heuer ...125
9. *Four Songs Away* by Reilly Carroll ...139

WE ARE KEEPERS OF LIGHT
10. *Unwavering Faith* by Jessica Varian Carroll ...147
11. *The Walk Home* by Kerry Bray ...157
12. *What I Didn't Know Have Been My Greatest Lessons* by Maureen Spataro ...171

WE ARE THE EPITOME OF LOVE AND GRACE PERSONIFIED
13. *Beauty for Ashes* by Wendy Laffey ...185
14. *Living Life Intentionally* by Brenda Karinja ...199
15. *The Love Model* by Jazimin Garrett ...209

WE ARE BOLD AND COURAGEOUS
16. *I'm In!* by Jessica Baguchinsky ...223
17. *A Very Little Key Can Open a Very Heavy Door* by Krista Lynn ...237
18. *#IHaveAVoice* by Nichole M. Palmer ...251

WE ARE WISE AND POWERFUL
19. *Prioritizing & Self Worth: A Mile Marker Moment* by Alicia Marie Geczi …275
20. *The Present is a Moment* by Stacey Anne Wade …289
21. *Having It All* by Tracey Hall …303

WE ARE READY TO SOAR
22. *My Year of Yes* by Emily Yablonski …315
23. *Fear Not: The Courage to Rise Up* by Frankie Winrow …329
24. *Learning to Fly* by Dr. Veera Gupta …337

WE ARE DEEPLY POETIC
25. *The Embrace* by Terisa Taylor …353
26. *Poetic Notes to Self* by Laura B. Ginsberg …363
27. *The Stars in My Chest* by Kayla Harris …375

WE ARE HEALERS AND HEALING
28. *Carrying the Weight of My World* by Brianna McCabe …389
29. *Healing Old Wounds of Worthiness* by Patty Lennon …405
30. *Looking Through a Different Lens* by Trisha Kilgour …417

WE ARE COMPASSIONATE, CARING, AND KIND
31. *Called to Serve* by Veronica Yankowski …431
32. *Prepare and Provide* by Risa Baghdadi …443
33. *I Wish He Would Have Known* by Kara Burke Manna …455

WE ARE
Magnificently Made

A BIT ABOUT THE STORIES

CONTENT ADVISORY

This book contains stories from women about their lives. Since our lives are layered and experiences varied, a range of topics are covered within the pages. There are so many things in our lives that are amazing and beautiful and still complicated. In the midst of magnificence, there can be trauma and grief and loss and pain. We wanted to provide a full picture of the human experience. As such, some content may be unsuitable for young audiences. Some chapters make use of strong language. Sensitive themes explored in the book include fertility, bullying, body dysmorphia, disordered eating, sexuality, alcohol and drug use, domestic abuse, sexual abuse, emotional abuse, racism, illness, violence, terroristic attacks, and mortality. Light shines through as these contributors crack their hearts open onto the page and vulnerably share their truths. Please read with care.

Magnificently MADE

CHAPTER 1: Journey to Dreams
by Susan Giacchi

In this powerful chapter, Susan Giacchi shares the story about how her dream came to fruition during the most unlikely of times. Filled with divine moments and surrounded by love, Susan identifies five keys that literally unlocked her dreams, and gives sage advice we all can learn from!

CA: *illness, cancer, mortality*

CHAPTER 2: Making Moves
by Jenn Garcia Mawson

When a dream calls out to us, sometimes we do things others simply don't understand, like moving 7 times in 5 years!! That's right, Jenn Garcia Mawson and her husband Gary did just that with a toddler in toe to pursue their real estate dreams. In her chapter, she's pulling back the curtain and sharing her absolutely mind-blowing story of living outside her comfort zone and following her intuition to make her dreams become reality!

CHAPTER 3: Turning Over a New Leaf *by Jessica Rojas*

Jessica Rojas is a strong woman who has been through many challenges, but never gave up on herself. In her chapter, she shares her battle with depression and how she reinvigorated her strength, rediscovered happiness, and redefined her dreams for life. She inspires and encourages all woman, at any age, to do the same.

CHAPTER 4: Let It Be *by Denise Cesare*

When times of trouble come into our lives, what is the one thing that can soothe our hurting hearts? In the chapter, Denise Cesare shares how music was the healing source, allowing her to connect to her higher power through the moment and just be. She writes about five pivotal moments in her life and the songs that literally carried her through.

CA: *sexual abuse, emotional abuse, bullying, mortality*

A Bit About The Stories

CHAPTER 5: Wearing Your Crown of Greatness *by Veronica Woods*

Sometimes in life, we meet people who want to dim our light. For whatever the reason, this can cause us to adjust ourselves for their comfort. Veronica Woods has experienced this, and with grace and immense wisdom she shares what she's learned to counter this dimming down. Veronica's chapter offers readers a chance for self-reflection with four important questions we all must ask ourselves.

CHAPTER 6: The Boldness of the In-Between *by Joy M. England*

This chapter is for anyone who has felt stuck in the waiting. Joy M. England is a woman determined to rise and help others do the same. Clinging to the Word through all the valley and mountaintop moments, Joy's chapter will inspire you to boldly step forward and live the life you dream of.

CHAPTER 7: Finding Our Superpower *by Chrisie Canny*

When we help others, we heal ourselves. Chrisie Canny does so much to put smiles on stranger's faces. She is a firm believer that we find strength by giving strength. She learned this at a young age when her family and friends rallied around her during the most traumatic period of her life, way back in 1995 when her son was born. Her chapter will inspire you to help others and use your unique gifts to be the hero that the world needs.

CA: *illness, mortality, cancer, strong language*

CHAPTER 8: Flipping Off Fear and Doubt *by Danni Heuer*

We've all had people say words that sting, sometimes even unintentionally label us. But these labels and words can stay long past their welcome. In her chapter, Danni Heuer takes us back to the aqua net days of the 80s when a gym teacher made an impact on her perception of herself, and how she finally let go of the words that kept her down for far too long!

Chapter 9: Four Songs Away
by Reilly Carroll

Moving can take its toll on us. But while our physical environments may change, the core of who we are does not. Reilly Carroll found a unique way to measure moves that ignited her spirit. In her chapter, Four Songs Away, she vulnerably opens her heart to share how a road and music became her source for stability in an ever-changing world.

Chapter 10: Unwavering Faith
by Jessica Varian Carroll

When faced with dying, faith prevails. Jessica Varian Carroll's mother does not know any other way. She walked in faith her entire life, and as the chapter title suggests, she is the epitome of Unwavering Faith. A beautiful account of her mother's final days, Jessica's story will serve as comfort for those thinking about life beyond our physical bodies and inspiration for all.
CA: *illness, mortality, cancer*

Chapter 11: The Walk Home
by Kerry Bray

This chapter details Kerry Bray's heart wrenching period of being a caretaker for her mother as she crossed over. Pulling on all her internal strength and spiritual tools, Kerry chooses loving kindness on this journey called life and in the complex relationship with her mother. Hers is a perspective that needs to be told, as we often hear of picture-perfect relationships or venomous ones, but there is a middle ground walked on by so many. Sharing her truth with such honest vulnerability, Kerry gives us a perspective on suffering, peace, and what it means to be "love in action" that we all can learn from.
CA: *illness, mortality*

A Bit About The Stories

CHAPTER 12: What I Didn't Know Have Been My Greatest Lessons
by Maureen Spataro

As she prepares for the approaching loss of her mother, Maureen Spataro embraces some of the experiences and truths that have taught her so much. Her chapter gives a raw account of what it is like to be her mother's caretaker. With so many unknowns, Maureen digs into the heart of what this precious circle of life is all about.
CA: *illness, mortality, cancer*

CHAPTER 13: Beauty for Ashes
by Wendy Laffey

This chapter details the inspiring story of Wendy Laffey's powerful testimony. After all she's endured, she remains a bright soul with so much love for others. She is bearing it all on the page in hopes of reminding even one person that no matter how far they think they've fallen, they have purpose, they are worthy, and they are never ever alone—God is right there with open, loving arms to heal and lift us all back up.
CA: *drug use, sexual abuse*

CHAPTER 14: Living Life Intentionally *by Brenda Karinja*

What do you do when you experience a profound, unexpected loss in your life? Brenda Karinja shares how her mother's sudden passing inspired her to live differently. In her chapter, Brenda splits open her heart to share about the woman who inspired her to live with such beauty, love, and grace, and how even through dark times we can still choose to see our light that shines from within.
CA: *mortality*

CHAPTER 15: The Love Model
by Jazimin Garrett

A journey through loss, pain, and love. In the face of life-altering events, Jazimin Garrett discovers the power of love and finds the strength to navigate the "how" and thrive. In her chapter, Jazimin reminds us that love transcends all, and that we love as a choice not as a response. She shares her story with grace and encourages us to be the love we all so desperately need.

CA: *mortality, racism, violence, incarceration*

CHAPTER 16: I'm In
by Jessica Baguchinsky

What do you do when a crazy opportunity presents itself? If you are Jessica Baguchinsky, you leap and let the net appear!! In her chapter, she shares both the tough times and the incredible ones that resulted from her jumping on board!! From her travels, her career, her adventurous spirit, her entrepreneurial endeavors to her resilience and tenacity, Jessica will inspire you to jump in for your next adventure.

CHAPTER 17: A Very Little Key Can Open a Very Heavy Door *by Krista Lynn*

Recognizing that with light there is shadow, Krista Lynn vulnerably shares how life will give you the keys of both sides. Her compelling chapter flashes back to her childhood experience as a latchkey kid and explores how life will also show you doors when you are ready to open them to keep deepening your human experience.

CHAPTER 18: #IHaveAVoice
by Nichole M. Palmer

In her chapter, Nichole shares how she was overcome with silence for 7 days following the George Floyd murder. She emerges determined to breathe as she recounts racial atrocities in America while believing for change. A poet, a word whisperer, and a creative midwife, Nichole M. Palmer uses her gift of powerful storytelling as she invites us into her upbringing, her childhood, and her experiences to deepen the human connection and ignite real change.

CA: *racism, violence, mortality*

A Bit About The Stories

CHAPTER 19: Prioritizing & Self-Worth *by Alicia Marie Geczi*

So often life takes us on paths that our soul knows is not the way. But in a blink of an eye, one connected moment, when our hearts are open, we can receive the direction we need. In her chapter, Alicia Marie Geczi takes us on a journey to a moment that allowed her to see clearly why prioritizing herself had less to do with time management and everything to do with a shadow she had to face. Her wisdom-filled words will inspire you to look within and awaken.

CHAPTER 20: The Present is a Moment *by Stacey Anne Wade*

For anybody who wishes to embody and embrace the ecstasy of being on your own, Stacey Anne Wade dedicates her chapter to you. Filled with wisdom and tools as she moves readers through five breaths in Tadasana as the key to self-discovery and unlocking it all, her chapter will be sure to inspire you to savor moments and take it all in.

CHAPTER 21: Having It All *by Tracey Hall*

Tracey Hall is a firm believer in women helping women, and she definitely does just that! She shares how a bad case of appendicitis lands her in the hospital where her laptop was on her lap all but during surgery. After an unexpected layoff and epiphany, Tracey wonders why she put her health on the line for a job. This is a thought-provoking chapter that dives into what the phrase "having it all" really means.

CHAPTER 22: My Year of Yes! *by Emily Yablonski*

For the woman who is pushing through life, taking care of everything and everyone with little time for herself, Emily Yablonski wrote this for you!! Hers is a story every human needs to hear. Written with beautiful honesty, Emily's chapter reminds us that we, too, matter, and that people pleasing and hiding from ourselves will lead to a breakdown or physical ailment (or both!) if we don't acknowledge our own needs.

CHAPTER 23: Fear Not: The Courage to Rise Up *by Frankie Winrow*

A dedicated woman of the church, Frankie Winrow is a weekly communion steward, who many community members immediately recognize as soon as they see her radiant presence and giant smile. But what many may not know is how she is able to lift others so high, with her big heart, endless generosity, and helping those in need. Frankie works tirelessly to give back and spread love. In her chapter, she shares about how she developed the courage it takes to rise in ways big and small.

CHAPTER 24: Learning to Fly
by Dr. Veera Gupta

If you've every questioned your potential as a human being, Dr. Veera Gupta will remind you that you can do anything! You are built from stardust! You are a miracle in motion. In her chapter, Dr. Veera shares how to feel weightless, free, and centered in this very moment. She offers three amazing perspectives on how she learned to do this herself.

CHAPTER 25: The Embrace
by Terisa Taylor

A poet at heart, Terisa Taylor's chapter, takes you into her world using metaphor and rhythm beautifully. For the inner child in awe of nature and the freedom we take for granted in our youth, this chapter was written as a means to acknowledge all the humiliation, fear and hurt we surrender to as teenage girls. Terisa reminds us that through it all, the fairytale is possible.
CA: *sexual abuse, rape*

A Bit About The Stories

CHAPTER 26: Poetic Notes to Self
by Laura B. Ginsberg

A brilliant balance of light and darkness, Laura B. Ginsberg's thought-provoking chapter, provides short phrases that you can use at times when you need them most. Laura will inspire you to listen within for the words your soul needs.

CHAPTER 27: The Stars in My Chest
by Kayla Harris

Kayla Harris is a poet, a creative, an activist, and a beautiful soul who uses words in the most captivating way to express herself deeply. Her chapter shares a raw, profound account of her experiences shifting surrealism and reality with such lyrical rhythm. Like so many of us, her history paved a way for what could have been her future, but instead she took a deeper look to forge a new road ahead.
CA: *sexual assault, rape, domestic abuse, alcohol use, strong language*

CHAPTER 28: Carrying the Weight of My World *by Brianna McCabe*

Brianna McCabe shares the struggles she's had with her body and the impact it has had on her. In her chapter, she vulnerably details the stories and explores the depth behind her challenges with self-esteem, self-worth, weight, and their correlation to how she treated her body and mind.
CA: *bullying, body dysmorphia, alcohol abuse, disordered eating, sexuality, strong language*

CHAPTER 29: Healing Old Wounds of Worthiness *by Patty Lennon*

If you've ever felt like "not enough", this chapter is for you. Patty Lennon shares how we can come to believe, at an early age, that we are not worthy or enough. If not dealt with, these feelings can manifest themselves physically in our bodies as well as in our lives. Her chapter gives us permission to dive deep into the trauma that caused this and wisdom to help us heal.

CHAPTER 30: Looking Through a Different Lens *by Trisha Kilgour*

There are times in everyone's life where a shift in behaviors leads to an incredible shift of perspective. In Trisha Kilgour's chapter, she shares how a wake-up call during COVID leads to a moment of clarity. From this personal awakening, Trisha embarked on a new path and transformed her life one choice at a time.

CA: *fertility, alcohol use*

CHAPTER 31: Called to Serve *by Veronica Yankowski*

Whether it be a longtime friend or a stranger she just met, Veronica Yankowski jumps in to help in any way she can. Nurturing comes naturally to her. Her chapter will open the hearts of so many to see all as an extension of oneself, to value the human connection above all else, to listen and learn without judgement, walls, or boundaries, and to help others without question.

CA: *drug use*

CHAPTER 32: Prepare and Provide *by Risa Baghdadi*

Have you ever tried to create the illusion of being in control when your situation is completely out of your control? Sometimes creating lists, organizing, and preparing is all we can do to feel better about a situation or circumstance. But on a deeper level, Risa Baghdadi's chapter shows us that when we do this for those we love with love, our caring heart shines through at all times. Risa weaves her incredible personal stories with important life lessons that remind us of what matters most.

A Bit About The Stories

CHAPTER 33: I Wish He Would've Known
by Kara Burke Manna
Kara Burke Manna shares her stories and wisdom with such humble grace. With thoughtful reflection on her experiences as the little sister often not listened to, it is clear that she wants nothing more than for others to know how amazing they are. In her chapter, Kara writes about her brother Pat's struggle with realizing how he, too, is magnificently made.
CA: *alcohol use, drug use, mortality*

> **JUST A NOTE:**
> We love writers who write in their unique voices. Grammar and punctuation may not always follow traditional rules so as to support the writer's tone, style, and personality.

SECTION 1

WE ARE DREAMERS

JOURNEY TO DREAMS
by Susan Giacchi

MAKING MOVES
by Jenn Garcia Mawson

TURNING OVER A NEW LEAF
by Jessica Rojas

> LET YOUR DREAMS BE YOUR WINGS AND BELIEVE THAT YOU WILL SOAR.

JOURNEY TO DREAMS

BY SUSAN GIACCHI

This chapter is to inspire and give hope to anyone who needs an example of how to overcome adversity and a diagnosis and still perseveres to obtain a DREAM.

From a very young age, I was an entrepreneur. I did whatever I could do to earn some extra money. But at the time, I didn't even know what the word meant or that the title of entrepreneur would someday be part of my life.

I grew up in Brooklyn, New York, in a three-family home with my aunts, uncles, and cousins just a flight of stairs away. My mom (Josephine Rose), brother (Sal), sister (Celia), and I lived on the third floor in the attic apartment, which had three rooms. We made it work, even though in those days, it wouldn't be fathomable to sleep in the same bed with your adult brother. For me it was normal. My parents were divorced when I was three, so I never lived with my dad that I could remember. He remarried shortly after the divorce, so I also had a stepmother (Bea).

I learned early in life that I had to work for the things I wanted because, unfortunately, my mom didn't have the money to support all the designer clothes or shoes that were popular, and hand-me-downs were primarily the way I got new clothes. To be honest, I loved getting other people's clothes. No shame in my game.

I had a number of jobs growing up. I worked stamping cigarettes and packing gum for a candy company. I worked at a place called Cardiopet; we took electrocardiograms of animals over the phone, and it was a very interesting job. I also sold jewelry and became a consultant at Home Interiors & Gifts, and I took up chocolate-making. Chocolate-making was the one I enjoyed the most, which has remained a favorite hobby to this day. My friend Joann was making chocolate for Easter as well as beautiful Easter baskets. One day, I started to help her, and I discovered that I really enjoyed doing it. For a while we did it together, and when Joann decided she didn't want to make chocolate anymore, I thought, *I could do this myself*, so I started to make chocolate for holiday bazaars and all kinds of favors and gifts for family and friends. It became my escape and therapy. I was thirteen years old. The funny thing was, I thought I was going to run out of ideas for chocolate-making! Was I ever wrong! It has evolved over the years, and the ideas still keep coming. So cool.

While working a full-time job in New York City, I started selling candles with Home Interiors & Gifts. I went to a house party at my friend Patty Zdep's and lo and behold, I signed up to only sell candles! That lasted a short time, and then I began to do house parties even though I really didn't want to. It was a fun time helping the ladies choose seasonal items, and I enjoyed putting centerpieces together for my clients, and I also picked up a couple of real estate clients. I was a go-getter, and I was always overlapping jobs a little. I had this candle business for eight years before I realized I wasn't going to be a Macy's and that I had too much inventory.

So real estate it was! When I started in real estate, I worked with a lot of rental relocation clients because no other agent in the office was interested in rentals. Within the first year I worked these transactions, I was awarded the MCAR Circle of Excellence for the first time, Bronze level. I had fun taking these clients out, and when I got paid, I would get more than one check, so, jokingly, I started to say, "I receive checks every day, sometimes more than one!" This mantra has stuck until today, and now I get my agents to say it or choose a saying that fits them best. I decided to get my broker's license in 2010, and when anyone asked me if I wanted to open an office, I would respond with, "No, it's too expensive!"

I did interview with another real estate franchise to be a manager, and by the time the meeting was over, I had the job if I wanted it. That was exciting, and I was honored to be given such an opportunity. Yet, at the same time, I knew

I didn't want to do that. I would lose my independence and flexibility because it would be a 9-to-5 job, and that didn't interest me. So, I remained at my RE/MAX office for the next few years until I had an opportunity to release that limiting belief of it being "too expensive" and unlock my dreams. But you know what they say about dreams: they don't come without some challenges. And I was faced with a big one—cancer.

THE DIAGNOSIS

In 2014, I was diagnosed with anal squamous cell cancer. It's actually skin cancer. It's come to light recently that it was a direct result from 9/11. This is for another chapter, but my heart sank when the doctor told me it was cancer. No one ever wants to hear it, but the one thing my wife Pam and I held on to when the doctor broke the news was that it was VERY TREATABLE! Truth be told, I thought I had hemorrhoids, but in fact it was a tumor, and because I was afraid and embarrassed to get it looked at, I let too much time go by without proper care, so it developed into the cancer. So, while we get scared at the thought of going to the doctor or you think *I'll wait to get this exam*, make it a yearly activity to get yourself checked out. Early detection really is the key.

Almost simultaneously, I was asked to attend a meeting to learn about a RE/MAX franchise and what they offer. I already worked in a RE/MAX office, but I didn't know all that was involved in owning a franchise. There were a few of us who were interested. I was a little confused as to why I was being asked. My friend replied, "It's better that two people listen to the information so we can decide if this is something that we would want to do." Made sense, so, with my fanny pack of chemo, administered for ninety-six hours, off I went to the meeting.

As soon as I saw the business plan and franchise information, I said out loud, "I'm in!"

My friend replied to me, "Hey ... what about us doing it together?" Of course, I did want to explore that option too. All of a sudden, I could see opportunity and possibility, except for one thing: I was just diagnosed with the "C" word.

Never one to shy away from a challenge, I left the meeting on a mission and laughing to myself thinking, *You have some pair of balls thinking you could do this.*

Every day for the next six weeks, I went to radiation, and all I could think about was opening a real estate office. At the end of the day, even if I didn't open

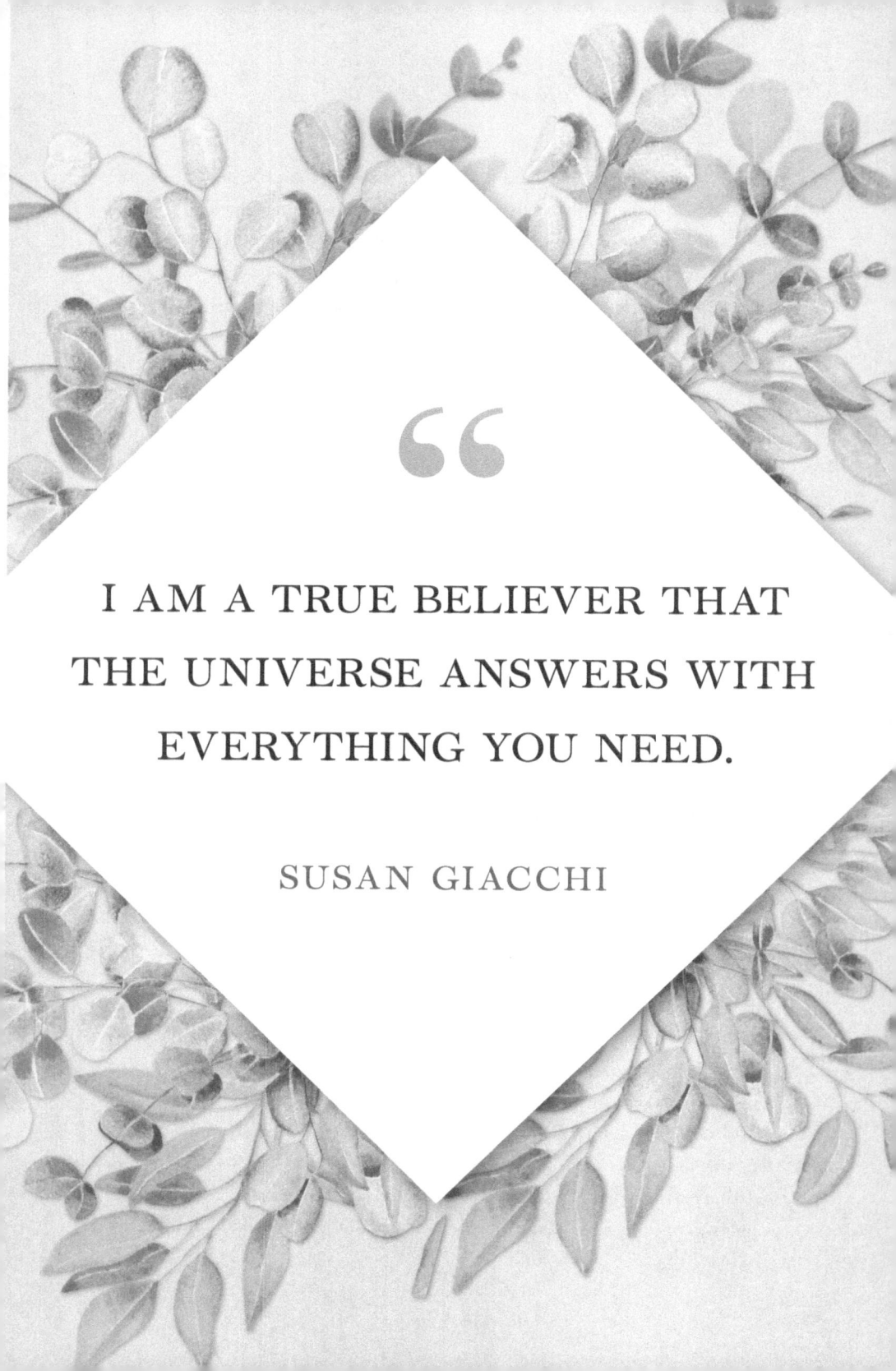

an office, it definitely helped me to have something positive to focus on during a very scary time. I could see a future when there was so much uncertainty. Ultimately, I did open that RE/MAX Dreams office! Many people asked me how was it possible that I could do that while being treated for cancer?

Now, I could write an entire book around this period of my life, and I just might! But, looking back, I think there were five key things to opening the door to my dreams during this challenging time that helped.

KEY #1 ALWAYS HAVE FUN

My first key is to always have FUN, even in a scary time! Put positive vibes out into the universe and laugh along the way. I am a true believer that the universe answers with everything you need. I continued to say I was "in," even though I really couldn't make any major decisions while going through this treatment—or at least waiting until I got an all clear from my doctors that I was cancer-free. But I still had FUN and kept dreaming.

In real estate, it's hard to be sick because you are a one-person business even when you're under an umbrella of a company. So I didn't really tell many people about the cancer, including my clients, because I didn't want it to seem like I was weak and couldn't conduct my business. Believe it or not, I worked throughout treatment and found ways to make it comfortable, like wearing men's bike shorts under my dresses for maximum relief.

Unfortunately, during the treatment process, I became a burn victim from the radiation and had to use creams and a product called *Domeboro*. To use this product, you dip a gauze pad in the solution with cold water, and you put it in the area of burn, which draws the heat out. Pam did this for me every day to minimize the discomfort of the burn I experienced. Even this, we took in stride!

Adding lightness, fun, and laughter lifts your spirits during the heavy times and I believe that attracts more goodness into your life.

KEY #2 SURROUND YOURSELF WITH LOVE

I found a person who loves me and would do anything for me, my Earth Angel, Pam! Pam stood by my side when I needed the most support and love. She also made light of every aspect within the process, like making me pictures of piña coladas when I had to drink something that probably didn't taste very good for a test I needed. She'd wrap the glass with this picture of a piña colada, and wouldn't you know that's what it tasted like—so amazing the power of the mind! We had signs all over the house, and one that read "VERY TREATABLE" with a Buddha face.

The love of family and friends was incredible during this difficult time, and one person who started out as a business associate became another amazing Earth Angel, my friend Lisa Mathews. Lisa prayed for me and with me every morning during my treatment. I couldn't have made it through without her care and concern and her daily prayers. It was an experience of a lifetime and one I will never forget. I thank Lisa from the bottom of my heart for her love and prayers.

LOVE FROM THE OTHER SIDE— THE DIVINE INTERVENTION BY "MOMMY ANGEL"

So, first I want to explain that I lost my mom when I was twenty years old. I was always very independent because Mom got sick when I was eleven years old, so I guess it was good that I had an independent way about me from the start, because I needed it. After she passed, I can't say we spent a ton of time focusing on our grief because that's not what our family did. Of course I was sad, but life went on, and other than remembering her on certain occasions, I can't say we had a huge connection to her after her passing. I didn't want to open up that hole in my heart. I kept it moving, so to speak. I didn't realize how much having her presence with me could help, so I guess I never opened my eyes to it after she died.

But she was there the whole time, and I really needed her.

Two weeks before I even knew I was having surgery, I happened to take out my high school yearbook. Looking back, I'm not sure at the time what made me do that. I graduated in 1981, and I just flipped through the pages that day and didn't really see anything in particular.

I found out two weeks later on April 27, 2014 that I needed surgery, and everything went so fast after that. The day I came home from surgery, the first thing I asked Pam for was my yearbook … it was right on my desk since I took it out just a few weeks before (as I write this, I'm getting the chills). As she handed me the book, I knew it was my mom telling me to get the yearbook, (crying and the chills continue), so I proceeded to find her last message to me before she died. When I was a child, my mom was the most comforting when I was sick. Who doesn't want their mom when they are sick? At this time of sickness, it was no different; she was there for me, and in every aspect of the process. The message in the yearbook had more to do with the person she knew I would be than anything to do with being sick this day, finding out this tumor was cancerous, and that I needed treatment. But just her words were a comfort, and I knew she was with me. I stopped worrying and embraced this moment in time and did everything I could to get back to a normal life, but it would definitely be a new normal.

As I read my mom's message over and over, I allowed myself to cry for myself and her loss. It also made me thankful that I had this message from her. The meaning it had on this day was certainly different than on the day she wrote the message for me for my high school graduation in June 1981, forty years ago.

Mom's Message:

Susan,

May your wisdom be as great as my faith. May God bless you with patience and knowledge unending. I am sure with all these qualities, your expectations are many.

As you enter college, may you succeed in all your endeavors.

Always remember what I have written will be the road to your happiness in the future. You are loved by many. Do not use it as stepping stone.

Decisions that you will come across in life should never be conducted abruptly.

Loving you,
Mom

Throughout this journey to dreams, my mom showed up in many ways, in addition to this yearbook message. She even used other people to get her point across that she was with me! My mother-in-law, Rose, bought me a Saint Anthony Alex + Ani bracelet. Saint Anthony was my mother's patron saint, and it meant so much to me. Having my mom's love come through was huge, and to this day I see and feel her presence with me when I need it most.

LOVE EXPRESSED IN SPECIAL MOMENTS—MY BROTHER SAL

Crazily enough, my brother Sal was diagnosed with Stage 4 lung cancer in 2013, a year before my diagnosis. When I found out about the diagnosis, I thought, *This is not possible. He's too important a person to me to lose him.* OMG, my brother was so many things to me. A brother, a father figure, a mentor, a cheerleader, and a BEST friend. We would talk every morning. We were thirteen years apart, but we were more similar than different even with our age difference. Even though Sal was sick himself with lung cancer, he never let that stop him. He even came to see me when I got home from surgery with lunch in hand ... roast beef. Roast beef was a little joke between us because while visiting Sal, and his family (Carol, Dawn, and JR) years ago, I fell asleep at their house because I wasn't feeling well and when I woke up, I wanted *roast beef!* Very specific request, I know, but I was craving it! So now it became a funny moment and inside joke between us, and we also laugh when we say roast beef and remember that moment.

There was so much meaning in his visit. He always made me feel special and loved.

KEY #3 FIND YOUR OWN VOICE AND TAKE CONTROL

I remember the first week of radiation. One of the nurses asked me how I was doing, and I said, "Great!" and she proceeded to tell me, "Well, wait until the end ... "

WHAT? You didn't just say that to me. Aren't nurses supposed to be supportive? I thought.

She happened to be the nurse taking my vital signs that day, and as we sat side by side, I told her, "I only want POSITIVE people on my team!" She never said a word to me about it. The strange thing was that she was never there again to take my vitals. I saw her after all my treatment was complete on my last visit. Coming from a place where children should be seen and not heard, I felt like it was a big deal for me to speak up and use my voice.

Using my VOICE and taking control in an unknown situation was empowering, and I got to practice doing this throughout my treatment. Before I started chemo, both my oncologist and surgeon said it was possible I would lose my hair. Instead of waking up one day with clumps of it on my pillow, I decided to cut my hair short so I wouldn't be so devastated if I did lose my hair. I really felt good about that decision; it gave me back control over a situation I felt so out of control of.

When strands of my hair would fall out, as they do for everyone, I would be tickled by the hair falling on my arms and I would think *Is this the start of my hair falling out?* I am thankful to God that I never actually lost my hair, but taking control over the situation made a difference to me. And I looked good with the new cut. I embraced my short hair!

Feeling the strands of hair was bad enough because there was always a possibility it could have happened. But the key of using my voice and making decisions that empowered me made this otherwise uncertain and uncomfortable time much more palatable and even propelled me into actually opening that real estate office. In the past, I might not have spoken up or taken control the way I did when I faced this diagnosis. It was an important lesson I'll never forget. Don't let your voice wait until a scary time; use it now and empower yourself now. You can thank me for it later!

KEY #4 KEEP A POSITIVE ATTITUDE

I never once accepted that I was sick! I came up with ways to be positive, so I named the radiation "Rays of Sunshine," and my chemo was "Love Potion #9!" When you have radiation, every time you go, they have to line you up with the marks they tattoo on you to make sure that you are in the correct spot for treatment. It takes about five minutes to do that. During that time, instead of letting my mind play the "wander and worry" game, I said affirmations to occupy my mind and stay in a positive mindset. (Connect with me and I will provide a copy of them should you want to adopt them as your own.)

During the treatment portion, I would just be thankful for everything in my life—always staying positive. I believe being positive truly helped me get through an uncertain and scary time.

When I started treatment, I started to read *The Power* by Rhonda Byrne, and it talks about having a good team as the medical staff. Well, that I did! It was so great that on the last day of radiation when I got off the elevator the two receptionists clapped for me as well as the nurses at the nurses' station. Plus, it all came together like it talks about in the book; my team was cheering me on!

Wow! What an accomplishment to have behind me... no pun intended.

KEY #5 KEEP DREAMING

So, this one is an important one for me. When you are facing a diagnosis with unknowns, it may be easy to put everything on hold until you are on the other side. But I say, "Keep Dreaming!" Throughout the time of my treatment, the dream of being my own broker kept me going, and it ultimately came to fruition on April 6, 2015. I believe this was a direct result of all the other lessons I shared, and combining together these five keys made such a huge difference during my treatment and after.

I opened my office in April, just shy of a year after my surgery, which is kind of crazy to think! Six months later, on October 9, 2015, I had my grand opening of RE/MAX Dreams, and guess who showed up for me that day? Yes, it was my brother Sal (crying). He was still in his own battle with stage 4 lung cancer, so he wasn't comfortable driving alone. But he wanted to be there. So, he asked one of his Knights of Columbus friends to bring him, and there he was. What a special gift for me! He was able to be a part of the ribbon cutting, and I loved having him there. To think, we both had cancer at the same time. We used to share the same war stories about chemo and how we felt. Sadly, my brother passed on November 1, 2015, only twenty-three days after my grand opening, but the memory of him being at the grand opening of Dreams will live in my heart forever. He was my hero.

As I just crossed the seven-year mark with RE/MAX Dreams, I reminisce about what it was like taking this risk to open my own real estate office. It was a very exciting time and, thankfully, I was cancer-FREE! At the same time, I was finally moving forward with a dream I had for my life, to open my own business. When I was younger and wanted to open my own business, my dad would never support it (especially financially) because he feared that I could get robbed if it was a cash business. But, as it turns out, we only deal with checks in real estate, so it's a win/win on that level!

They say, "If you build it, they will come!" So, that was the approach I took; just keep moving forward. It gave me butterflies to think of all the possibilities of owning something while facing the cancer that was trying to own me. I didn't have all the answers, and I didn't even have a staff! I honestly didn't know who would become a part of my Dreams family, and when we opened, I was the only licensed agent. A week later, I hired my assistant Shalondra "Shie" Kurtzman to be on my Dream Team, and from there we began to grow.

I would say to her, "Shie, when are they coming?"

Thirty-plus agents later, a second office, a real estate school, and growing... we're here!

It took a little time for us to get established, but we have grown, and we will continue to grow. With the help of our agents, we really have a beautiful family environment and culture that is built on mutual respect and care for each other. I get the most joy out of seeing my agents succeed. I love being a mentor and coach to them as well as helping them solve their problems. We have meetings to strategize so I can help them build and grow their businesses. In real estate, in general, you wear many hats: as a broker/owner, you can add even more! I'm a recruiter, a broker, an owner, a coach, a networker, a cheerleader, a connector, and even a therapist sometimes, just to name a few. I thrive on helping people achieve their goals, helping my clients with selling or buying a home, and helping individuals create a career in real estate.

I am proud that I have established good relationships and I that created an amazing reputation in the real estate business, long before I knew I would open my own real estate office. It was a foundation piece for me, and one of the reasons that I was confident that I could be a success with opening RE/MAX Dreams.

I participate at the Metro Center Association of Realtors (MCAR) on various committees to build relationships with agents. After seventeen years I was inducted as a 2022 Board of Director at MCAR and CJMLS. I have been a member of BNI since 2005, and I have been on the leadership team many times. This year, I am the Vice President of the BNI Hawks Chapter. I have been recognized over the years by MCAR as a Circle of Excellence Award winner, and in 2021, I earned the Silver level. I have also been awarded by RE/MAX year over year.

But all of these accolades are nothing compared to the joy I see when one of the clients we serve closes on the home of their dreams or sells their home to go pursue other dreams. For me, dreams are everything. Dreams shouldn't just be "maybe someday" passing thoughts. They are like directions; if we follow them, they will put us on the path of a lifetime!

Now, I encourage you to look at your own dreams, shed those limiting beliefs and follow the five keys – always have fun, surround yourself with love and support, find your voice and empower yourself, focus on the positive, and keep on dreaming, no matter what!

ABOUT THE CONTRIBUTOR

Passionate, optimistic, and driven, Susan Giacchi has found her true calling in real estate. Prior to working as a real estate agent, Susan worked at *The Bond Market Association* for more than fourteen years. She started as an office assistant, and shortly thereafter she was promoted to office manager. It was in her last three years with the company that she developed an interest in real estate, assisting the president and CFO with locating new offices in Midtown, as well as procuring two offices and a conference center in London. After finishing up these projects, Susan decided to engage her new passion for real estate by becoming a residential agent. Working with various real estate companies over the last several years, Susan decided to pursue her dream and took the necessary steps to get her broker's license. Susan opened up a RE/MAX Dreams office in Sayreville, New Jersey shortly thereafter, and she has been thriving since with a second office and Dreams Real Estate Academy. Most recently, Susan was selected as the 2023 MCAR Realtor of the Year.

Bits of Her Heart...

Susan Giacchi

What you think about, you bring about ... so always Dream BIG!

FUN FACT...

Sue is obsessed with Brink's trucks! Her agents often send her photos of them!

2

MAKING MOVES

BY JENN GARCIA MAWSON

Dear Reader, I want you to know that in life there are times that we need to step out of our comfort zone to get the things we desire in our heart. I hope this story gives you the courage and inspiration to take that first step. And when you do, you may not know how it's going to work out but trust that the universe will provide what you need to get there, even if it is filled with lots of twists and turns. It's all part of the process.

I remember once reading a quote, "Life begins outside of your comfort zone." It definitely resonated with me. Something about it spoke to my soul, and it ended up being my mantra for the story you are about to read. It is my hope that you find your life begins outside of your comfort zone as well!

Let me explain. One day, when I was at the park with my five-year-old, I struck up a conversation with another mom. We talked about where we lived and realized we were practically neighbors. She inquisitively asked where we moved from. Such an innocent question, but I fumbled with my words and jokingly responded, "All over!" I then explained to her that we had moved several times since my son was born, and we were new to this neighborhood. It's funny. Until I was asked that question so innocently, I didn't stop to think about how many moves we actually made since my son was born. I paused to think about it more in depth later and counted all the moves we had made; I realized we had moved seven times in the past five years with a small child in tow! You must be thinking, *Why on earth would anyone do that willingly?*

Our journey outside the comfort zone began when my son was born in November of 2015. We yearned to set ourselves up for financial stability so we could provide him with everything he needed and more. Together, my husband and I have always had big dreams of becoming successful real estate investors. We worked as real estate agents for a living and were recovering from the real estate crash of 2008. We would daydream about the homes we would love to buy, the locations where we would like to own said homes, and of course fantasized about the way we would design them. We were HGTV junkies and had such big dreams (thanks Chip and Joanna!). So, after our son was born, we made the conscious decision to follow our dreams for him. We had no idea how this was going to work out exactly, but we knew if we had any shot at making it work, we had to make some bold moves.

WHERE WE STARTED– DREAM BEACH RENTAL

So, as I mentioned, my son was born in November of 2015. At the time, we were renting a cozy three-bedroom home in an idyllic beach town in New Jersey called Avon-by-the-Sea with a beautiful beach and a charming main street. We had been living there for a few years, and the house was perfect for us! It had a guest room with a full bath for our friends and family, and it even had a sky-blue wraparound porch that was perfect to just sit on and enjoy the breeze. We loved living there, and right before our son came, we set up his nursery. The room was small but bright and had a rocking chair, changing table, and crib—everything we needed.

We didn't want to think about moving, mostly because we enjoyed our dream rental and its location, but also because the last time we had invested in real estate, we got burned. Like many homeowners and investors during the crash of the real estate market in 2008 and through 2011 we dealt with a couple of bad investments. First, we had to sell our condo as a short sale in 2010, so there was no profit. And then, shortly after, we lost even more money when a home we intended to flip for a profit sold for a loss. It took us years to recover. And yet here we were in 2015 eager to do this again! We licked our wounds and learned from our past mistakes. My husband and I worked together as realtors since 2008, and over the years we had successfully helped dozens of our clients buy homes. We knew the economy was stabilizing and it was a good time to get back in. We had to trust ourselves and our intuition. We had to trust the lessons we learned in the past. We had more experience and more knowledge. Plus, we had the burning desire to do it again. But this time, we were going to do it bigger and better.

So, we came up with an initial plan. We decided we were going to spend all our money in savings to buy real estate and move out of our comfort zone and our sky-blue piece of heaven. We knew we were risking it all again. Now with a newborn, the stakes were even higher, but the reward would be even sweeter. Our son was our biggest motivation, and, right before his first birthday, we moved out of our dream rental and in with my parents.

MOVE #1—MOVING INTO MY HIGH SCHOOL BEDROOM

Once we made the decision to invest in real estate, we started looking at all options that would maximize every dollar of our modest savings account. Instead of doing the practical and safe option of buying a reasonable move-in ready home, we did the opposite and bought two fixer-upper properties that we knew would be great long-term investments. This meant the results would not be immediate, but they would pay off generously, in time. One of the properties we bought was a two-family home that needed work but was rented out, and the rent covered the mortgage. We didn't have to do anything to it, at least not right away. The other property we bought was an abandoned single-family home that was in desperate need of complete rehabilitation inside and out. This sad looking home had a broken garage door, old frayed carpet inside, and scuffed up walls, and it was filled with junk from the previous tenant who lived there before. We bought it completely as is, with the junk and all. We had the vision! We knew the location well—it was just a mile away from our dream beach rental, and we knew it would be nice once it was done.

The renovations were extensive though, and the house needed everything from a new bathroom and kitchen to new flooring, plumbing, and electrical. The project was going to take several months and lots of money to make our vision a reality, so thankfully my parents took us in. We talked about our dreams to become successful real estate investors with them, and they supported us, even though at times they questioned why we couldn't just buy a nice home and wondered why we were going through all the stress of renovating an ugly house.

We put all our furniture, all of our belongings, and all of our son's toys in storage. We just kept some clothes and literally lived out of a suitcase for months! We slept in my old high school bedroom. My husband and I slept on a small, full-size bed, and my son slept in his Pack 'n Play. We made the best of our situation and enjoyed the company of my parents who went above and beyond for us by cooking us dinner, tending to our laundry, and spending quality time with our son. We were so grateful my parents allowed us to move in with them, but after a few months, the three of us in one tiny room was getting old. Plus, we missed our own space and all our things from storage, so just shy of four months later we moved again into our new home before it was completely finished.

MOVE #2 – CRAFTSMAN-STYLE FIXER-UPPER

In March of 2017, we moved into our fixer-upper, an old craftsman-style home that we transformed with a beautiful new kitchen complete with granite countertops and white cabinets, a new bathroom with ceramic tile, gleaming wood floors, and tranquil new paint colors throughout. We were reunited with our items from storage, which was amazing, but we also lived in the middle of a work zone for a little while. Some more trim needed to be hung, doorknobs were missing, closet organizers were not installed, and we were missing bathroom mirrors. You don't realize what a difference these seemingly small things make until they're missing. I mean, brushing my teeth and washing my face without a mirror for the first couple of weeks sucked! We managed, of course, and after tending to the finishing touches inside we set our focus to fixing the outside.

The outside of our new home was a complete and neglected mess with overgrown bushes, faded pink siding, and a yard that had no grass. So, our first summer there was a labor of love, with us removing a lot of bushes and weeds, taming the grass, and just trying to make it look somewhat decent to have our friends over for a BBQ. We also tackled the project of repainting the old pink siding ourselves. Our neighbors must have hated it though, because it was half pink and gray for weeks as the project took us longer than anticipated since we could only get to it on nights and weekends! Once it was done, the outside looked great, and finally

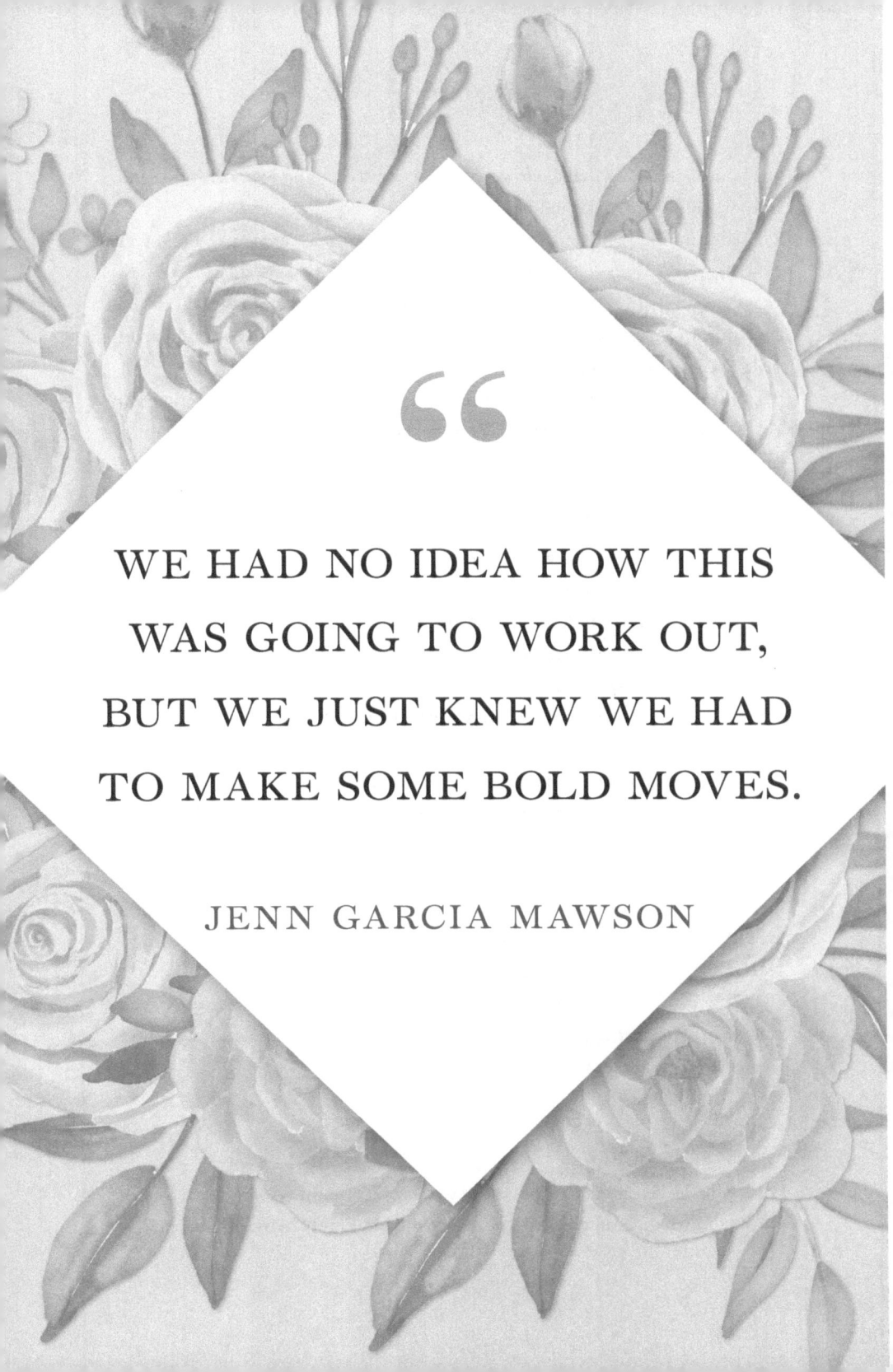

"
WE HAD NO IDEA HOW THIS WAS GOING TO WORK OUT, BUT WE JUST KNEW WE HAD TO MAKE SOME BOLD MOVES.

JENN GARCIA MAWSON

the house was taking shape. However, just as it was coming together inside and out, we decided to make another bold move.

Since my husband and I were real estate agents, we were seeing first-hand how the prices were going up in our neighborhood. We were excited and saw the opportunity to cash out and buy more real estate. Our plan was to buy more investment properties, so we followed our intuition again and sold our craftsman-style fixer-upper for a nice profit!

Once we put our home on the market, we got eight offers and settled for one $40,000 over our list price! We were shocked and happy, but our family and friends started to think we were going crazy. After all that work, we were walking away from a beautiful home and a place our son loved. He had his own room and a playroom full of toys, but he was just two years old at the time, and we knew as long as he was with us, he would be just fine.

We asked the new buyers to give us three months to close, and they agreed. So, we spent the summer of 2018 plotting out what to buy next. We used our child's chalkboard easel to write down numbers and calculate how we could maximize every dollar of our savings and make a profit again. We liked the idea of buying a multi-family home so we could have more rental properties, which would, in turn, get us one step closer to our goal of financial stability.

We found another two-family home to buy in a desirable location close by. It had a large apartment downstairs and a small apartment upstairs. We would have loved to live in the apartment downstairs but the tenant who lived there wanted to stay, so we honored their lease with the previous owner. The upstairs apartment was empty but had old carpet everywhere that smelled like cat pee! It needed work and, since we were going to be redoing the floors, we decided to redo the kitchen and bathroom too while we were at it!

We knew this project would take some time, and we had to move out of the craftsman-style fixer-upper since our closing was imminent. Thankfully we found a great short-term rental by the beach.

MOVE #3—SHORT-TERM RENTAL BY THE BEACH

We live by the beach in New Jersey, and in the winter months some beach homes are offered at a discounted rate to rent since they are empty in the off season. The catch was the home was already furnished, so we had to put all our stuff back in storage. This was move number three. We took this inconvenience in stride, though, and focused on the positives; the location was great. It reminded us of our dream beach rental when our son was born. It was close to the beach and a block to the main street with lots of great restaurants, a bakery, coffee shops, and new brewery, and we took advantage of it all! Plus, it had a new kitchen with an island, something I had never gotten to enjoy before.

Our time there was great, in fact much better than we had anticipated. We didn't want to leave, but it was only supposed to be temporary (September to May), and we were eager to buy more real estate anyway!

As our lease there was coming to an end, we saw the demand for Airbnb in our area. We were supposed to move back into the brand-new renovated apartment that had once smelled like cat pee, but our investor hearts told us to do what any smart investor would do and seize the opportunity to Airbnb that home for the summer of 2019, which is exactly what we did, but it also left us in a predicament again... where would we live?

MOVE #4—FUNKY LAYOUT APARTMENT

An option presented itself. It wasn't ideal, but it was the best option we had. Remember that two-family home that we first bought that needed work but was rented out? Well, now it had an empty unit. It wasn't ideal because it was an old home built in 1904 and had a funky layout. I mean really funky. Picture a bedroom next to the kitchen that led to a long skinny hallway to another bedroom and a small living room. And, on top of that, it had no central air. Plus, the kitchen had cabinets from the 1950s and needed to be updated desperately. We didn't have time to renovate everything though as our short-term lease was coming to an end, so we just redid all the floors and painted the walls, and we would get to the kitchen later.

The most attractive thing about living there was that the upstairs tenant's rent covered the whole mortgage, so our payment would be nothing. How could we pass that opportunity up, to live somewhere rent-free? And, since it needed to be renovated, we could complete the project without taking a big hit on our expenses. So, it was settled! We had the crazy idea to move into this funky, old two-bedroom apartment without central air with our three-year-old for the summer of 2019. No air during a hot, humid Jersey summer would be a push out of my comfort zone for sure!

I focused on the fact that living there rent-free would allow us to have more money to invest in real estate and fix up this apartment that needed updating desperately. Plus, the location wasn't bad; it was a short bike ride to the beach and a five-minute walk to Main Street. But things took a turn for the worse just one month in when I discovered a mouse right before bed. You should know, I am petrified of mice and was horrified. We subsequently found several more and called the exterminator right away. They took care of it, but to our horror again there was also a roach issue in the walls. At this point I wanted to run far away from this place, but we owned it and we were the landlords, and it needed to be fixed. The previous tenant never told us of these issues! We couldn't believe we had blindly agreed to move in, unaware of the severity of these problems. We vowed to make it better and managed to get the mouse and roach situation completely under control, but I was still scared every time I walked the hallway at night. I wanted out in the worst way and remember counting the days till we could move again. Looking back, it was a blessing we lived there to experience these issues and fix them properly. But while some blessings have beautiful wraparound porches, other blessings come wrapped in rodents and bugs!

We were actively looking for a new house to buy, and this time not a two-family but a single- family that needed work. As investors, we obviously love projects! We started to get addicted to seeing the transformations we were making on the homes we bought. And we often envisioned what we would do to our new home as a family. To us location was important, as we loved being so close to the beach. So, we didn't want to compromise too much on that. We looked high and low, but the inventory of homes for sale, even in 2019, was starting to dry up. Our best option was to buy a short sale in a great neighborhood that we liked close by. (A short sale is a home selling for less than the mortgage owed and usually less than the full value of the home because it is in pre-foreclosure, but it also means an open-ended closing date.) We went into contract with the short sale not knowing when we would be able to close. We had to trust it was going to work out and that the universe would provide.

Making Moves

As months went on while we were under contract with the short sale, it became clear we were not going to be closing on that short sale anytime soon. Our only other option at this point was to move into the renovated apartment that had once smelled like cat pee but had since been transformed into a beautiful Airbnb.

MOVE #5 – SMALL AIRBNB APARTMENT

Is your head starting to spin from all the moves we made? Ours was, and this was just move

number five! We moved into the beautiful Airbnb but there was just one thing: it was only six-hundred square feet, and we were moving in with a very wild and rambunctious four-year-old! Our downstairs tenant must have hated us. We settled in and waited and waited to hear back from the short sale home we were hoping to buy. The closing date kept getting pushed back, and we had no choice but to hang in there since home prices were going up and we knew we were getting a good deal.

Finally, the time came, and we closed on the short sale at the end of February 2020.

We were so excited, but the house needed a ton of work. Avid smokers had lived there, and the paint was yellow from it. In addition, the bathroom was dated, and the hardwood floors had to be refinished. Then, just as we got started on the renovations COVID hit. It was not only a crazy time in everyone's lives but in ours as well as we were locked down in a six-hundred-square-foot apartment with a four-year-old. I cried a lot! But these are the choices my husband and I made for our family. We chose to move with our young son in tow, so we knew that it wasn't always going to be easy. Thankfully my husband gave me a pep talk, in which he reminded me of our dreams and why we had set out on this journey. This "unconventional journey," which many of our friends and family couldn't comprehend, made it hard to talk about all the highs and lows with anyone. No one understood except for my husband, and I am so grateful he and I shared the same vision. I had to push through and remind myself this was part of our bigger picture. I had to dig deep within to keep going through with living out of our comfort zone. That's the thing about dreams—people won't always understand the dreams you have, and you will be tested time and time again to see if you really are committed to the dream. But if you focus on the "why" and you have just one person who can dream with you, it makes the wild adventure so worth it.

But we weren't at the "this feels totally worth it" part just yet. It was getting close but there were still more growing pains ahead. As the COVID lockdown dragged on, we started getting inquiries from people who had used our apartment on Airbnb the summer before, and we realized there was a big demand for it. Plus, we had a home to renovate, and the costs were adding up, so renting it out on Airbnb made total sense for us as investors.

This left us with a dilemma of where to live again?! Our new home wasn't ready, and the renovations were getting delayed from COVID restrictions, so back to my high school bedroom we went!

MOVE #6—HIGH SCHOOL BEDROOM PART TWO

This was move number six for us. This time my younger sister moved out so there was an extra bedroom for my son, and my son absolutely loved spending quality time with his grandparents, which I am eternally grateful for! Thank God for my mom and dad, who have been supportive every step of the way. They may not have always understood what we were doing, but they believed in us. They have helped us with moving, given us shelter, and lent a hand to fix up our homes.

So, we waited patiently for our short-sale home to be completed, and this time I was pregnant with our second baby and the nesting phase was really starting to kick in! By the end of June our short-sale fixer-upper was ready, so on to the next move!

MOVE #7—SHORT-SALE FIXER-UPPER

This is the move we were waiting and waiting for! We moved from my parents' house to our new home, which was move number seven. This move was big for us. We finally had a home again with space to run around and enjoy. It had three bedrooms and even had a bonus room that we made into a playroom. It was nice to settle into a place that we could see ourselves enjoying for more than just a few months.

Making Moves

Once we were settled in, I reflected back and couldn't believe the last five years! We moved seven times with a young child. He was one when we started this journey and was now almost five. He enjoyed the adventures, and if you ask my son now if he wants to move again, he would say, "Yes, but this time to a home with two floors!" We live in a ranch, so I guess the real estate bug has gotten into him too!

We're not done yet. We have a couple of more moves in us, and our family and friends have now started to ask, "So when are you guys moving again?" I think they might be half joking but half serious! We know how crazy it must have looked to everyone. A young family in their thirties, hopping around from home, to parents, to an apartment, to another apartment, back to parents, and then to another home. It was trying times for my husband and me, especially the constant packing and unpacking. And it was hard mentally, as while our peers were leveling up to bigger homes, we were shifting around from a starter home to a small apartment. But thankfully my husband and I kept our vision and dreams alive. We would talk about it often to get us through. We truly believed in the big picture, and at the end of living five years out of our comfort zone we attracted the attention of other real estate investors to partner with and we were able to invest in several flips (that we didn't have to live in) and buy more rental properties. AND we have more real estate projects are in the works! The dream is coming into fruition.

It all started because we believed in ourselves, and even in the most trying times when I wanted to give up, we made it work and found a way. And remember, there is always a way! Sometimes you have to get creative like we did, and take the leap and not worry about the details. Because if I had stopped in the beginning, when we were comfortable in our cozy beach rental, I would still have this longing to go after our real estate dreams. And I know that longing would eat away at my heart. Yes, people will try to talk you out of it, but whose life are you living? Don't let others' opinions or your own fear of what they will think dictate how you will live.

This journey has given me confidence to keep going and growing our real estate investment portfolio. This is just the beginning, and I was able to build this foundation since I listened to my heart and followed my intuition. I didn't have the answers of how this was going to work when I started. I just had faith.

ABOUT THE CONTRIBUTOR

Jenn Garcia Mawson is a wife and mom of two amazing kids and a rescue dog. She has a long career in real estate and real estate investing. She cherishes her friendships and family and lives for spending quality time with those closest to her. Her favorite things include wine, the beach, and palm trees!

Jenn is a graduate of Rowan University where she studied history and developed her love for writing thanks to never-ending required written assignments. She dug right in to researching lots of fascinating topics and people. She's grateful for her degree, which also led her to meet her husband, Gary.

Jenn has been a real estate agent since 2008, working with Keller Williams and now EXP Realty. She and her husband started their own real estate team called *The Jersey Property Group* in 2019. They have a passion for helping people buy, sell, and invest in real estate. You can also hear Jenn weekly on her podcast called "Mom Boss Chronicles" and, at this time in her life, along with Inspired Girl Books, she is excited to have this opportunity to write and share her work with others!

Bits of Her Heart...

Jenn Garcia Mawson

Life is about creating memories with the ones you love...

FUN FACT...

Jenn sometimes wishes she was Barbara Walters. She loves interviewing people and getting to know about them.

TURNING OVER A NEW LEAF

BY JESSICA ROJAS

Dedicated to anyone who wants to see a change in the world. Believe in yourself, have faith, and enjoy the journey.

"I choose to make the rest of my life the best of my life."
Louise Hay

Whoever said that life is like a roller coaster was one hundred percent correct. With its ups and downs, I can absolutely equate my life to a roller coaster. I find it very ironic to compare it to a roller coaster ride simply because I was not the biggest fan of them, that is until I had a life-changing experience at Disney California Adventure Park! I once heard from a friend and mentor named Jessica that the way you celebrate your birthday sets the tone for how your year will be. So, for my thirty-first birthday, I wanted to treat myself to an amazing celebration, because I deserved it. I booked a trip to California in November 2021 and took my daughter with me for the adventure.

The birthday prior was a huge milestone for me because I turned thirty. I think thirty it is bittersweet for a woman, at least it was for me. It was like this little voice said to me, "Oh my goodness, you are leaving your twenties, and you should have figured out what you want to do with your life!" or something like that. It just felt a little better to say I was twenty-something since I'm so small and look younger. It felt better to lie about my age, plus people are simply shook because of my petite size! Regardless, the little voice in my head tormented me about this turn of the decade. I'm not going to sugar coat it—I struggled with who I was and what my purpose was. I had to do something about it. I was tired of feeling hopeless. But I had to get back up and find my motivation and inspiration. I had to look deep, and I know I couldn't let my family down. I wanted to do something different. I also realized I did have something incredible to bring to this world, and I needed to celebrate ME! I had to trust and believe in that, and even more so, I had to believe in myself. A big step in believing and just going for it was booking the trip to Disney. You'll hear all about this transformation and the trip a bit later.

I know I am not alone in feeling a little lost. Sometimes, we have to reflect on where we came from, memories from our childhood, what we've been through, and what we dream of in order to realize exactly who we are. I promise it's so much more extraordinary than that nasty little voice in our heads tells us.

I am inspired by my roots and the tough skin that runs through my blood. My mom, at the age of ten, left her home in order to provide for her parents and her younger siblings. She taught herself almost everything, and she was a hard worker. One day, at twenty-two years old, this brave, young woman decided to start a new life in the United States so that her unborn child in the womb (me) and her new family could have a better lifestyle. Growing up, my mom did most of the parenting. She cooked, she cleaned, and most importantly she gave me a happy childhood. She also raised me to be humble, to be strong, and to work hard.

Education was very important in my household, which I was not a big fan of back then. I remember how my mom made me study and practice my times tables out loud while she was sorting out the dirty laundry. I hated it. I never understood why I had to do that, but now as an adult I totally get it. My mom was teaching me to become better at math, to become better than yesterday, and it's no wonder I became the best at multiplication times tables. Her encouraging me and being rigorous with my studies helped me to become a competitor through my education and in life. Winning was my favorite part.

Being born in the first generation, I was raised with lots of responsibilities like translating and speaking English for my parents, doing many chores, and getting good grades through my elementary and high school years. I became a very well-rounded student—that was my "job." My mom also taught me to be independent; I had a lot to figure out on my own like college essays and life advice. She also gave me the freedom to dream big and to achieve my goals. I had a dream of continuing school and graduating college since it was expected of me. For my career, I had a dream of being a television sports anchor or journalist. I also set high standards for myself because being the oldest (and both my parents immigrating to this country), I wanted to accomplish a lot of things for mi familia, and, most importantly, for myself. I wanted to make them proud. By the end of my high school year, I was ready to embark on the next chapter of life—leaving for college and enjoying my new journey. It was exciting, and off I went.

However, love can be a dangerous game, and I played it. I fell in love, and life took a different direction—I found out that I was pregnant. I did not know what to do at first. I had my whole life planned out already, and a baby wasn't in my life plan just yet. But everything just completely changed when I decided to become a mother at the age of twenty-one.

I still had my dreams and goals; I was a driven young woman. But I was in this new chapter of my life called "Motherhood," and there was no way of turning back now. Some of my dreams didn't seem possible, at least not at that time. On top of that, my relationship with a man became very sour. There were so many red flags that I was blind to at the time. So much was happening so fast that I was losing myself. I was blessed to become a mommy, but I also had my biggest fear realized: becoming a single mom. I never wanted to raise a child alone. That wasn't in the plan. That wasn't the dream.

Do you feel like you are on a roller coaster yet? Just wait.

I hit a depression, not realizing that I was truly depressed. I was trying my best to be a really good mom, but something inside me was still off. I loved being a mom. I was blessed with a beautiful baby girl. I named her Antonella, and I recently came to believe that I had manifested her without even knowing it. I was mesmerized by her beautiful, big, hazel green eyes, and my main focus was to become the best mom (and dad) ever to her. Antonella became my life, my world, and I was just focusing on us. I am grateful for my family because I couldn't have done it without the help of my mom and my sisters. Like I mentioned before, not only did my mom teach me great things, she also taught my sisters the same, which we applied into my daughter's life. Trust me, in a household with six females, well, there's a ton of strength right there. While I was worried about being a single mom, my baby Antonella had hit the mom jackpot because she's loved by and learning from all of us. Over these early years, I learned how beautiful it was to be a woman; we create life, and we teach life. We were raised to be strong and to not give up. All of these valuable lessons my daughter was absorbing and continues to absorb.

So, while there was all of this girl power, there was also the weight I felt without understanding why or what it was. To escape it, all I could do was to dream. Dreaming helped me to escape my reality sometimes and imagine how I wanted to live and to imagine my daughter's life in the future. I was lost. I wasn't really motivated. I wanted more for us. I sometimes felt like life wasn't always fair.

Why are things going wrong for me?

Why me? Why us? Does my daughter feel this pain that I am feeling?

Why does it seem like others are achieving so much more than me?

I had so many questions but never had the right answers. I was at my lowest point, but I kept going because deep inside I knew I was built for this. I knew I was chosen to go down this path. There were plans for me and Antonella. I was exhausted, but hope still whispered in my heart. So, I started to set new goals for myself because I was tired of living a life I wasn't happy with. Ever felt that way? Ever had that feeling? I wasn't sure what I wanted to do exactly. So, I decided to go to dental school. I was hopeful this could be the career path for me. So, I tried it, but when COVID hit and shut down the nation I had to stop my schooling. By the time it was reopened, I was not feeling it anymore. So, I was back to square one again.

I should fight harder. I don't want to let my daughter down.

These thoughts and those nasty voices invaded my head, squashing the whispers of hope. On the positive side, when the world went into a lockdown and we all had to stay home, I decided to be more productive with my stay-at-home time and make some serious changes. This led to changing up my lifestyle and adding some new routines into my life. I always admired those who read books. They had always inspired me! So, one of my goals was to become a reader and fall in love with books. The other was to take care of myself more by meditating, breathing, and adding a skincare routine in the morning and in the evening. With continuous work every day, I was seeing progress (Yippee!) and changes in myself, mentally and physically. I developed a new lifestyle, but I fell back into

> I WAS EXHAUSTED BUT HOPE STILL WHISPERED IN MY HEART.

— JESSICA ROJAS

the train wreck of depression. During all of these ups and downs emotionally, I tried to cling to my roots of being raised as a strong woman with big dreams. The glimmer of who I really was kept me going still. I wasn't going to give up on me—Antonella needed me, and I needed me.

I sought a therapist and went back to the gym since it helped me so much in the past. I fell back in love with this new fitness lifestyle again, and my life felt easier once I started implementing what I was reading in lots of self-help books, personal growth books, and money learning books. I listened to podcasts. I surrounded myself with growth-minded people. I was discovering a new world. I made changes; I was learning a new way of thinking and I was feeling so great about it that I noticed that I started speaking differently and thinking differently.

Ever heard that consistency is key? Well, I realized it when I started seeing my body goals coming through. I made it my goal to show up and be one percent better than yesterday. That was my new way of thinking. Mentally I was there. That's what changed me. I dedicated myself to my new lifestyle and woke up at 4 a.m. throughout the week to hit the gym at 5 a.m. This took self-discipline. Learning to wake up every morning and to be grateful the first thing in the morning really helped me to make serious changes and get things done. When I started seeing serious changes, I was looking at myself differently. I was seeing results and the gym became my self-therapy. I was happy with my body results, and this led to changing my diet and tracking my foods because protein is very important. I was looking sexy and guess what? That made me happy since I had been insecure about my body before, and I've never worn a two-piece ever! So that was my other new goal: to look good naked. I'm a woman, and we women should be proud of our bodies and not compare ourselves to others because we are all different. I was loving the feeling of how sore my body felt knowing it was a good sign, since the soreness simply meant growth. I became stronger mentally and physically because I was determined to help the world, my friends, and my family. Seeing my body grow muscles gave me so much confidence. I was also feeling like Wonder Woman, and she's my inspiration. I was releasing a lot of my old demons from the past, literally releasing them out of my body, so much so that I began to sleep better at night.

I learned that if you want serious changes, check yourself and show up to do the work. Have faith because it will get you through your journey. It is always you versus you. I began to see drastic changes: I was looking good, I began to feel like myself, I was happier, and at this point I was unstoppable.

So, here's where I learned to love roller coasters.

For my thirty-first birthday, I wanted to celebrate in a big and adventurous fashion. It had always been a dream of mine to go to California and do Disney since I was a kid. I wasn't really a huge fan of Disney like most people, and I really did not "get it" before, but my life had changed for the better, and why not celebrate that by being in the happiest place on earth? Let me tell you, everything changed even more for the better after the trip as well. I really enjoyed my vacation birthday present in California. The vibes were everything to me. I fell in love with it. This is the lifestyle I had dreamed of when I was a young girl, and now I was living the moment. I visualized myself on more trips and was manifesting my life while on the plane ride there. I was seeing myself living in California.

This trip was one for the books since it was so memorable for my daughter and me together. I had a blast in Disneyland and Disney Adventure Park. I rode all the roller coasters because I wanted to let go of my fears and try something new; I wanted to explore the beauty of my life and enjoy the fun. I danced in the performances at Avenger Park and simply lived in the moment. I was enjoying the freedom of living my dreams as an adult, and I booked this trip for my daughter to enjoy her childhood being in Disney. I was not given these types of moments when I was a little girl because we couldn't afford trips such as this. So, while she was having fun being a kid, I was also having an amazing time as an adult! I found myself again, reliving moments that I remembered having when I was a child. Fascinating feelings started growing in my soul; I was feeling alive all over again. Nothing and nobody was stopping me.

I kept visualizing and dreaming while I was there. Reliving my dreams brought me pure happiness, and I was up in the air, high in the moon with my hands up on the most wonderful, fun roller coaster ever—The Incredicoaster. I was more in control of my life, and I felt the power I had all along that was finally fully manifesting in this moment. It felt pretty extraordinary, and sharing it with my daughter meant everything to me.

We both experienced life like a roller coaster with its ups and downs, but at the end, I know our life is going to end up with pure happiness. Everything happens for a reason, and becoming a single mom was my biggest flex since I really enjoy teaching my daughter in a different, unique kind of way. Fast forward to now, and I am grateful for being a single mom because it made me that much stronger. It made me realize the beauty and gift of being a woman, knowing I am worth a lot and teaching my daughter *her* worth. These are the lessons I am teaching her, so she knows how amazing it is to be a savage woman and how we are capable of doing lots of things in this world.

I am very proud of my daughter; she has inspired me. She is my pride and joy. I was supposed to become a mom first. It is my appointed life to enjoy her while we are both young and to make her the superstar she was born to be. Antonella is my best friend, and I want to make my daughter proud of her mom. Again, the old Jessica fell into depression, but the depression saved me. It had me search for the truth of who I am, and I became a new, healthier version of myself. The way I see it now, you have to fail in life in order to succeed. I am a mastermind, but life tested me. The tests were not very kind to me. At times I was heartbroken. But making it through the tests, we come full circle to who we are born to be. Life is a prize, and I am amazed at how far I have come.

I started with this ambition from my mother's pure love. I became this tough woman warrior because of her and past generations. Wonder Woman became my mom's favorite superhero. She is tough, gorgeous, and smart, and she became my favorite superhero as well. Being a woman is beautiful, as is being sexy while being strong, and knowing what you like and not taking anything less for an answer. It is all about being confident, classy, unique, and a diva. It's not giving a damn what others say but following the path you know you were chosen for. It is about you inspiring some people and knowing you're going to piss off the rest, so do it anyway! I learned that I could ignore my negative thoughts and think sexy because having confidence is everything, Honey! I am so proud of myself and proud of my Mexican Heritage. Our journeys are our own, and we all can win at this gift of life, so do not compete or compare yourself to others because YOU can make your own path, you can find your own happiness, and you can inspire others at any age. Age is nothing but a number. I repeat, age is nothing but a number. You are never too young or too old to learn something new, so don't give up on yourself or your dreams no matter how often that nasty voice comes into your head. Keep learning. Learn something today and believe that dreams do come true. I have learned this, and I am blessed. You are too. When you are ready to become the powerful woman that you are designed to be, when you are ready to make a change in the world, remember it all starts with YOU.

Repeat after me:

I am a boss.

I am strong.

I am unique.

I am different.

I am becoming the woman I was always destined to be, and this is only my beginning.

I'm just getting started Baby, and so are YOU.

Xoxo,
Jessica Rojas

ABOUT THE CONTRIBUTOR

Jessica Rojas was born in New York, raised in Asbury Park, and this combination of big city dreams and small-town love has shaped the woman she is today!! Jess loves to teach and spends much of her time teaching the future generation.

She is very kind and loves to help others in any way she can. Whether volunteering or in her community simply lending a hand, Jess uses her gifts to serve so many.

Jessica is a mother to a beautiful eleven-year-old daughter. She is a driven, independent woman, with a passion for this miracle of life. Having faced many obstacles head on since she was a young girl, she is determined to help and inspire other human beings to believe in themselves and become the best version of themselves possible!

Bits of Her Heart...

Jessica Rojas

You only live once, so make it count!

FUN FACT...

Jess loves to eat! Her guilty pleasures are cakes, pastries, and strawberry ice cream. She would love to share a meal with Beyoncé.

SECTION 2

WE ARE TORCH-BEARING BELIEVERS

LET IT BE
by Denise Cesare

WEARING YOUR CROWN OF GREATNESS
by Veronica Woods

THE BOLDNESS OF THE IN-BETWEEN
by Joy M. England

> WE CAN EACH CHOOSE TO BE THE MAGNET FOR AND THE LIGHTHOUSE TO ALL THAT IS GOOD.

4

LET IT BE

BY DENISE CESARE

This chapter is dedicated to anyone who has ever felt the need to heal.

"Music is a therapy. It is a communication far more powerful than words, far more immediate, far more efficient."

Yehudi Menuhin

THE POWER OF MUSIC.

What is on your playlist? Do you have a life soundtrack, or is there simply a song that touched you in some way during your life?

Music heals us, reminds us, and brings us back to a moment in time. Music is a motivator, a mood elevator.

Music has helped me on my journey, even during the most difficult, at times horrific, events and situations in my life. Music is a constant steady rhythm in the day-to-day of my life. Music is with me to dance to through the highs and to cry with through the lows.

Why music?

For me, it is an outlet. Just listening to a soothing accompaniment calms me. Sometimes it is the lyrics that speak to me. Music has saved me throughout many dark times, no matter my age, seven or fifty-seven. To this day, music reminds me that I am not alone; songs and their words speak directly to my heart. Sometimes it feels like the songwriter wrote the song just for me! Music connects us, weaving our hearts together.

Music gives me strength. Music is the balm to my soul. The words, lyrics, poetry put to music, the beat, the instruments. Even nature is like music to me. Listening to the sounds of Mother Earth, nature healing us through all the moments of feeling, breathing in all of the beauty in the world. The rain, the ocean, the wind, the birds, the trees swaying and leaves rustling through, the thunder and lightning.

How did music heal me?

Music healed my broken heart. Music brought light into the darkness I experienced through molestation, sexual assault, loss, death, betrayal, grief, sickness, emotional abuse, harassment, bullying, discrimination.

Have you ever experienced any of these situations?

Although a song may bring you back to a memory that brings up a lot of sadness, the memory is now connected to a new message, with song lyrics woven into the memory like strands of a thread weaving beautiful patterns together. While the memory itself doesn't go away, you can heal and be transformed by the power of music. Music can tap into the emotions and be a powerful tool, especially during times of sadness or angst. Music can help get you through the day.

My story is a collaboration of mind, body, and the spirit of music. I want to take you with me on a journey to understanding what it truly means to "Let It BE" and how music can be a symphonic companion during five pivotal experiences in one's life—the passing of parents, the union of marriage, the birth of a child, the hurt of feeling invisible, and the beauty of receiving divine signs.

Following are these stories in my life and the songs that carried me through.

"WIND BENEATH MY WINGS"

When I woke up that morning, I felt so numb. It was a gloomy, rainy morning in November 1987, the day of my father's funeral and burial. I just wanted this nightmare to end; it could not be true. I remember during the mass, the priest said, "Don't be sad. He is with God now, but you can feel his wind beneath your wings."

The mass ended, and off to the cemetery we went. It was such an intense feeling, and my tears could not stop the feeling in my heart. As I walked away,

Let it Be

I wished he was still alive. Then, suddenly, I felt a slight breeze that reminded me what the priest said to me in church, my father was the "wind beneath my wings." I never heard that expression before, but I found out the phrase was also lyrics from a song. The year following my father's passing, 1988, the song became popularized by Bette Midler, but it actually had been recorded by several artists, even Gladys Knight & the Pips in 1983.

I was twenty-three, and my dad forty-six when he passed away. November 8, 1987. He always was the life of the party, and he lived life to the fullest. It is sad that he died so young. Everyone loved him. His death was the saddest day of my life.

I get my love of Disney and Mickey Mouse from him, and now I share that love with my husband and son.

I am always thinking of him, feeling his love, and always believing there is more power from heaven, he is always protecting me. "Wind Beneath My Wings", always looking up moments. Whenever I hear this song, it's always my sign, and ironically, it's the song dedicated to my father at my cousin's Sweet 16? Can you believe it... that's the song played for him!

No one you love is ever gone. They are in your hopes, dreams, memories, and songs.

I AM MY FATHER'S DAUGHTER
a letter to my father on the anniversary of his passing.

Thinking about you and wondering how did 35 years without you move so fast and so slow at the same time?

I remember your laugh, your kindness, and your heart. I remember you singing and dancing, always wanting to celebrate holidays or any day with your family. Disney, Sunday foodie and football fanatic. Beautiful moments etched in my heart forever!

I also know the sadness you hid from those you loved as well.

I love sharing stories about you, with everyone, Dan and especially to Daniel.

Blessed with your protection from above... always looking up moments!

"

TO THIS DAY, MUSIC REMINDS ME THAT I AM NOT ALONE; SONGS AND THEIR WORDS SPEAK DIRECTLY TO MY HEART.

DENISE CESARE

Let it Be

Thank God for you ... The wind beneath my wings. I am my father's daughter.

The journey and the healing are like a song, and the beat will continue with love.

"NATURAL WOMAN"

Thank you, Aretha Franklin, for giving me my anthem for healing and love. You make me feel like a natural woman!

After all of the relationships that didn't work out, was there really anybody who I wanted to be with? It was a long road of healing from past relationships that were abusive and unhealthy. In fact, when I met my husband, I was dating someone who couldn't commit, and an ex-boyfriend wanted to get back together because he found out I was dating again.

I met my husband at a bar in Belmar, New Jersey. Belmar is a beach town, and I didn't think anything would become of it, because does anyone really marry anyone they meet at the shore? But there was something about him. Danny was just such a nice guy! Of course, I instead went back to the old boyfriend ... but I did save that nice guy's number, and eight months later, after being cheated on by my ex-boyfriend, I decided to call Dan. Wow, I was brave! He answered my call, and the rest is our history.

We shared stories of losing our fathers at a young age. We also talked about hurts we experienced in past relationships. We had so much in common. We talked about how these experiences had a profound impact on us, and we agreed that life was precious. Being honest and kind mattered to both of us. We were meant to be together!

We married on June 24, 1995. Our wedding day was so beautiful, and music was intentionally an important part of the day. We chose songs to capture our love and feelings for each other and that day. "Natural Woman" was my secret song, and he picked "Have You Ever Really Loved a Woman?" by Bryan Adams.

"SUNSHINE ON MY SHOULDERS"

John Denver sang lyrics that would become a constant reminder of the love and bond between me and my son. But it was a longer road to get pregnant than we ever expected. It was over four years since we were married and years of testing, and trying, totally unsure if I would ever get pregnant. After all the researching, reading articles and books, even learning that tea could help make you pregnant—yes I tried that big cup of tea made delicious like a cappuccino—along with lots of crying, hoping, and praying. Finally! We were having a baby!

I remember feeling so in love with the little boy I was carrying. It was an unbelievable feeling I had never felt before, kind of like butterflies in my stomach. I even told my mom, "It is like a tiny flutter that fills my heart so."

The day my son was born, it was a sunshiny, windy December day in 1999. We took him home on Christmas Eve day. What a gift! He literally felt like sunshine on my shoulders, and I would sing those lyrics to him. As he got older, I would listen to the song with him.

Now, whenever I hear "Sunshine on My Shoulders" it stirs up all that love. I cannot listen without just stopping and taking it in, thinking of my wonderful boy! It brings me right back to that sweet baby and mommy moment!!!

"FIGHTER"

I lost my voice in May 2006 after a car accident left me with a condition called spasmodic dysphonia. I had to learn how to navigate and survive during this extremely difficult and dark period in my life.

One afternoon, as I was driving home from an extremely difficult day at work; I just thought I couldn't take another day there, being bullied as an adult. It was just so heavy, and I really wanted to give up fighting ever single minute!

Every day was a challenge, but this day seemed just a little more difficult. I was in the hallway and a co-worker began talking about me, right in front of me! She asked another coworker, "She still can't talk?" It was as if I was invisible. I couldn't speak, at least not very well or for more than a few words at a time, but I could absolutely hear. So, I pulled up all my courage, took a deep breath, and I mustered the words, "No, but I can hear you."

The insensitivity was astounding, hurtful, and shocking. Here I suffered a traumatic accident where I had to heal inside and out. I had post-traumatic stress, and on top of all this, I was a Speech Language Pathologist with no voice. Oh, the irony! The way I was treated felt like harassment and discrimination, and it was all so intense. I felt I was under a microscope as supervisors would come in and out of my room, and I was even observed for over two hours. It was difficult to go to work every day. I would wake up every morning and look at myself in the mirror and smile, and I would smile all day. I loved the students, and that's why I was there. But my heart couldn't take the heaviness of feeling singled out and made fun of for something that was beyond my control. I would cry myself to sleep at night and then wake up and do it all over again.

The bullying turned into a battle, and I had to fight to keep my job. I even hired a lawyer so I could stay in my career. But on my drive home this one particular afternoon, the song "Fighter" by Christina Aguilera came on the radio. I pulled my car over and stopped, cried, then listened to the words. Could they be any more fitting? I don't think so. This, and the song "Brave" by Sara Bareilles became my go-to songs if I was having a bad day at work. It reminded me of my strength and purpose. And to all those who seemed to kick me while I was down, I thank you for making me a Fighter!

"LET IT BE"

"Mother Mary comes to me."

I've experienced many signs from Mother Mary, losing my voice in 2006 was an extremely difficult and dark time in my life that had me search for signs of *why me?*

Mother Mary and the lyrics to "Let It Be" had always been a lifeline, a healing comfort to my soul. And receiving any divine validation comforted me even more than you can imagine. I remember one day in spring of 2008. I was picking my son up from school. We were in a parking lot and a random woman I did not recognize handed me a Mother Mary holy water bottle! Yes it was in the shape of Mother Mary. I wish you could see it, blue and clear.

The woman said to me, "I see your struggles. Please take this. I know you need it."

I still have it, and yes, I needed it! Believe and Let it Be. Listening to and speaking "words of wisdom."

It is a combination of the beautiful lyrics coinciding with my life that have touched my heart and connected with my soul through this song.

"SOMEWHERE OVER THE RAINBOW"
Israel Ka'ano'i Kamakawiwo'ole Hawaiian version

I wake up to the sound of music.

On my fiftieth birthday, my mom was diagnosed with a brain tumor and cancer. A few weeks before, she wasn't feeling well and told me about her symptoms. My mom was a fighter and suffered with rheumatoid arthritis since her thirties. She never complained, but this time it was different.

"We are going to beat this!" she said, after having brain surgery and healed. A year later the lung cancer took her life.

It seemed she was doing ok. The week before she died, she even had more energy. I wasn't sure if we should go on our family vacation to Disney, but she said, "No worries, Denise! Go, have fun, and I will see you when you get back!" On the ride home from Florida, I received a call from Hospice.

How could this be? She was okay yesterday. My thoughts were cloudy; my heart hurt so very much.

My mom took a turn for the worse. We worried we would not make it home to be with her. My son was fifteen, and he was so close to her. She loved him so much! We arrived, and she was sleeping, but for an instant she opened her eyes for my son—the strength and love that took.

My mom passed away on July 8, 2015.

I was with her when she crossed over. Playing music to soothe her, "Somewhere Over the Rainbow" and" Imagine." It was the only way I knew how to ease her transition. Music transcends, and its beauty and power were a gift that night.

And I had a "Let It Be" moment when I held her in my arms and brought her close to my chest. I had her to listen to my heartbeat, as I said to her, "You gave me life, and I listened to your heartbeat from your womb, now listen to and feel mine. It's ok, you will always be with us." She passed that morning. Always looking up...

"Though they may be parted." I believe souls who have crossed, like my mom and my dad (thirty-five years earlier), have more power where they are.

WISDOM IN THE WORDS

We often hear advice about letting things go and moving on, but it doesn't get to the heart of the matter to heal. When we let it be, in my experience facing many obstacles throughout my life and overcoming them, we let it be by faith and love and "believing" in a higher power. The "Be" in believe is how we

Let it Be

connect to that higher power, in each moment. Letting something go may not always be feasible, at least without the proper healing to actually release it. But we all can "let it be" by being present. I am still on my journey of learning to be human, being kind, and believing! I am still learning what it truly means to "let it be," and I am grateful for the wisdom that comes through musical exploration. The lyrics are messengers.

"There will be an answer" for me in the music, lyrics, and sounds that soothe my soul!

ABOUT THE CONTRIBUTOR

Denise Cesare is a published author, keynote speaker, and social emotional learning specialist focusing her efforts to serve the needs of schools, organizations, and communities. She has worked as a Speech Language Pathologist and Special Education/Social Emotional Specialist for over twenty-five years earning two master's degrees.

In 2006, she lost her voice due to a condition called spasmodic dysphonia from a major car accident. Since that time, much has come to surface for her about the meaning of life, the importance of being present, the gift every moment offers, and the power love has to heal. Combining her vast education, continued learning, and personal experience, Denise delivers research-backed talks on regulating emotions, mindfulness education, and kindness initiatives. Her wisdom has been featured online, in print, on podcasts, and through live streams in outlets around the world. Her book, *Moments in Motion with Love*, is available wherever books are sold.

Born and raised in Brooklyn, NY, she currently resides in Staten Island with her husband Dan of twenty-eight years years. She has an amazing son, Daniel, working and living in Pennsylvania.

Bits of Her Heart...

Denise Cesare

 Kindness moments matter.

FUN FACT...

When Denise was in her twenties, she held three jobs at the same time. She taught driving school, she was a dance teacher, and she was travel agent.

WEARING YOUR CROWN OF GREATNESS

BY VERONICA WOODS

This chapter is dedicated to the loving memory of my father. Thank you for teaching me that confidence is not just a feeling but a strength that grows within us when nurtured by the unwavering love of those who believe in us.

> "I am not dimming my light. I am just going to have to hand you a pair of shades."
>
> **Lisa Nichols**

Not everyone will be able to appreciate your light.

As a freshly minted college graduate, I had the opportunity to participate in a management trainee program on Wall Street with other new grads from across the country.

My light was fueled by the fact that I stood on the shoulders of my ancestors. My parents grew up in the rural South before moving to Philadelphia. Both made groundbreaking achievements in their respective families by pursuing higher education and business. They inspired me to want to continue to extend this tradition.

They sacrificed financially to send me to a highly ranked university. I responded in turn by racking up educational accolades.

While I was excited to take on the trainee program, getting along with all the characters while I rotated through the different departments was challenging. As an introvert, I was not as skilled at small talk with people I didn't know well. When in doubt, I often jumped right into questions about how things worked. I was genuinely curious and wanted to look smart like I did in school.

With limited emotional intelligence and experience, I didn't see it coming when I essentially got a "no confidence vote" during one of my rotational assignments. One of my mentors shared that I had rubbed some team members wrong. This report shocked me. He helped me understand how my attempt to look interested and intelligent could have been misinterpreted. He encouraged me to keep my ambition but to be more selective about with whom I shared some of my goals.

This feedback confused me. Was I expected to adjust my light up and down daily depending on who I was around? And how would I know who to shine bright for and who to dim down for? His words prodded my insecurities about whether this was the right job for me.

As I reflect on the experience, I see how I almost let the perception of a handful of people cause me to second guess whether I could be successful at the company. Eventually, I did connect with one senior leader who liked my inquisitive nature. He saw my potential and was willing to develop my natural talents further.

From this early lesson, I understood that you have to shine a light on your gifts no matter what. It is the only way that you can reach your full potential. Yes, I believe outside feedback is valuable, but I give myself more leeway in judging how to put it in context. Then, I learned to throw some of it right out to the trash.

This chapter reviews four self-reflective questions to calibrate how well you are shining your light. The questions help guide me when I feel off-course or may be at risk of shrinking within a situation.

QUESTION #1: AM I RUNNING MY OWN RACE TO GREATNESS?

After business school, I did the typical thing and worked for a few large corporations. Each year, I reached toward a new promotion or company award. I learned a ton from my peers and leaders, but I never felt fulfilled. When I got laid off, I thought this was my time to forge a new path—to entrepreneurship.

I thought entrepreneurship would be a straight path to time and financial freedom. Instead, I made a few sprints and some unexpected turns. I didn't know that this journey would force me to question myself daily. For most entrepreneurs, it leaves you quite vulnerable when you put yourself out to the world as a creator, owner, or expert and the world doesn't immediately fawn over you with attention or money.

After experimenting with working on various projects as a business consultant, my dad illuminated a path that was not remotely on my radar—real estate. He had pivoted into real estate brokerage, ironically around the same age. He told me that he saw some talents in me that would allow me to excel in the field if I allowed myself to explore.

On one hand, I had a new appreciation for the opportunity to take over the family business after I saw that it was not easy to keep one open and thriving. On the other, I thought to myself, *Should I have considered this path earlier?* Did I miss out on working side by side with my father in his prime to chase a corner office that I was likely not meant for?

Each "path change" requires some distance before you feel fully grounded without looking back at the other paths you walked away from. Although the new direction can bring fresh passion and drive, you can still have some self-doubt.

For example, someone asking me, "Are you still in real estate?" could be a trigger. Now, this person could genuinely want to confirm what I am up to. However, if I am feeling more vulnerable about whether I am on the right path, I may hear a few other questions like:

You've changed paths quite often, just wondering if you're finally sticking to one.
Are you having much success with real estate?
You don't have a real job by now? I thought you would be back in a corporate job.
You are only helping people buy and sell homes? I thought you would be building entire communities of luxury condos by now, too.

Of course, this was my self-talk. I was being overly critical of myself. I did have a little nagging question about the level of success I could achieve.

However, sometimes these questions come out of people's mouths directly. You have to be careful to recognize whether they are genuinely just curious or if they are projecting their vulnerability or life experiences on your journey. You can still choose to use this confrontational inquiry as a chance to reinforce your convictions. You can respond with, "I understand that you are playing devil's advocate, but I am good with my career right now."

Equating speed to achievement to doing the right thing can be problematic. When things appear to be moving slowly for you, or as compared to others, you fall into the comparison trap. Just because someone got married, bought a house, or made their first million before you, does not negate your path. All these things could still be on the way but in due season. We can second guess ourselves too soon to see the gift. When we compare ourselves to others, we stop running our own race to greatness, and the path becomes muddled with insecurities.

QUESTION #2: HAVE I GIVEN MYSELF PERMISSION TO STRETCH AND NOT BE PERFECT?

Entrepreneurship can test your boundaries of what you think you are capable of in a very unique way. Ironically, you find success when you stretch beyond what you thought was possible.

At the beginning of the entrepreneurial journey, most people have to wear a lot of hats. For me, the role that felt the most unnatural was that of a salesperson. In my head, a salesperson had to be some stereotypical cheesy, pushy, and loud character to be effective.

I remember I used to have a habit of saying, "I am not a salesperson." I said this phrase so much that my cousin, also an entrepreneur, told me to quit saying that. He showed me examples of how I had effectively sold my ideas and services in the past. He cautioned me to get that used car salesman image out of my head. Then, he assured me that I would feel more comfortable over time.

When it came time to launch my YouTube channel, I delayed hitting the record button for a full year fearing that I could not convey the grace of Michelle Obama on camera. Despite people telling me that they thought I would be great on video, I feared not looking polished enough.

I recorded my first video only after committing to an accountability buddy that I would record a video by the end of the month. Honestly, if I did not have the date on the calendar where I would have to report the results, I might have dragged out my timeline further.

"

A GOOD SUPPORT SYSTEM CAN HELP YOU RECHARGE A FIRE THAT IS ALREADY THERE. IT IS NOT SO MUCH THAT YOU FIND VALIDATION OUTSIDE OF YOURSELF, BUT A GOOD CIRCLE CAN SERVE AS A MIRROR.

VERONICA WOODS

I got in front of the camera with all my fancy unused equipment and shared my knowledge. It was only about seven minutes of tips for home sellers.

After I watched the replay, I was horrified. I saw the fear in my eyes. I looked like a deer in headlights. I shared the video with another entrepreneur friend and braced for her to cosign, "Just take the video down and start over."

Instead, she said, "Yes, you look a little nervous because I know you. You shared some useful information and looked like a true expert."

I asked her, "Do you see how stiff I looked during the first two minutes? I am taking it down."

She responded, "You act like you completely froze. Just post it. You will get better over time." I went on to record more videos, and I even got new clients as a result.

What I learned was to trust that I can get better. I would limit my success if I were not brave enough to try a new skill and start awkwardly. You may mislabel something as a weakness when it is just a lack of experience. You must catch yourself to avoid giving up early or worse self-sabotaging to prove that you were destined to fail anyway.

One of my favorite quotes from NBA legend Pat Reilly's book "The Winner Within" says it best: "Repeated choking is the essence of defeatism, which is the acceptance of defeat without struggle. Losing becomes a part of your identity. You begin playing to avoid a loss, rather than playing to score a win."

Giving myself permission to not be perfect was quite literally a game-changer. I encourage you to stretch yourself and trust that you will get better as you go. It is the only way.

QUESTION #3: DO I HAVE THE RIGHT VILLAGE AROUND ME FOR THIS SEASON?

Although inner brilliance may come from within, your village can help amplify it. It is not surprising why many people who have at least one person who encourages their talents early in life become so successful. I was fortunate to grow up with parents who reassured me that "Whatever you want to do, we have your back." This was truly a blessing, something everyone may not have been able to experience growing up.

I am thankful for the financial support, but I am even more appreciative of the emotional support. I took on challenges that were "the road less traveled" for many in my neighborhood crew. For instance, I attended journalism camp at sixteen over seven hundred miles away from home where I didn't know a soul because I read something in a magazine. This was only possible with supportive parents like mine.

As I have gone through life, I have had various other support circles come together whenever I struggled to the point where my light dimmed down to a flicker. Whether breaking free from a toxic romantic relationship or launching a business, I always seemed to attract the right circle.

For example, when I got laid off from my job in 2012, I felt mixed emotions. On one hand, I had been preparing for this day for some years. I ran an online beauty venture by night and joined networks of other ambitious women around New York City. On the other hand, I questioned whether my business was scalable as a full-time operation. Going in with the expectation of a decent but not amazing severance package, did I have a chance? On top of everything else, my mother's health was failing. It was a real reminder that tomorrow at full physical steam and acumen is not promised.

About one month after I turned in my corporate badge, I decided to attend a national conference in Texas for women entrepreneurs. After starting to feel some anxiety about my decision not to look for another job, I entered a room of a thousand women on fire to thrive and felt a new confidence.

One of the conference's highlights was an activity facilitated by one of my virtual mentors, Lisa Nichols. In groups of about five women, we formed a physical support circle where we took turns feeding our truths to each other through words of affirmation.

"You are a powerful connector."

"You can build a business that transforms lives."

"Nothing can stop you."

The women would repeat your affirmation over and over with one physical hand on your back and shoulder, providing support.

My circle said the words that I wrote down about myself. The words landed differently when I heard them from others. I wanted to embody these words so badly. At once, I felt the tears well up in my eyes.

This exercise was a reminder that a good support system can help you recharge a fire that is already there. It is not so much that you find validation outside of yourself, but a good circle can serve as a mirror. Find your village that will support and lift you up.

QUESTION #4: DID I UNAPOLOGETICALLY OWN MY GREATNESS IN THAT MOMENT?

Many people feel like imposters despite having something special to offer the world. We use weak labels like having a "little business" or add unnecessary qualifiers like "beginner" to feel more comfortable with the masses.

Now, I am not suggesting that we should all stretch the truth beyond believability, but we owe it to the world to give a more accurate reflection of our talents.

I remember the moment I felt I would call myself a real estate expert with my full throat. It was in the middle of a consultation with a new client. I told story after story about how I helped clients dodge all kinds of landmines and bullets. I could also share about advising clients through good deals that left them excited to take on the next one. These anecdotes just flowed out of my mouth. I just know what I know. One of my favorite clients always teases me, "Let me stay in my lane."

There is a time to be humble in acknowledging God and your support circle, but not owning that you may be a little more gifted or accomplished robs the world of the chance for you to inspire others.

I wish I could report that I sprinted to this place of confidence. The reality is that it came after some gut punches. I routinely undercharged for advice that made my clients five figures because I didn't think I had enough experience. I also allowed others to leverage my experience and education to demonstrate their credibility and benefit more than I did.

My big aha moment came when I brought a roller coaster deal to a close and learned that the other agent had negotiated terms to get paid more than me. And it was more by a significant amount. I called my dad to vent, and he told me, "Well I guess she believed she was worth it. Her client knew she was hiring an expert." *Ouch!* This motivated me to claim my expert status more often than I once felt natural.

I have come to terms with the fact that owning my expert status is not bragging. You are just sharing facts about who you are that would be valuable for others to know. I practice saying my "I ams" about my knowledge, experience, and talents in a calm and confident tone. It helps when I replay the stories in my head that I would tell a new client. Some people may want to write these down as a brag book.

Owning your greatness has broader application than just your career. How often do you slip to say, "I do a little cooking" or "I am an okay mom." You can't inspire others if they don't know who you are. Own your greatness in all aspects of your life, and those who need your light will be drawn to you.

We all start with a unique crown of greatness that is part of our birthright. The challenge is that we have to figure out how to wear it.

Recently, I donned a tiara for an event. When I first put the crown on my head, it felt awkward. I shifted it from left to right in search of a comfortable position. Quite frankly, it hurt. I felt very self-conscious. My head seemed too big to keep the crown in place for an entire luncheon. In the middle of my tenth micro-adjustment for the perfect fit, a friend walked by and remarked, "Don't we all look amazing?"

I answered, "Yes, girl, we do."

I would tell my twenty-three-year-old self in the training program it is okay to acknowledge your gifts even in the face of self-doubt. You can draw people into your light even while figuring out how to navigate your life's purpose. You are more in control of how intense your light can shine than you think. Surround yourself with a village of support, and unapologetically own the greatness God put inside of you.

ABOUT THE CONTRIBUTOR

Veronica finds joy connecting people for everything from hair salons to jobs. After 20 years working in Corporate America in Finance and Product Management for companies like Dun & Bradstreet, Merck, and Merrill Lynch, she turned her matchmaking skills to real estate. She joined the family real estate business—her first job.

Today, Veronica is the Broker/Owner of Daniel Woods Real Estate, founded by her father. Veronica is passionate about helping her clients create wealth, legacy, and lifestyle through real estate. Her firm represents clients buying, selling, and managing properties in the Philadelphia metro area.

Veronica earned her bachelor's degree in economics from Northwestern University and her MBA in finance from The Wharton School. Veronica lives in suburban Philadelphia and serves on several nonprofit boards. She is a proud Life member of Sigma Gamma Rho Sorority, Inc.

Follow her on her YouTube channel for real estate wisdom for rental property investors and real estate investing in Philadelphia.

Bits of Her Heart...

Veronica Woods

Lift as you climb.

FUN FACT...

Veronica's go-to karaoke song is Janet Jackson's "Control." Two books that changed everything for her were **Simple Abundance** by Sarah Ban Breathnach and A Millionaire Mind by T. Harv Eker.

THE BOLDNESS OF THE IN-BETWEEN

BY JOY M. ENGLAND

This chapter is dedicated to anyone who has felt stuck in the waiting.

L ife is a journey."
We all have heard or made this declaration at times in our lives. I would agree that life in all of its complicated glory is a journey, one unique to every traveler. My individual journey often includes aimless wandering through my what-ifs when I am not on solid ground and when I am in darkness.

What if I don't?
What if I can't?
What if God doesn't?

What-ifs will cause an avalanche of fear, effectively smothering hope with doubt. When I allow my what-ifs to control my mind, they trap me in the darkness of doubts. It is this place of darkness that I refer to as the "in-between." The place where choices are made, beliefs solidified, and journeys expedited or extended. The "in-between" is a place of both wonder and fear, pressure and pursuit. The in-between is always a gap between where I am and where I believe God is bringing me. The existence of the in-between is an indication that I need to shore up my bravery by being bold in my faith.

Getting from where I am to where God needs me to be is hard work; much will be required to whom much is given (Luke 12:48 NIV). The times where I have felt my weakest, where I have decided I had no ability to overcome, where surrender to fear was all I could see—those times, my friends, were plentiful. I did not know during those times what I am about to share with you. I had no idea how to harness the power of the truth of who I am. I was way too consumed with the lies I was believing about myself. There is work to be done in the in-between. There is surrender and grace, there is revelation and refinement, and, above all else, there is love and redemption. Will we be able to choose to stand and allow the in-between to do the work it needs to do in us, so we can grab hold of the beauty of the life God wrote for us?

Life is a blessing. The ability to have your heart's desires realized is a testament to amazing grace. But let's be really honest for a second. Life doesn't show up every day *looking* like a blessing. There are days when life is downright unfair and traumatic. When life shows up like this, it is hard not to succumb to the in-between pressure. Don't get me wrong; I live a life blessed with grace and favor, with love and protection. I am honored that I was called on this unique journey. I am also simultaneously fearful that the most challenging parts of that journey will endlessly repeat themselves. The in-between for me is fraught with land mines, typically taking shape as a what-if. My what-ifs are effective tools to keep me from moving forward. Their sole purpose is to point out all the potential dangers of whatever I am reaching for.

I have carefully curated my what ifs; they range in tenacity and cruelness. I needed them. I relied on them to remind me of my life's genuine and imagined dangers:

What if you heard God wrong, and you look like a fool?

What if you aren't good enough to see it through?

The old standby ... *what if you fail, Joy?*

My what-ifs also served to keep me constantly aware of what was missing from my life. The fear of lack in all its forms is something that attempts to torment me daily. My what-ifs did a great job at keeping me shackled to crippling fear, which perpetuated the likelihood that lack would flood in. What-ifs try to eclipse your joy and force your focus on the shadows of what is missing. I had to find my way to not just exist in my in-betweens but to honor that time as a place where miracles are molded, and hearts' desires are fulfilled. How do we identify these what-ifs and release them because they no longer serve to protect but instead imprison us?

Let me share with you something that all my time in the in-between has taught me: *boldness is the antidote to what if.*

Boldness. What is it, and how do we wield it? Merriam-Webster defines bold as being fearless before danger, showing or requiring a fearless, daring spirit. The biblical view on boldness embodies confidence, fearlessness, and freedom of speech. Boldness requires fearless confidence in action and speech. The weight of the in-between always tempts me into silence. In silence, I am comfortable; it feels like safety. I often thought, *Okay, Joy, just shrink back and try to be as invisible as possible.* When you grow up in a never-ending series of in-betweens, silence and invisibility are the only way to survive. These tools kept me safe, physically and emotionally. When we are out of that immediate danger and we keep using the same protection tactics, they serve to only shackle us to fear. Learning through experiences that required me to lean only on God's grace and protection was how I realized that I needed to embrace a new way of dealing with the "in-between." These same experiences taught me that the "in-betweens" are where I have the power to find my voice. I could begin to use it to bridge the gap between my heart's desires and my current situation.

Looking back now, it seems evident that the way to build that bridge is through thoughts and words. At the time, I was still learning that the power of my voice (and the words I spoke over myself and my circumstances) was the power supply to the "in-between." Taking a stand, making the decision, over and over, choosing life over death, choosing faith over fear, and choosing power over people's opinions will always determine the course of the "in-betweens."

I know you must be thinking that this all sounds great until the fear outweighs the hope, and we are being dragged to the ground under the weight of what is *not*. The real heaviness of the in-between is in the weight of the what-if. When we are hoping for the outcome God has spoken, but our natural vision can only see the circumstances shouting defeat; that is when the in-between has the propensity to smother us. Knowledge, however, is power. Let's try and remember that.

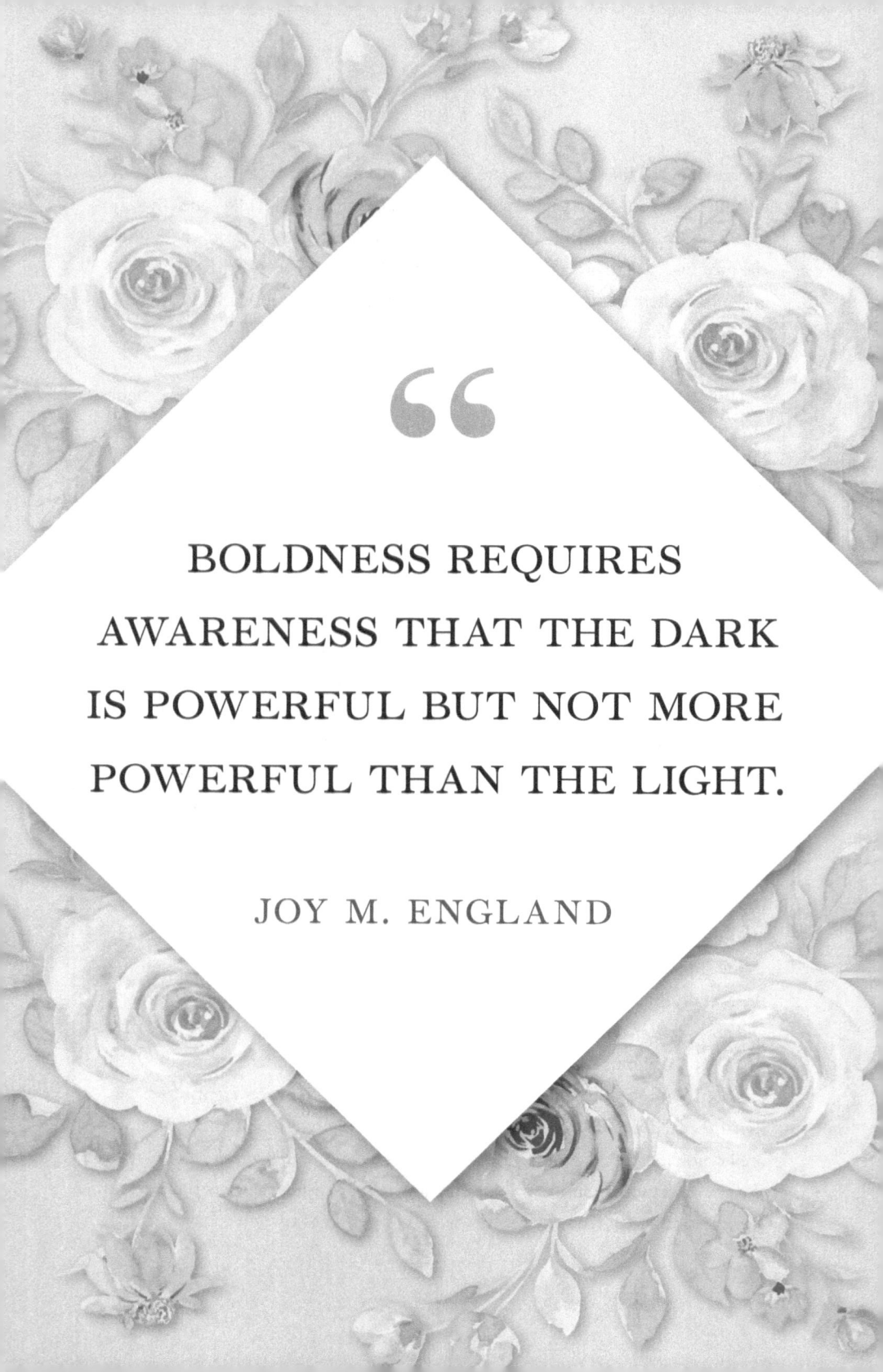

"

BOLDNESS REQUIRES AWARENESS THAT THE DARK IS POWERFUL BUT NOT MORE POWERFUL THAN THE LIGHT.

JOY M. ENGLAND

The Boldness of the In-Between

When we are aware of the truth, and we know that we are victors, that is where the embers of boldness smolder.

The darkness of living in the shadows of our heart's desires is not where boldness is born. Boldness requires awareness. Awareness that the dark is powerful but not more powerful than the light and understanding that the always-present light of hope fuels our boldness. Clinging to fear and standing firmly on doubt is a sure-fire way to stay stuck in the in-between— stuck between where your fear says you belong and where God is calling you to be. The in-between and all of its glorious pressure are where we need to choose. We have to decide to command our thoughts and speak life with our words. The in-between is an opportunity for you and me to surrender the fear to the authority of faith.

How bold is the cure for the in-between?

Choosing to command how we think is a bold move made even more forceful by the addition of life-breathing words. Getting there will take a conscious decision to move past the paralysis of fear with faith-forward confidence. Now that we know we have the power to kick the butt of the in-between, how do we do it? Our words and thoughts have the power to condemn and set free; they breathe life or compel death. It all comes down to choices, my friends. Words kill, words give life; they're either poison or fruit—you choose (Proverbs 18:21 MSG). Learning to speak life to ourselves takes conditioning. It is not a natural response, especially if you have lived under the lies of condemnation and defeat.

What does it look like to speak life over yourself? Let me show you. Here are some defeating thoughts common to the in-between:

You are not smart enough to overcome this.

You have made too many mistakes; this will never turn around.

You do not have the support you need; you cannot do this on your own.

Now, choose boldness, and re-write these defeating thoughts:

I have all that I need within me to accomplish my goals.

My past is behind me, and it has no power over my destiny.

I am powerful and called; I can do all things through Him who strengthens me.

You see how easy that was! Those, my dear friends, are seeds of hope planted in the opportunity of the in-between. I would love to say that you say these once, and they take root and free you from your lifelong doubts. God is more than capable of ridding us of the thoughts immediately. However, He is more interested in the lessons and the conditioning of the in-between. As we looked at before, the in-between is where miracles are molded; it takes time to mold something into its most potent form. So, we practice and we repeat the life-giving over and over. We keep at it; we speak it even when we barely believe it. Our belief in the statements comes with time. The boldness of the declarations gets us out from under the pressure of the in-between.

We are now welding boldness in the form of our words and thoughts. We are actively fighting against the what-ifs and the doubts by commanding them, subject to the power of the truth. Consistency is where the victory comes. When we can continue to recognize where we have limited ourselves with the lies of doubt and fear, we will continually face the opportunity of the in-between.

There are so many lessons that we learn when we allow ourselves to be present in the in-between. Lessons about who we are and who we are not, and perhaps the most important lesson we can learn: who we were created to be. There is something so freeing about truly knowing who we are. My experiences in the in-between have absolutely shown me the reality of who I was trying to be versus who God created me to be. That knowledge has become my litmus test when I am facing the weight of life and the self-doubt I still battle. We keep moving forward toward the prize of this life through bold choices.

Boldness is the key to living the life we dream of, living the life that defeat has incorrectly taught us will never be a reality. I encourage you today, instead of wandering through your own what-ifs, to embrace the opportunities to be bold. Embrace the in-between and the power we yield when we speak life and encouragement, especially over ourselves. Boldness will always provide you with the opportunity to be stronger. Boldness is where your faith is encouraged and your voice is empowered.

ABOUT THE CONTRIBUTOR

Hi, I am Joy England; I am the Founder of Advocates in Action, The Pink Marker Movement, and The Influentials Podcast. I have been blessed to "be" many things in my career; the ones who hold the truest in this season are writer, creator, and minister.

As an entrepreneur and a proud mother of two phenomenal young men, "has been an adventure, to say the least. I have learned some valuable lessons through the years, and I spend my time penning those adventures through blogs, books, podcasts, and ministry.

"We go through to bring others through" is my motto and focus for much of my writing. What is the point of all the struggles, heartaches, accomplishments, and accolades if we do not share the insight with people?

As an ordained minister, I commit myself to leading with love. I truly believe that all things are possible—not easy, but possible with love. I use this perspective to do advocacy. Advocacy requires humility boldness, and bravery.

I pray that through my work and words, the world can see a little brighter the light that is Jesus. —Xoxox, Joy M.

Bits of Her Heart...

Joy M. England

We go through
to bring others
through.

FUN FACT...

Through her work with Advocates in Action, Joy is on a mission to be the voice for the reform we desperately need in the welfare system and with women's equity, especially in the Church.

SECTION 3

WE ARE JOY SEEKERS

FINDING OUR SUPERPOWER
by Chrisie Canny

FLIPPING OFF FEAR AND DOUBT
by Danni Heuer

FOUR SONGS AWAY
by Reilly Carroll

THE LENS YOU CHOOSE TO LOOK AT THE WORLD THROUGH CHANGES YOUR EXPERIENCE IN IT.

FINDING OUR SUPERPOWER

BY CHRISIE CANNY

This chapter is dedicated to all the moms and dads out there. Please don't despair or give up hope. Your child doesn't need the best things in the world; they need you, your love to help them grow, and your example to teach them to be kind and compassionate. There are days that life will be challenging, there will be days when you don't know how you will survive but know you will get through them. You are not alone in your doubt so reach out and lift another and you will see you will be lifted too! You can and you will!

It was 2013, and I was attending the Atlanta Gift Show. My old company had a wholesale space there, and I was going solo to work the show. I had never flown alone before in my life. I always had a friend next to me to keep me sane. See, I was terrified of flying. I needed to ask for water as soon as I saw the steward. I'd be sweating, wanting to puke, loaded up on Dramamine, talking a mile a minute, and getting ready to stab someone with a plastic fork. You get it. I was scared until the day I flew home from that show, and I met someone who beat me by a mile. Hell, ten miles!

The route from Atlanta to New York City is known for turbulence. So, the fasten your seatbelt light was destined to come on. That light came on, and so did the pilot as he prepped us with an "It's going to be bad" speech. Well, bad was an understatement. As my rear end lifted off my seat, and I was preparing myself for death, my attention turned to the young man next to me. He was sweating and in full panic mode, gripping the chair in front of him, crying, and muttering that he didn't want to die. And in two seconds something snapped in me as I turned into a fearless flier and talked that kid off the ledge. We became airborne about ten times that flight. I comforted him and made him laugh all while I remained peaceful and calm. We made it safely to New York, hugged goodbye, and I noted that doing for others really helps you do for yourself. That sentiment has always been a part of me. Helping others calms me and makes me stronger. Helping someone pushes me through my own fears. Helping others—that's my superpower. And I believe it's yours too. You just have to tap into it so you too can become fearless!

I realized when I flip my focus to helping someone else, that in turn it will help me, and I can get through anything going on in my life. Even when I just share my stories about work, or home, or I share the doubts in my head, it helps someone else feel less alone. The one superpower we all have is sharing. It's a two-way street after all. I share a lot, and others share their journeys with me. So many times, just by connecting in this way, I have felt encouraged and inspired to keep going. Even when life hit me with some enormous things, it was my community of loved ones that gave me strength. They gave me the ability to see the good in the bad and to turn lemons into lemonade.

NORMAN AND HIS SUPERPOWERS

I can't say the word lemon and not think of my dad, Norman. He had a huge lemon tree on his porch in Brooklyn that he loved. And even though it wasn't very fruitful, he never gave up on it. He was like that with everything. Norman had the ability to make everyone feel special, beautiful, and talented. He taught me to live life to the fullest—smell the flowers, give accolades, surround yourself with friends, help strangers, love your family… the list goes on and on. My dad was an inventor and creator, and from him I inherited my beliefs that life is great, there is always a solution, and there is good in everyone.

Finding Our Superpower

I lost my dad in 2003 to lung cancer. The strong man he always was—who could roller skate down the block with one foot in the air at age sixty-five, the man who could garden all day, the man who could hit a black diamond on the slopes and beat a twenty-year-old, was now relinquished to lying in bed all day. The cancer deteriorated him to nothing, robbing us all of that strong man he was, robbed him of his love for food, and robbed us of our walks in the botanical gardens. I fucking hate cancer.

Norman really was adored. His wake was packed, and, in my opinion, it wasn't long enough. I could have stayed for hours because I wanted to continue hearing all of the amazing stories people were sharing with me. He was even more incredible than I thought. And then see... there's that superpower again that we all have—everyone used their stories with Norman to heal our broken hearts and ease their own pain. Sharing is healing; sharing is (as corny as it sounds) caring.

In loss, we must keep those we love alive by continuing to share their memories and stories. My daughter, Cate, was not even three years old when Norman died, but you wouldn't know it. I know he lives on in her as she knows him through me, and she definitely inherited his people skills. She knows his likes, his cooking skills, and his charm. When Dad died, monarch butterflies started to appear in my life. If you doubt the connection between myself, Cate, and Norman you needed to witness the day my little dyslexic girl... just like Norman... had to go for a brain scan. She was so scared as we walked toward the office. I assured her she would be okay, that Grandpa was with her, and she just needed to think of him. And then not two seconds later, in the middle of Brooklyn in a cement jungle, a monarch butterfly not only appeared in front of us, it landed on Cate and kissed her on the nose. I can vividly remember the feeling, my heart stopping as I looked around because it seemed to vanish. My little girl looked at me with the biggest smile and said, "I got this!" And she did.

THE POWER OF FAITH, COMMUNITY, AND STRENGTH

I'm certain if you look around, you will witness these little miracles too. After this little miracle, my faith grew even more. But this was not my first trip with faith. I learned all about the power of faith, community, and strength when I was twenty-two years old. I was pregnant and married, and I had no idea what was coming. My husband, Mike, and I had nothing. We had no money in the bank, no health insurance, nowhere to live, no furniture to sit on... nothing. But our family, friends, and strangers showered us with house gifts, showered us with baby gifts, and helped us find a cheap apartment ($650 for a two-bedroom!!). It was amazing how generous everyone was. We could focus on learning to become adults, a married couple, and soon-to-be parents. It was time to grow up fast!

Our son needed to be evicted from my womb as he was huge, I was huge, and he was a week late. I was hooked up to Pitocin from the early morning, just waiting for him to come. The contractions had started around two in the afternoon. I endured them a few hours and then asked for the magical epidural. I felt no pain after it. I could only see the contractions on the machine. He was just starting to descend but everyone felt nothing would happen until the morning.

As I was just closing my eyes to go to sleep a nurse ran into our room and to the machine. She started to move the heart monitor across my belly that was tracking the baby's heartbeat. Then she went back to the readout, then back to the monitor on my belly in a frenzy. Then there was another nurse, and another nurse, and Mike and I were just screaming, "What is going on?!!!" The next thing I knew there was a team of surgeons rushing in and an oxygen mask placed over my tear-streaked face. They told us our baby's heart had stopped, and I needed an emergency C-section. I was prepped for surgery and rolled into the emergency room.

The anesthesiologist sedated me, and tied me down to the table like Jesus on the cross. I prayed for my child's life, and for strength. This wasn't what we signed up for. I was just a baby myself. Mike sat next to me holding my head as I went in and out of consciousness. I was trying so hard to stay awake to see our son raised out of me. The OR was eerily quiet, the lights were spinning, and then I heard him. Everyone was relieved, our baby was alive and breathing. But I wasn't relieved. I felt something was wrong. I looked to my left as Mike held our son with the biggest smile, that smile I fell in love with. He stood tall and proud for his first moment as a father. And then they whisked our son away to check all of his vitals, and I gave in to my drugs and slept again.

I woke up to Mike and my mom talking around me in the recovery room. I was shaking so bad, and I was so nauseous I couldn't open my eyes. I finally found the strength to speak.

Finding Our Superpower

"Where is our son? Is he alive? Is he okay? Something is wrong!"

And Mike stood by me, with all the color drained from his face and said, "There is something wrong, they just don't know what it is. He has been put on oxygen. They think there is something wrong with his heart, and we are waiting for a specialist." And with my own heart crushed I was back out of it yet again.

The next time I came through I was being shaken awake by Mike. I was in a room now, and a hazy figure of a stranger stood in front of me. His head was low as he started to explain what was going on with our son. I tried as hard as I could to grasp it. There was something wrong with his heart... no oxygen going to his body... his heart was backwards... he needed open heart surgery... he needed to be transferred right away via ambulance to NYU... your husband will go with him... they are taking you now so you can see him. It was just too much to take. Days later, I would finally grasp his diagnosis—transposition of the greater arteries.

And just a few hours after my C-section, and still being so sick, the nurses stood me up as I screamed in pain, and they got me into a wheelchair. From darkness into the light of the ICU with its beeps and alarms, I went to see my son. There was an air of pity and sadness as those amazing nurses knew the journey our big boy was about to go through. The table he was on was taller than I could see sitting. I mustered as much strength as I could to stand to see him before he was taken from me. I rose, afraid to touch him, and my heart sank to levels I had not yet ever experienced. To have so much love for someone in such a short time, and to have so much grief in an instant. The room started to spin, the sweat started to pour down me, and I had to sit. I couldn't even stand to see my child as guilt overcame me. I felt I was already losing the race of being a good mother.

Back in my room, writhing in pain, I once again struggled to stay coherent. Mike stood before me with papers that needed to be filled out before our son was transferred. His name needed to be decided. Mike was adamant that he did not want our son to be named after him. And through tears I looked at him and said, "Mike, he needs to have your name for strength." So, our nine-pound eleven-and-a-half-ounce boy was named Michael Shane.

I kissed Mike goodbye. He looked heartbroken and exhausted. I just wanted to make everything better for him. I composed myself, sat up higher, told him I loved him, smiled, and assured him I would be okay. I needed to be taken off of his worry list as I knew he was devastated leaving me in my condition.

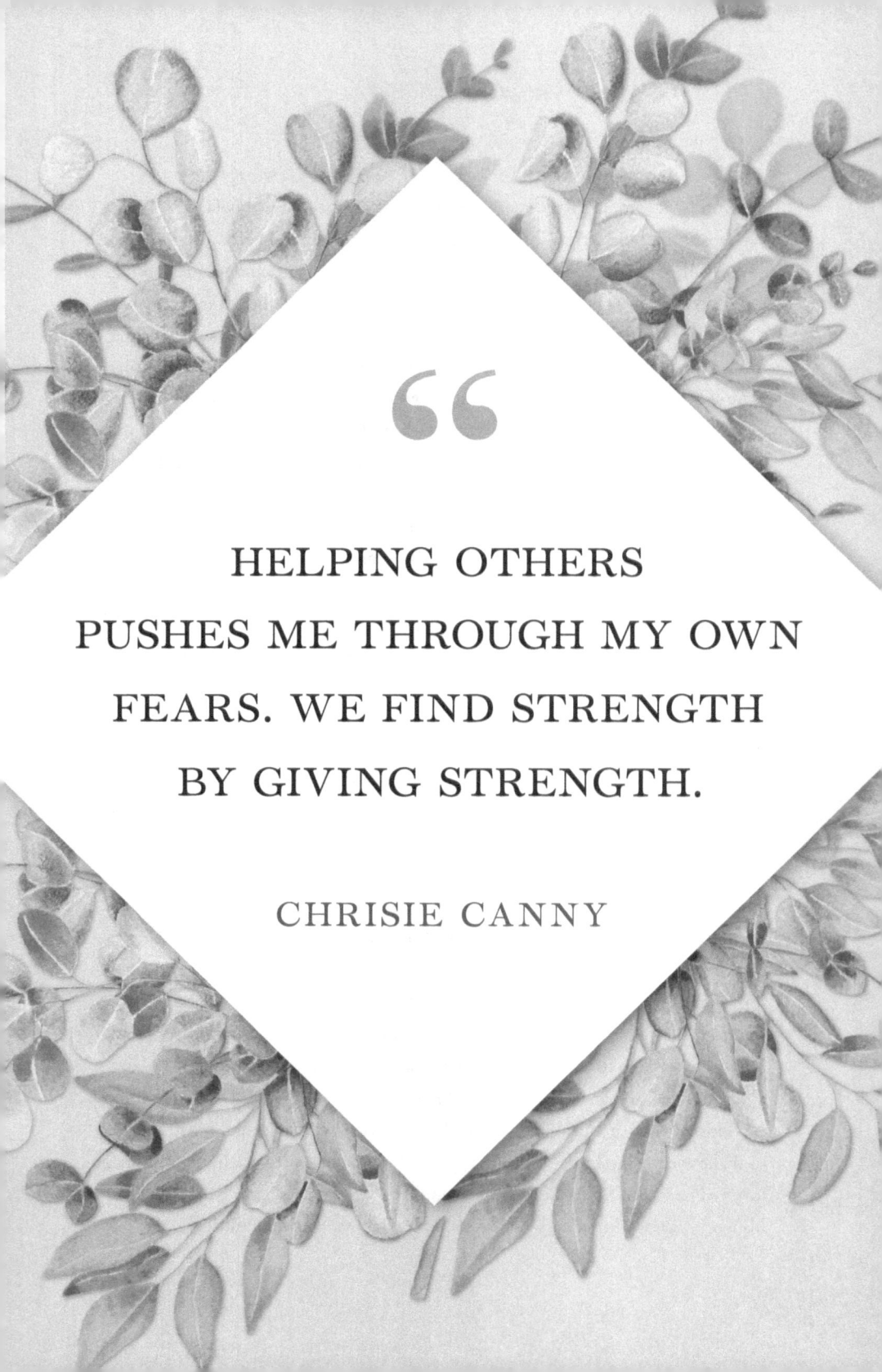

> "
>
> HELPING OTHERS PUSHES ME THROUGH MY OWN FEARS. WE FIND STRENGTH BY GIVING STRENGTH.
>
> — CHRISIE CANNY

Finding Our Superpower

And when he was gone, and I was on my own in my room with an empty bed next to me, I cried and prayed, "God If you need to take him today, I can endure the pain but after tomorrow please let him be mine and let him be saved."

TOUGHNESS AS A SUPERPOWER

My mom arrived back later Saturday to help me look a little nicer when Mike got back. She brushed my hair, helped me put on the nice PJs, put some makeup on me, and we started walking around the corridor. The goal was set—I wanted out as soon as possible. We both understood I could not be away from Michael Shane. We were going to make me look as good as possible to help Mike feel at ease and help me get the hell out of there.

My mom Mary Ellen, aka Nana, is a tough lady. She has instilled this toughness in me. She is someone you want on your side. She will go out of her way for any friend and would probably kill for her family. As we walked, she told me how when Michael Shane was taken out of the OR, she was waiting outside those doors. She sensed something was off. (Okay, she may have trust issues about people doing their jobs correctly.) Anyway, she followed closely behind and watched his assessment from outside the nursery. She watched as the nurses evaluated him and watched as the doctor came over. She looked at their faces as they spoke, and she watched their body language and saw that they were in disagreement. The nurse was saying something was wrong with Michael Shane and the doctor was refusing, insisting he was fine. Nana knew she had to defend my son. The doctor walked out of the nursery and my mother pinned her right to the wall demanding to know what that nurse was saying. My mother pressed the doctor further, "If that nurse with twenty years of experience thinks there is something wrong with my grandson, then I want him moved to ICU now. Don't think because you are a doctor that you know more than her!"

And the doctor walked back into the nursery and had him moved to the ICU. They gave him much-needed oxygen, and this saved his life, and they made the determination to call in a specialist. That doctor could not look us in the eye later that afternoon, but hopefully she learned to listen to the people with more experience moving forward. So basically, Nana saved our son's life that day. I was never so grateful for her being her as I was in that moment.

About thirty-two hours after having a C-section I was released. It was Mother's Day after all, and I would have signed myself out if they didn't release me. I was still in a lot of pain and nauseous, but I needed to be with my son. I pulled up my big girl panties, combed my hair, and put on lipstick and a smile filled with determination. My staples and incision had different plans as I can remember screaming and wincing over every pothole we hit as we traveled from Brooklyn to NYU. If you have been on the FDR here in New York, you can only imagine my groans.

Upon arrival to NYU, I was greeted with a wheelchair and rolled up to the NICU, the neonatal intensive care unit. The NICU was a small, rectangular room flooded with the rhythm of monitors and alarms but yet eerily quiet as the parents prayed over their children. Most of the babies were in incubators and premature. Michael was immediately to the right of the entrance. I had no problem finding him as our parents were surrounding him, and he was at least triple the size of every other baby in the NICU. Our family was praying, looking to see if he had any signs of brain loss from the lack of oxygen, and looking for a glimmer of hope. I looked at my son who had been taken away from me. His swollen hands were in diapers from line attempts, he had an IV in his head, he was laid out like a frog that you would find in biology class, and he had monitors all over him that led to a machine with all of his vitals.

I took it all in and found my voice to say his name, "Michael Shane, it's Mommy. I am here." And with that, he opened his eyes and seemed to search for me. Everyone around me gasped with relief as he finally seemed aware. The silent tears poured out of all of our eyes and then sobs from the pit of my soul hit me uncontrollably. I collapsed into my father's arms for what seemed like forever. Was it fear or gratitude? I am still not sure... but I knew God was on our side.

A YOUNG DOCTOR AND SCHEDULING A MIRACLE

The next day we met with someone from the surgical team. We crammed into the small hallway as a young doctor started to explain everything to us. He went into a long explanation of rerouting and moving ventricles. Of course, it was in much more detail than that, but I was totally clouded over thinking, *How old is this kid who is going to be assisting in mending my son's broken heart?* From everything he said, we got this—it was a very long surgery, and success was not guaranteed. And we shouldn't be offended by Dr. Colvin, the lead surgeon, when he came to talk to us, because he was not a people person. But he was here to save our son's life.

Dr. Colvin came to talk to us after that, and it made me appreciate that young Doogie Howser spoke to us first. Doogie was gentler and kinder in his approach. Dr. Colvin made us realize how dire the situation was. It was a new surgery, only about ten years old, and it could have complications. We were told he may need more surgeries down the road and that he may never play sports or be in the military. We also didn't know if he suffered from oxygen loss and if he would have learning disabilities. Our hearts were heavy with uncertainty. We had faith and the support of so many. We were blessed—we even had friends who created a divine prayer circle at church. I believe in the power of prayer—it gave us strength during this devastating time.

Surgery was scheduled for Tuesday, and we were told to stay home. In the evening as we sat around on our tenth pot of tea, the phone rang. It was young Doogie Howser. The surgery went well, and Michael was stable and sedated. His big size was an advantage. Yes, the next forty-eight hours were critical, but the mend to his heart was a success. His blood was flowing to all four chambers of his heart and circulating in his body correctly. We hung up, praised God, and spread the good news to our family and friends.

We made our way into NYU to see Michael Shane on Wednesday. It was yet another dull, rainy, cold day. That was all it seemed to have been since the morning I was induced. The weather fit our feelings; it was May, and we should have been celebrating that, but winter had not yet left us.

We ran into Dr. Doogie Howser in the hallway that day and stopped to thank him for the miracle the doctors performed. He told us how the team was preparing for yet another little boy to go into surgery. He asked us to pray for him as he was smaller than Michael and he had a hole in his heart. We said we would and went in to see our boy with a prayer in our heart for that other child.

We walked into a huge recovery room with those damn beeps and alarms and oxygen running. There we found him on a regular stretcher with a clear cake dish on his head. His body bloodied and stained with pre surgery wash and a scar down what seemed like his whole body. It went from the top of his chest all the way to his belly button. There were IVs and monitors all over him as he laid there motionless.

We stayed on the side of the bed as much as they allowed us that day as we waited for him to be able to step back down to NICU. There was a lot of waiting, a lot of praying, a lot of reactions to his oxygen levels, but we somehow knew he would be okay. We left him that night on that stretcher with a little more hope in our hearts. We walked into the hallway with smiles on our faces.

On our way out, we again ran into Doogie Howser, this time with his head against the wall, fists in a ball, with tears running down his face. I looked at him and said, "The other baby didn't make it did he?" He could only shake his head no. The loss for such a young doctor was not yet something he had learned to cope with. I will forever hold on to this moment for the rest of my life. I was so happy that my child was alive but mourned so deeply for the baby's mother and that child. I kept thinking how that could have been Michael. It made me realize how close to death he was, appreciating his life even more. Why did God choose him to live and the other boy to die? I promised at that moment to help him fulfill his purpose in life.

Mike and I mourned that little baby and provided the strength that we each needed. We were such babies who had to grow up in a matter of days. It wasn't just being a young parent; it was being a parent to a child who was sick. But our love for each other and the love of our family rallied us through the days. Finally, a week after being born, Michael Shane had his oxygen removed. Also, he was eating, I got to hold him, and the skies finally seemed a little brighter. He was living up to his newly minted nickname *Miracle Mike* as the days passed.

A MISSION TO GIVE BACK

Michael turns twenty-eight this year. He gets an echocardiogram and an EKG annually to make sure his arteries and ventricles grow with his body. We worry every year as it approaches that he will need surgery again. But every year since, he has received a great report. He was granted permission to play sports as a child and a teenager and never had any of the restrictions they warned us about. When he told us he wanted to be a fireman, we worried that he may not pass the physical because of his heart surgery. But all six feet two inches of him trained like crazy, and he passed. He became a member of the FDNY in 2021. I may have secretly hoped he wouldn't pass as it's such a dangerous job, but I always knew God placed him here to save others. Michael was always a child who couldn't understand why people didn't get along and he wanted the world to be better. First, he was an EMT, and now he runs into fires. People ask how I sleep at night, but I know God has his back, and I know he is fulfilling his purpose.

Like Michael, I have always been a people person since I was little. I loved making others smile, even when I had my own stuff going on. But ever since this experience, I vowed to always do whatever I could to help strengthen another struggling human being. I saw how making others feel better in turn made my own problems seem less intense. This experience as a new mom brought me closer to my husband and closer to our families. It was a gift that helped us appreciate life and made us realize that helping others, the way we were helped, is so easy to do. We all have the superpower of giving strength to others, and this helps us find strength within ourselves.

I can't tell you how much living this way has strengthened me. It is my mission to give back and help others whenever possible. And guess what I've realized? It's ALWAYS possible. You find strength by giving strength. Even when I was diagnosed with breast cancer in December 2021, I knew I was going to need strength leading up to my double mastectomy, so I turned my attention toward others and used this superpower to bring people together for fundraising! At Christmas I asked my friends to lift up a waitress with an extra big tip! We surprised her with a tip of $1,000! I then asked everyone to donate a bracelet to the nurses, (obviously you know how I feel about nurses) patients, and staff at Sloan Kettering, where I was having my surgery. Because of my community rallying together, I packed over four hundred bracelets, hand wrote over four hundred thank you cards (with all of my friends' names who donated), then walked in on surgery day and gifted others. Once again, through praying, giving strength, and helping others do good, I was able to walk into surgery with a smile on my face.

As I sat here and figured out how I wanted to end this chapter, a thought came to me, which might be morbid for some. Me? Nah! I want to live my life so that my grandchildren enjoy my funeral. I want them to hear from complete strangers about how wonderful their grandma was. I want them to hear tales of how I helped others through a tough time in their lives, how I may have inspired them to start a business or maybe even how they started a fundraiser. This is the person

I want to be. I want them to enjoy my wake in the way I enjoyed my dad's so they can treasure the tales for years. I want to be a hero in their eyes.

So, how about you? The next time you are on a plane, and you see someone who needs some love, will you give it? The next time you hear of a young mother who needs financial help, will you help? When a friend loses a loved one, will you let her cry and pray for her? When you hear a mom stressed out and worried that she is failing, will you fill her with all of your mom fails so she knows she is not alone? How do you want to be remembered?

Go dust off that cape, give yourself a high five, and be the hero that changes the world.

ABOUT THE CONTRIBUTOR

Wife, mother, serial entrepreneur, inventor and FUNdriser Chrisie Canny is a Brooklyn native and CEO of Vented In Brooklyn®, a company that designs and sells aromatherapy diffuser jewelry and products with a mission helping you Feel Good, Smell Good and Do Good! After losing her father Norman to cancer years ago, she made it her mission to help cancer patients know that they are not alone and to raise money for as many organizations as possible.

Chrisie believes in sharing her life's "lessons" to help others and surrounds herself with other amazing women who want to help others, who leave jealousy behind, and who realize that we all can succeed! She interviews different women and business owners weekly on her Vented Uplift series on IGTV Live to help spread their stories.

Chrisie left Brooklyn after forty-seven years and made that first hop over the bridge to Staten Island three years ago. She lives with her husband Mike, her FDNY firefighter son Michael, and her college graduate daughter Cate. Family, music, and hosting parties and fundraisers are their priorities!

Bits of Her Heart...

Chrisie Canny

Just be nice!

FUN FACT...

Chrisie almost got on Shark Tank ten years ago. She got cut just four weeks before filming in California. She was chosen out of over 40,000 contestants!

8

FLIPPING OFF DOUBT AND FEAR

BY DANNI HEUER

This chapter is dedicated to those who have ever cringed at a part of themselves, fought an inner critic, or carried around someone else's impression of themselves—even after high school. I hope my story reminds you that you can use all of this as fuel to find courage to do the things that frighten you!

I also dedicate this chapter to my Pop Pop, who I told to be patient because I had big plans. I know you have been cheering me on and, yes, waiting; I feel you. And to my high school gym teacher whose relentless, exhausting attempts to find my inner athlete helped me instead to find the courage to do the things that frighten me, to find my passion for lifting the souls of others, and to bring my very first story to print.

I read somewhere that each of us has approximately twelve social interactions a day. The way I see it, we get about 360 opportunities a month, 4320 times in a year to make a difference in the life of another human being.

With each interaction we have with another human being we are gifted with an opportunity to connect and to make a difference in the life of another, even if for a moment. In the busy, often mundane, ordinary days of our lives, we often miss the magnitude of this opportunity.

There are countless stories of people who have decided to change the course of their lives simply because of the smile or kind words from someone in a grocery store line, at the bank, or at a fast food checkout. There are even more stories of people touched by the mentorship and guidance of a person who has helped catapult them to a new level of achievement or success. And sadly, there are too many stories of people who have felt the weight of another person's unkindness or cruel remarks, even coming from a seemingly normal interaction, that resulted in unfathomable consequences.

We often don't consider the impression we can have on another human spirit, even in what looks like a fleeting or inconsequential moment in time. But each of us has the power to change a life. The words we choose, the sentences we string together, the energy we carry with us all have the power to ignite reactions in others. Knowing that our words can either lift a soul or crush a spirit has been something that fascinates me. I believe that each of us on this planet is emboldened with this great power—and with that, great responsibility—but the question is, are we using this gift?

What inspired my awakening to this great power, you may ask. To that I credit some compelling interactions with a gym teacher in high school back in the 1980s. But first, I'll take you back to the more recent September of 1998.

I can still feel the sun fighting to shine through the tree-lined street. I was biking in a 300-mile marathon. As I was admiring the adorable brownstones on either side of me, I realized I had lost the pack and was getting a rare moment completely alone, which felt great after the last three days. I remember this amazing feeling of accomplishment at that moment, while also feeling the sadness that comes when something is ending. I also remember being all alone on that street and feeling really emotional at that moment. At first, I thought I might burst into tears, but then my face did the exact opposite. I found myself smiling instead. Smiling really big. And probably looking a bit goofy, biking alone on this street with the hugest smile that people who are alone don't often wear, but I didn't care. I felt the weight of this accomplishment in my chest.

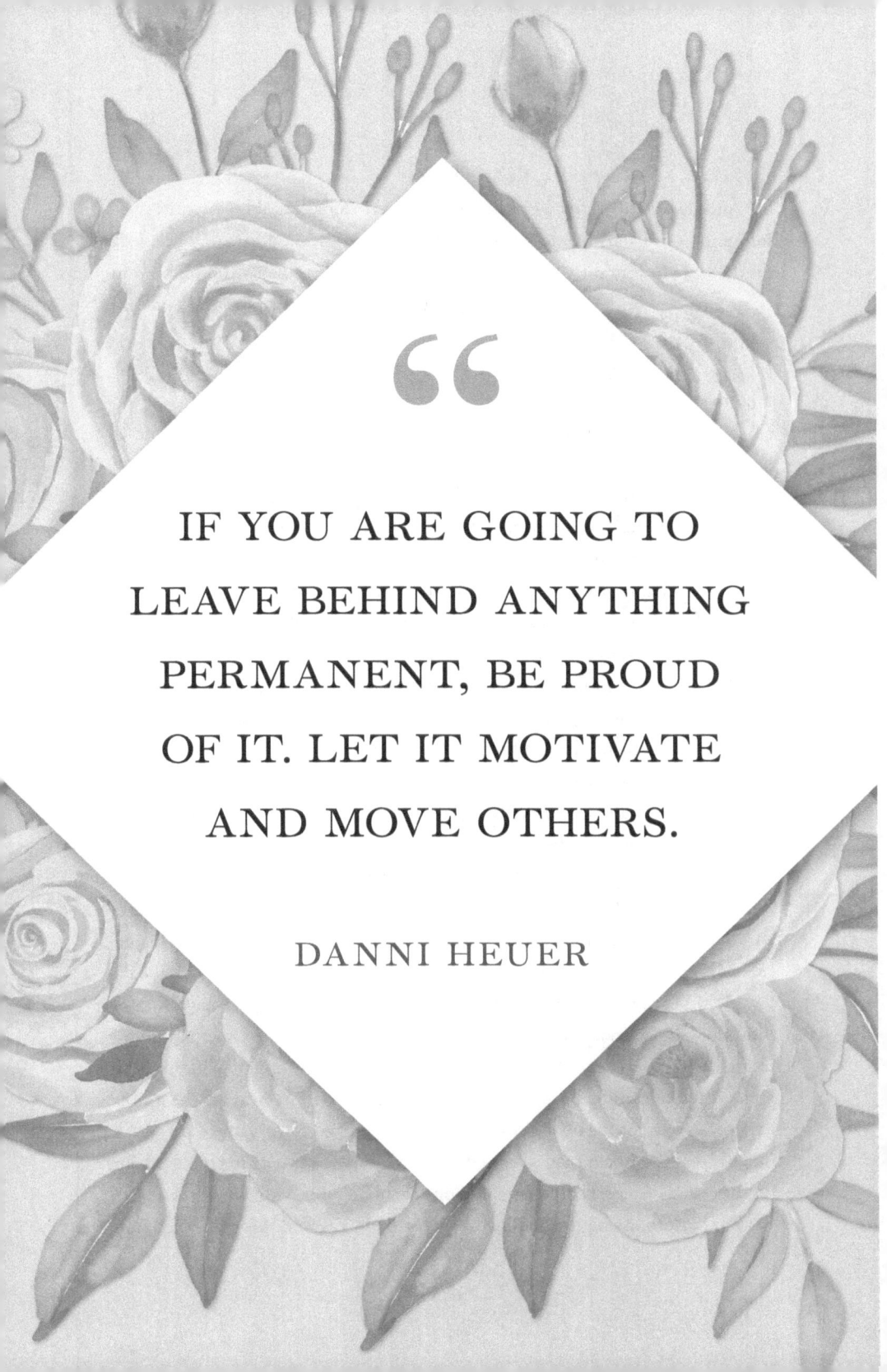

> IF YOU ARE GOING TO LEAVE BEHIND ANYTHING PERMANENT, BE PROUD OF IT. LET IT MOTIVATE AND MOVE OTHERS.
>
> DANNI HEUER

I did it. I freaking did it. Aha! Yes! Yes! Yes!!

And they didn't think I could. Heck, I didn't think I could. My smile grew into a full-on, hands-in-the-air, solo cheer to myself, while I carefully balanced on the beaten, very dirty road bike that just carried me almost 300 miles from Boston to New York City. Then I flipped the world the bird and yelled out loud, "Take that Mr. Vorp!"

"Who's My. Vorp?" you may ask. Well, that requires a trip back to my high school years from 1985 to 1989.

High school is that glorious period of your life when you feel perfectly imperfect. I imagine that even the most popular, well liked, academically inclined student would admit that it's an interesting four years. There is so much going on inside of our heads; we are trying to figure out the world during this phase of our lives, and even figuring out where we belong in it. I did not belong in first period gym class—that I knew for certain. I don't think anyone should be in first period gym class. In fact, I still feel strongly about this. Who makes students take gym first thing in the morning? Who wants to feel sweaty all day? And in the '80s in North Jersey at the peak of the teased, permed hair phase, you can imagine how risky sweat and humidity was to my "look." With my exceptionally fine hair, every piece of hair on my head was strategically held up, defying gravity and seriously at risk of not making it past first period gym class. In fact, I remember relying heavily on that fabulous grape-scented, all-powerful Aussie Sprunch Spray to maintain my look. That spray is a literal time machine. If I were to smell that hair spray right now, it would immediately transport me back to high school.

But that would mean I had to face gym class again, as well as a gym teacher who I was convinced planned gym activities geared toward my personal inabilities. Mr. Vorp, my gym teacher in high school, apparently mistook my dislike for any physical activity that ruined my perfectly sculpted hair as a personal dislike of him and what he stood for as a gym teacher. We did not hit it off. Our relationship in high school was very bumpy, at least to me. It didn't help that I did not have an athletic bone in my body. No exaggeration here. You can even ask the judges at cheer tryouts, or the poor girl who stood opposite me as we warmed up with a friendly toss at softball tryouts. But I digress. Why an unathletic girl even tried out for softball is an entirely different question. Thankfully Mr. Vorp wasn't the coach!

But back to my high school nemesis. I strongly disliked this man, rued him, and cursed him under my breath. In my eyes he deserved my full-on teenage eye rolling hatred. He called me out in gym class, announcing it to my classmates when I stunk at something—which was about daily. He commented on my lack of form when we ran laps (apparently, I ran like I was asleep), and he even sent me down to the principal when he felt I wasn't putting my all into a gym activity. He even did this more than once! As a straight A, National Honor Society member, and honor roll student, my visits to the principal only occurred when the main office staff got a request for a tutor, needed a school tour for a new student, or to try to get me to rat out my classmates. Don't even ask. I was a vault.

And yet, Mr. Volp had to take the one thing that revealed my insecurities and make sure as many people as possible knew, even the administration. So off to the principal I went "to explain myself."

What did he want me to say?

So, I told the principal, "Mr. Vorp hates me, picks on me, and is making me feel very insecure." I remember the principal playing mediator between Mr. Vorp and me. I also remember thinking, "How childish of this grown man, to keep this up in front of our principal, saying that I had an attitude? Me? He had the attitude."

Fast forward thirty years, and now as a parent of my own children, I will admit yes, I was feeling incredibly insecure, and it definitely felt like he was picking on me, but I doubt that the emotion I was feeling from him was hate at all. But, at the time, it was the only thing that made sense. He must hate me. His sole purpose in life was to reveal my feelings of gym inadequacies for my entire class to see.

As a result, gym was my least favorite part of the day. I know some students look forward to the gym period, relishing the tiny space of freedom that comes with the break from learning. Not me. I lost sleep worrying about being picked last for the next day's team activity. I dreaded having my athletic abilities on display. One vivid memory of my gym abilities being displayed involved a dodgeball to the head triggering the bouncing of my head into the cement gym wall. Ignoring the game and talking with my girlfriend in the last row of students was my strategy for not being noticed in the game. Huge fail. Another awful gym memory came from my odd inability to kick the ball during the kickball tournament. Apparently striking out in kickball is rare. But as I can attest, it is not unheard of.

I doubt that Mr. Vorp would have had sympathy for me had he known my high level of gym anxiety. He did not appear to have a soft side.

IN MY TWENTIES

As the years passed after high school, memories of gym certainly didn't consume my thoughts. But I also didn't realize how much those memories were clinging to me. At some point, without my realizing it, those memories became catalysts for how I would stretch and challenge myself in the future. The first time I noticed this was in my twenties when a friend and I completed a three-day bicycle ride from Boston to NYC, raising money for AIDS, while biking almost 300 miles, sleeping in tents (that bikers had to set up on their own, in the dark, after a long day on the bike), and showering in groups in these tractors that followed us down the east coast. Remember that unathletic girl I described? Well, she did all of that. And she was unsure, scared, and determined not to be picked up by the van they called the "Sweeper".

So, while crossing into NYC on a sunny, Sunday afternoon, sunburned, exhausted, and aching all over, I suddenly yelled out, "Take that Mr. Vorp!" I nearly laughed out loud when I heard my voice say it. Ha, look at me! I was feeling pretty darn proud of myself. I was so proud that I even signed up and did that ride again the very next year.

IN MY THIRTIES

After the bike ride, it was a few years before I recall myself actively thinking about Mr. Vorp again. This time it was when I participated in a women's learn-to-surf weekend. I upped the challenge here, because I now added two fears on top of simply doing something very physical. I have a bit of a fear of the ocean and, with that, a fear of being eaten by sharks. This was going to be a challenge for me! Riding a bike is easy compared to balancing on a moving, slippery board in the middle of the scary ocean, which in my mind is filled with sea creatures waiting to eat me alive.

But on that last day of the surf weekend, after countless attempts, when I finally stood up on that board, coincidentally at the same moment my girlfriend stood up about ten feet from me, I yelled to her, "Take that Mr. Vorp," and actually balanced while flipping the middle finger of both hands. My high school girlfriend had joined me for the surf weekend, so she was familiar with Mr. Vorp and also knew that he was not one of my fond high school memories. We both laughed out loud and afterwards toasted to Mr. Vorp when we celebrated our amazing surf weekend, complete with surfing, yoga, meditation, and once again mentally flipping off my high school nemesis. Ha, he wasn't going to hold me back.

TWENTY YEARS AFTER HIGH SCHOOL

Each time I challenged myself physically, Mr. Vorp showed up in the back of my mind. I wasn't consciously thinking about him the entire time, but he continued to be this odd internal cheerleader showing up, typically right as I conquered a challenging event. Flipping him off mentally with each accomplishment was now motivating me to tackle these challenges head on and prove to myself (and to the memory of Mr. Vorp that I yelled to each time I accomplished another goal) that I was capable of doing some things that the high school version of myself probably never imagined. The girl who avoided run days with every creative excuse possible ran several 5Ks and even got to a 10K distance once. Yep. And would Mr. Vorp be surprised that I even competed in a triathlon, forcing myself back into the scary ocean, facing that fear again, but this time swimming 300 yards for one of the legs of the triathlon? It was probably the scariest thing I have ever done besides that time I hiked up the side of a waterfall in Costa Rica, and ziplined through the jungle with howler monkeys sitting in trees within an arm's reach of me. How about that, Mr. Vorp?

Ha, I even joined a summer volleyball league. Ok, I admit that was more for the social aspect, but I had to face down some very serious teams those summers. And to this day, when I rotate to the front row in volleyball, and I am eye-to-eye with a competitive parent opponent, looking through those intimidating squares in the net, I try to put on a brave face, but inside I am fifteen years old in gym class all over again! Since high school, I have faced several other scary moments that challenged me to dig into my inner athlete and competitor. I participated in a few seasons of couples tennis where my poor husband ran around that court playing his side and mine, while I reverted back to my high school ego-protecting strategy of laughing and goofing off. The ego doesn't seem to grow up like the rest of us, and it still responds like it did in those teenage years.

So, I focus on growing athletically with solo events, but I no longer avoid the social team events. I slap on a smile, embrace my inabilities, and attempt to make up the difference with tons of heart and effort. Overall, my thirty-plus years since I graduated high school have provided me with a lot of opportunities to grow and a lot of time to accept myself for all of me, even the parts I struggle to understand. I mean really, couldn't I have been given an ounce of athletic prowess please? But despite this, I have flipped off Mr. Vorp quite a lot! And, I have flipped off that voice inside me that says, "You can't do it!" so I guess I've been busy doing the things I wasn't sure I could pull off.

Oh yeah, "Watch me!"

This story does not end with me growing into a new athletic version of myself or tapping into some hidden athletic abilities that I didn't allow to surface because I was stubborn teenager. Not for a moment. I am incredibly ill-fitted for most physical events, especially those including other people. And I am the biggest scaredy-cat and the queen of fear. I was petrified doing some of those things. I almost backed out of the triathlon swim a million times, even the very moment on the sand right before I dove in.

I am still that unathletic girl. I have accepted that I won't be the fastest, the most skilled, or the one with the best form. I doggy paddled some of the ocean swim, even taking a break floating on my back for a second. But what I have come to accept and even appreciate about myself, is that I don't aspire to be the fastest or to come in first. I guess in addition to not being super athletic, I am also not very competitive. But I am really interested in seeing what I am capable of and in doing my best.

For that, I say, "Thank you, Mr. Vorp."

Now, when I am critical of myself, I am addicted to flipping off my inner critic. When my inner voice says things like, "Who do you think you are?" "You have no business doing this," "You will be laughed at," or "You aren't strong enough," I flip it off.

I also giggle a bit when I think back to how Mr. Vorp influenced this more confident version of myself, flipping off self-doubt and taking on big, scary challenges, especially those physical ones. I was convinced, for many years, that Mr. Vorp hated me, that he designed gym activities just to make me cry, and that he actually wanted me to fail. When I think of Mr. Vorp now, as an adult with kids of my own, I smile, knowing how he unknowingly impacted many choices I made since high school. And when my kids come home from school complaining

Flipping Off Doubt and Fear

that their teachers have it out for them, one even complaining about the gym teacher—yes, true story—I respond with, "I guess they see something in you that you haven't discovered yet."

You see, we all have those inner voices that tell us to stay small as these voices hide behind the façade that they are protecting us. We may see some of our interactions as attempts to call out what we fear, to uncover what we may be hiding about ourselves. We are afraid to fail, afraid to try even, because we could fail. But, since gym in the '80s, I have done my fair share of failing, falling, and climbing back up. Figuring it out and seeing what I am capable of have been some of my greatest moments.

Looking back at that teenager who hid behind excuse after excuse to not let the world see her not be good at something, I wonder what I would tell her, if I could go back in time? Would I tell her that when she grows up, she will still be scared of objects that fly at her, and that she will never figure out the whole hand-eye coordination thing? Would I tell her that it just doesn't matter in the scheme of the beautiful life she will live? Or would I instead tell her that with every interaction she has, she will get messages; she will sometimes be told things about herself. But I would tell her it's her story. Those words are only her reality if she lets them be.

In my experience, fighting other people's reality of us can follow us past those teenage years. In fact, I work with clients on this constantly. So, if you have been fighting that inner critic, or trying to make sense of comments other people said about you, try these strategies to help you be in charge of your own story!

Embrace the opportunity in the moments. You will encounter people (approximately 4,000 times a year) who may influence you and how you think and feel. Each of these interactions is an opportunity for you to internalize a moment and use it for your future. You get to choose how you use that energy. You can use it to build yourself up or tear yourself down.

Find the lesson in these experiences. If an interaction leaves you feeling challenged or is riddled with negativity, see how you can use that information to improve yourself. Maybe you can see the "truth" in the feedback. Can you apply the "Watch me," or "You haven't even seen me try yet" approach?

Use your moments to give others what they need. Can you share something that someone needs to hear to shine? I am really fond of the quote by Rumi, "Be a lamp, or a lifeboat, or a ladder." Can you be one of those for others you meet?

Remember your words are always leaving a footprint behind. Some footprints are light and hard to make out, and others are deep and leave a permanent indent. If you are going to leave behind anything permanent, be proud of it. Let it motivate and move others.

Flip off whatever is holding you back! Flip off the past, flip off the negativity, and flip off the naysayers.

ABOUT THE CONTRIBUTOR

Danni Heuer has spent the last fifteen years helping clients reach their potential, chart new journeys, and find their voices. Through her consulting and coaching on leadership, communications, and career pathing, she gets the opportunity to serve clients across the globe, in a variety of industries, and with goals that range from career impacting to life changing.

She is the also the author of the upcoming book *Joy Ride* based on her experiences coaching clients in their pursuit of careers, goals, and, ultimately, lives that bring them joy.

Her own pursuit of joy often has her baking, stalking bookstores, biking on her beach cruiser, perusing garage sales, practicing her piano skills, and teaching herself how to juggle. Danni is also a self-proclaimed, halfway decent tambourine player, and she often carries at least one tambourine with her at all times.

Bits of Her Heart...

Danni Heuer

Go for it!
If not now, when?
If not you, who?

FUN FACT...

Danni has a tribe of twelve women from high school who are like sisters to her. They call themselves The Dirty Dozen. *They have monthly lunches, annual road trips, holiday parties, and the longest messenger thread of all time.*

FOUR SONGS AWAY

BY REILLY CARROLL

This chapter is dedicated to anyone who is looking for something solid when everything around them is shifting.

When I was seven years old, I fell in love with a road. This impressive strip of black pavement stretches along the coast of the Atlantic Ocean and graces the towns it journeys through. Although I had enjoyed my summer as a seven-year-old, I was now onto my fifth move and was entering yet another school district. At such a young age I was accustomed to drastic changes. I was familiar with the strangeness I endured and had to resort to what comforted me. That comfort was Ocean Avenue. Despite constantly moving homes, I remained in proximity to the most sensational roadway in all of New Jersey. Driving southward on this road I could gaze out the window and watch the waves ebb and flow into the ocean. When I glanced in the other direction, I would see the livelihood of the towns and the residents that were fortunate enough to live on this extraordinary street.

Despite the transition into the cooler seasons, Ocean Avenue remained just as beautiful as ever. There were now fewer cars on the road and fewer pedestrians along the sidewalks. Lucky for me, I still lived roughly eight songs away. Just as life began to feel normal, I was burdened with a terrible, familiar feeling. I was now seven, and I began my first month of second grade in yet another brand-new

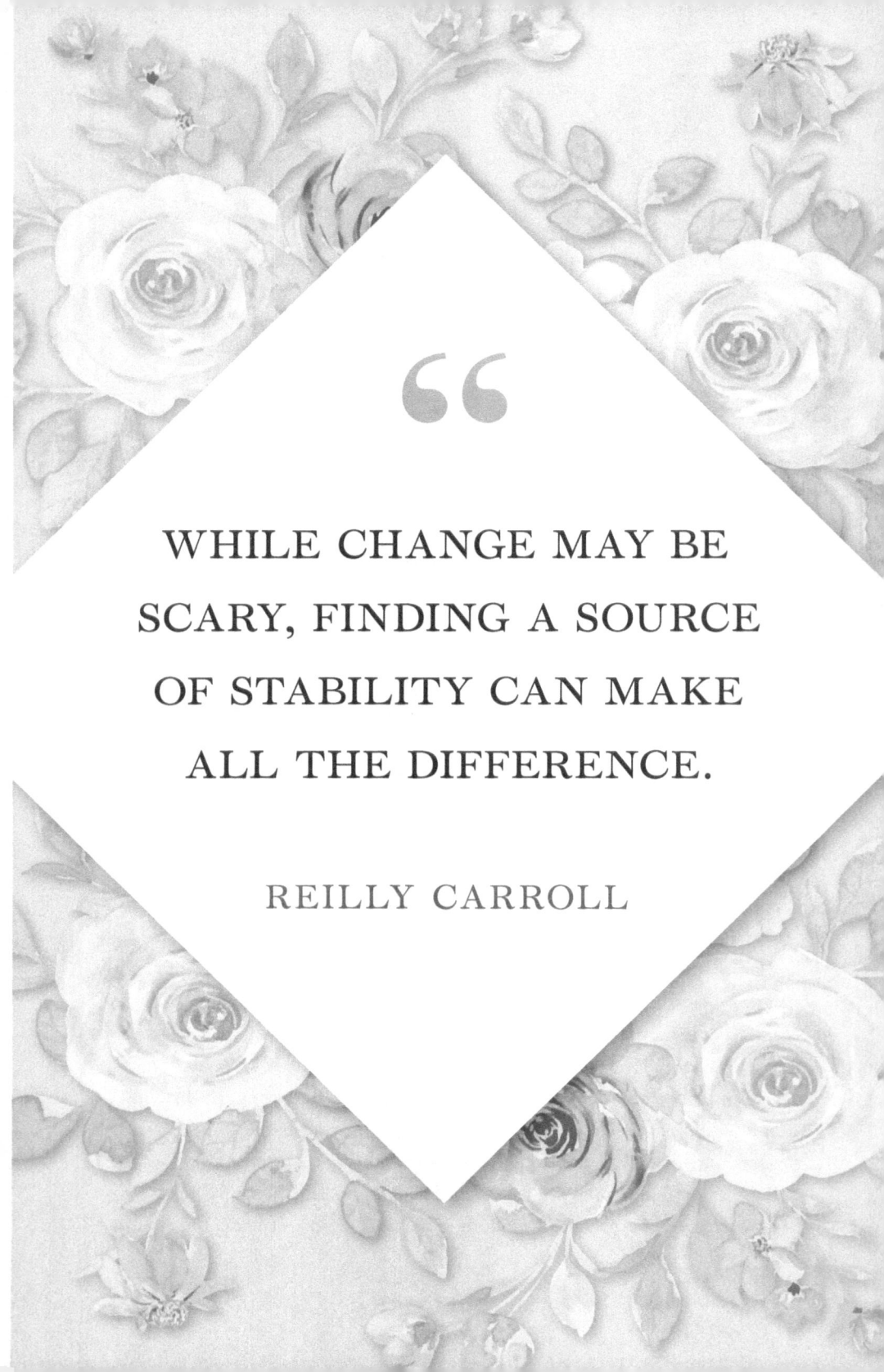

"

WHILE CHANGE MAY BE SCARY, FINDING A SOURCE OF STABILITY CAN MAKE ALL THE DIFFERENCE.

REILLY CARROLL

school. Little did I know more changes were about to take place, not just to me but to my beloved road. The month of October was not kind to either of us. We were rudely introduced to the monster, Hurricane Sandy. This monster brought hazardous conditions and complete devastation. My poor Ocean Avenue was ripped to shreds and was unrecognizable to all. The destruction of my comfort entirely overcame me. I had finally identified the true meaning of change.

At this point I had gone on to complete the fourth grade at my school. However, I was hindered by a sixth move and entered a third school district. I had to begin all over again. Now the drives to what was once my most precious road were limited. There were too many songs on the radio for me to count. The former beautiful stretch of pavement and the life around it was recovering, and I would recover too.

Life began abruptly as I entered the fifth grade with no sense of comfort to hold on to. As time went on, I began to adjust to the changes in my life. I was now entering the eighth grade at that once foreign school that I began to love. I would frequently join my mother for a car ride along Ocean Avenue and admire its rebuilt magnificence. Nevertheless, I began the moving process for the seventh time. I began my freshman year of high school living only three songs away from the exceptional roadway I now called my friend. I had overcome my hatred of change and began to respect the opportunities change had presented me.

Ocean Avenue was under construction for the majority of that year. The most familiar thing to me now had a new appearance. Even so, I realized that change was not necessarily bad. I entered into my junior year of high school, and I relocated for the eighth time. I currently live four songs away from my beloved road. Despite the changes my dearest avenue and I have undergone, we continue to prevail. We all may experience changes; it is part of the inevitable evolution of life. But while change may be scary, finding a source of stability can make all the difference. I will always look to this forty-something-mile strip of black pavement as my source of stability in an ever-changing world.

ABOUT THE CONTRIBUTOR

My name is Reilly Carroll, and I am a first-year college student. For the past eighteen years of my life, I have surrounded myself with a diverse group of people. Due to my frequent uprooting, I have grown the desire to travel the world. With an undergraduate degree in business and the ultimate goal of achieving my masters I hope to put myself in a position so that I can travel the world through my work. I plan to study abroad in Florence, Italy, my junior year as I am bilingual in the Italian language.

Bits of Her Heart...

Reilly Carroll

"Slow down, you're doin' fine. You can't be everything you wanna be before your time."—Billy Joel

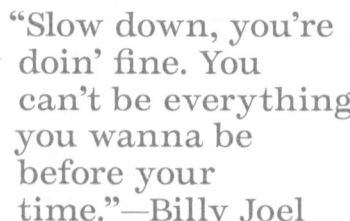

FUN FACT...

Reilly's favorite thing to do is to spend quality time with herself, that typically includes deep cleaning and reorganizing her room on a weekly basis.

SECTION 4

WE ARE KEEPERS OF LIGHT

UNWAVERING FAITH
by Jessica Varian Carroll

THE WALK HOME
by Kerry Bray

WHAT I DIDN'T KNOW HAVE BEEN MY GREATEST LESSONS
by Maureen Spataro

> WHEN PEOPLE INSPIRE US, IT IS BECAUSE THEY ARE A REFLECTION OF ALL THAT WE ARE BUT MAY HAVE FORGOTTEN.

10

UNWAVERING FAITH

BY JESSICA VARIAN CARROLL

The chapter is dedicated to those who may be losing a loved one to their final destination. May you have comfort in your final time with your loved one that they may be in peace even though you cannot possibly imagine how. Just be there to lovingly support them with the time you have left, sending them love & light all throughout their transition.

> "Our death is not an end if we can live on in our children and the younger generation. For they are us; our bodies are only wilted leaves on the tree of life."
>
> Albert Einstein

My mom, Mary Helen Gilliam, born February 4, 1963, was lying in Jersey Shore Medical Center Emergency Room on a stretcher just in from the ambulance that delivered her from the only home she's ever known on Grassmere Avenue in Wanamassa, New Jersey.

Her five-feet-nine-inch frame weighed barely one-hundred pounds. She was just fifty-seven years young. I could not believe she was calm and collected while in so much constant pain. Her unseen companion, her faith and love for God and Heaven, was right there beside her, with her. The doctors prescribed her pain medication, but it made her so ill, her body couldn't tolerate it, so she opted not to take it. God had her back.

It was late August, actually my birthday, and I reached out to Father Miguel over text. My mom was requesting last rites, a ritual practiced by Catholics before leaving this world. Having Father on speed-dial is one of the many benefits of working and volunteering at our family church for over a decade, not that I ever needed to use it before. Father answered my call and was on his way; my mom was immediately relieved.

Earlier that day my sister Tara, my brother Tim, and I were all in her small bedroom on Grassmere surrounding her with love. That bedroom was her parents' bedroom before it became hers. She wasn't doing well. Her words were hard to hear, her voice slow and shaky, but her stance was still clear as she had the talk with us on how to take care of all the kids and how to keep a close relationship with our aunts and uncles, our friends, and of course each other. Taking care of people was always my mom's biggest concern. She'd literally give the hamburger she just got to a complete stranger or run home to grab blankets for a man living on the side of the road. No pomp or circumstance, no cameras or fanfare surrounding her, she wanted just the opposite really. An angel, who fought her own demons like we all do, with her heart of gold shone like no other.

My grandmother, her mother, was the matriarch, and when she departed the world that role defaulted to my mom. My mother loved her four brothers madly. Each one of them was so different and required different forms of communication, and she kept in touch. Bob, Mike, Joe, and Ted always knew where home was: right there on the back porch of Grassmere.

This small bedroom, where we stood that day shoulder to shoulder, contained all her worldly possessions. No jewelry, (well just the gold cross around her neck and her small gold earrings), no makeup, no pocketbooks. She had a few pairs of jeans, two pairs of sneakers, a couple sweatshirts, and a small drawer of shirts along with a few sentimental photos, and some keepsakes from my father, us (her children), and her grandchildren. Oh, and, of course, an address book of the people she cared for. She was known for writing them each notes but never having a stamp. And her most recent treasure, the hundreds of cards that were sent to her from loved ones and strangers from all over the States.

She was asked by a doctor in the hospital at one point during her illness, if

"

WE WASTE SO MUCH TIME KEEPING UP WITH OUR STUFF. MY MOM WAS PROOF WE JUST DON'T NEED IT ALL.

JESSICA VARIAN CARROLL

she was to go home, who would take care of her? She proudly held up the stacks of cards she kept with her and said, "These people will."

She was in the literal end stages of her life having everything that was important to her in that very room of her home. It all boiled down to the people she loved, not much more than that. Material items meant very little to her—she lived that way her whole life. Always giving more than she had, she lived by following her faith, taking care of others, and putting others first.

For a family that doesn't show emotion or cry, on this day, forever etched in my heart, there was no holding back, and trust me we tried. She was at peace and doing the best she could to comfort us. We understood what she was doing, but that didn't make it any easier.

Reflecting on it now, I wonder if the way my mom lived actually has been my own life's mission: to help people, including my *Organista Home* clients, live their best life with just what was needed. We waste so much time keeping up with our stuff. My mom was proof we just don't need it all. Had my mother taught me that from early on? It had been so ingrained in me for my whole life that I'm still doing it. Hundreds of clients and families, millions of items donated to charity and people living happily with less... I think so.

We called Wanamassa First Aid to take her to the hospital but without sirens, because she never wanted a big commotion made for her. She physically could not walk or get herself into a car. My brother tried to carry her, but it caused her too much pain. So I went with her in the ambulance. We held a pillow on her stomach so when hitting any bumps in the road it wouldn't jostle her, sending her into more intolerable pain.

We arrived at Jersey Shore Medical Center shortly thereafter. This was the very hospital she worked at while we were growing up as kids. She was an ER Tech. She loved her job, but again, she loved the people there even more. She made sure people from all walks of life were heard, listened to, respected, and taken care of—whether they were living or had passed.

It was time. We all knew, her especially, and so that's why my mom asked me if I could get Father to come and give her last rites.

My mom grew up in the Holy Spirit Roman Catholic Church her entire life and attended Holy Spirit Grammar school as her four older brothers had. My grandmother was a deeply religious woman, attending church with her husband and five children each week.

Father arrived. By that point, my mother's small frame was now writhing in pain. When she met Father Miguel's eyes, that was it. Her body may have given up but not her face and her unwavering faith. She knew where she was going—to Heaven to be with God, her one true love, and my father Tim and to reunite with all those who had passed before her.

Her hazel eyes just looked back and accepted Father's blessings. When he had finished the ritual, of course she took all the strength she could muster to make sure she thanked him and to let Father know just how much she appreciated him coming. I'll never forget that.

Here's a woman so close to the gates of heaven and making sure all those around her know just how grateful she is. For the people taking her vitals, the ambulance drivers, the nurses, doctors, and the janitorial staff. How is that even possible? When was the last time you went out of your way to really thank someone?

It was a little up and down from that day until the day she crossed over. My mother got slightly better, so she was sent home, but then she went back to the hospital a few days later. It was 2020 and COVID was still a very big thing at this time. When she was admitted to the hospital, she was in Hospice although the nurses and doctors didn't care for it. She was granted unlimited visitors, and that would be the only way she would agree to stay. COVID be damned, she wanted friends and family to be there if they wanted to be. And they were; she was never left alone. My mother, being a caretaker many times over, never left anyone to pass alone. She would share with us that it was always easy to find someone to take care of the babies but not seniors.

Within two weeks of her last rites on September 12, she passed peacefully. My son Noah (she called him an apostle) was the only one that hadn't been able to see her until that night. He finally arrived, and it was just the three of us. I gave them some time alone. Noah left and just minutes later, she left us. She waited for him. Being thoughtful and considerate up until her last moments with us, that's just my mom.

I waited a few minutes before calling the nurses to make sure Noah was no longer on the floor, so he wouldn't have to witness what would happen next. I pulled the major deal alert cord sending what seemed to be the entire staff on that level to her room.

She left us to go to the only place she knew she was going to be unafraid: home to Heaven.

My father Timothy Stewart Varian left this world in the same way my mother did, Stage 4 lung cancer. He was just fifty years old.

They had been together since the ages of fourteen and sixteen, high school sweethearts. Proud parents of three incredible children and grandparents to six at the time. Mary and Tim were inseparable. Only when he was working at his three jobs were they not together.

When my father was diagnosed, the doctors gave him a year and half to live. He stopped working, and from that moment for the next 547 days they spent every moment together. They were making up for all of those six days a week twelve-plus-hour days he spent at work to provide for his family.

My father did the treatments, whatever he could. My mother had knowledge of medical treatments and didn't want to lose him. She was squeezing in all the possible time with him and our family.

Sometimes I wonder if my mother could've fought harder, like my dad. She did try some of the initial treatments, but it was so difficult for her. Driving her every day, hunched over because she couldn't sit up straight all the way to New Brunswick.

The alternative? She would be reunited with the only man she ever loved that much sooner. She never recovered after my father's death. Could you blame her? I couldn't, but we all certainly could've used her a little longer. So, she stopped her treatments and let her physical body pass on so her spirit could live on in eternal paradise with my dad.

Ever since my mom's passing, I have thought a lot about this one precious life. I have contemplated what it all means. Admittedly there were times when I wanted more—a bigger home, a nicer car, that trip to the island. But when I look at how my mother lived, none of those things mattered at all. She had the same home she grew up in and was content. An island vacation was nothing compared to bringing someone in need a blanket or cheeseburger. And as long as the car ran to get her from A to B it may as well have been a chariot. She valued the handwritten note from an old friend and having a conversation with a neighbor, and a surprise candy bar delivery had her over the moon. You can only imagine how she felt when she received over a hundred thanks to good old Facebook.

But really, this is living—beyond credit scores and bank accounts, beyond six-figure salaries and penthouse suites. And if you want that, don't worry, there is an eternal paradise whose pearly gates has nothing on The Plaza Hotel. And faith is the only currency we need to get in.

I wonder, what if we all lived like my mom? What if we all helped others, even when it is uncomfortable? What if we lived with less and gave the rest to those who needed it? What if we connected with our higher power the way my mom did, looking Father Miguel in the eyes without fear? What if the things we left behind were small but mighty in the way they touched the hearts of those who receive them?

My mother left me a Mary and child statue her father had given to her when I was born, the Waterford guardian angel statue I got for her at the time of her diagnosis, and her two daily devotionals with her underlines, comments, and the smell of cigarettes. I couldn't be more grateful. But what she really left me was the gift of unwavering faith: an undeniable belief that God is real, our life has meaning and purpose, and that what we need more than any material thing of this world is each other.

ABOUT THE CONTRIBUTOR

Ever since Jessica was a young girl, she had a passion for helping people organize their spaces. Dating back to elementary school, she was in charge of the class bookshelf, and her room was always neat and tidy. Her mother's influence shaped the way Jessica viewed excess stuff, and she learned from a young age about the importance of giving to others just by witnessing her mom live this way. But her time spent working in a church basement catapulted Jessica into the mission she now lives through her award-winning company, *Organista Home*. Since 2011, she has worked with hundreds of clients to consciously declutter their homes and has donated over one million items.

    Jessica is also a published author, co-founder of SOAR Symposium, and a partner in Inspired Girl. In her personal life, Jessica's passions are walks in nature and spending time with friends. She is the mother to four wonderful children who make her proud each and every day. They are the motivating force behind Jessica's desire to create a legacy, showing them the power of using our gifts to help others and anything is possible.

Bits of Her Heart...
Jessica Varian Carroll

Do good, be good.
Jump and the
net will follow.

FUN FACT...

Jessica shares a birthday with Mother Teresa. She'd love to share a meal with her too!

11

THE WALK HOME

BY KERRY BRAY

This chapter is dedicated to anyone who has had a complicated relationship with someone they love dearly. May you choose the path of loving kindness and may the love you give be returned back to you always.

> "We are all just walking each other home."
> **Ram Dass**

It is a miracle when someone brings us into this world, but there is no greater honor and privilege than to be there when they leave us. I was able to help walk her home, where now her spirit flies free and she finally has peace.

We all have common threads in the fabric of life that connect us, and losing a parent is one of them. This was happening, and I could not stop it. I could hear myself thinking, *This is it. There is no yesterday. There is no tomorrow. There is only now; stay in this moment.*

I knew she was beginning her journey home, and I wanted to be fully present with and for her. But, in this process, time bends and blurs, sleepless nights living off coffee and tears—second-guessing all of your choices, their choices actually, that you need to carry out and begging for things to turn around. Willing to do anything to take away their pain—this is what it is like to live through someone dying.

I feel so profoundly as an empath; it is both a gift and a curse. It was a long and painful road for her, and I felt every moment of it. I knew this was my role. I knew that it was going to be the two of us, just the way she wanted it. It is so complex because the woman I am telling you about is my biological grandmother, but she raised me as my mother. My birth mother (who is her biological daughter) was sixteen. She could not care for me, so my biological grandmother Janet stepped in and adopted me. I was her doll; she even made my clothes when I was younger. But the relationship was not always perfect; there were many layers.

She always seemed like a mystery to me. I loved her so much; deep down, I knew she loved me. But with all her love, it seemed she had more jealousy and anguish too. And that would spill over into how she treated others, making our relationship very hard. It is sad to say this, but how she died was really like how she lived her life—complicated and full of hurt and pain that ran deep. In the end, eight agonizing days would reveal a new level of suffering as each day went on. She was scared. She wasn't tethered to any spiritual belief. She didn't know what was on the *other side* or who would be there with her. She was fighting death, not fighting to live, and there is a difference. I would try to help her focus on the positive, but it was futile.

She didn't like my optimism, often reminding me that I didn't understand because I was healthy. I would remind her that with this disease, she would have to fight the darkness that creeps in. My optimism was like a counterbalance if even to help keep her from spiraling too far down. It was still dark for her. I am unsure if she was denying her illness or couldn't accept it.

She had Parkinson's. She hid it from me until one day when she couldn't move and had to go to the hospital. They did all kinds of tests, even a spinal tap. Shockingly, I found out at that hospital visit that she had been diagnosed with the disease two years prior, in 2012. The neurologist in the hospital had been treating her, and my mother wasn't taking medicine. That explained these "freezing episodes." Can you imagine my surprise? She was sick and suffering from this disease for ten years until her final transition in April 2022.

After her passing, my daughter said to me, "My Mimi was a very loving grandma to me, but your mom, Janet, was very tough on you and did some really hurtful things to others as well. Do you think that is why she suffered so much?" Children see things simply as they are. My children were no strangers to seeing me having to apologize for their Mimi. They often went back into a restaurant after we left and gave extra tips when she would leave hardly anything. They would get embarrassed while my mom was fighting with someone in the store because she was often rude to people in the service industry. She was the only person I knew who could get into a fight with the gas station attendant. Perhaps she was suffering through her transition because she still had that fighting edge?

In the Buddhist tradition, they call this "karmic burn-off." A clear mind at death is important as the state of a person's mind determines the type of rebirth they will experience. Hindus also believe that suffering is an integral part of life and results from past negative thoughts and actions. By suffering, the person may satisfy the debt incurred for past negative behaviors. In Christian beliefs, it is called reconciliation, and in Judaism, to face suffering is a sign that a person will be rewarded in the afterlife. In most religions, suffering is innate to the human condition and possesses potential to assist an individual to learn and grow through it—in this life or the next. I do think it was part of her soul's journey to make some things right before she left here. I believe that we are all given this chance to right our wrongs before transitioning. For some of us, it happens throughout our lifetime; for others, it happens right before we cross over. I believe we are all innately good and desire to do the right thing. I know my mom was inherently good, but she just had some things to sort out.

I think this is what people mean when they say your life flashes before you when you are dying. If your conscience is clear, you will experience a peaceful transition. And if not, it will take some more time. Suffering is when we have attachments, and I believe she was firmly attached to her hurt, pain, and jealousy, none of which served her highest good. And her actions that were deeply tied to those feelings might have needed to be revised.

All the things she once enjoyed were slowly taken from her. She was so independent but could no longer move her body or bathe. She liked affection, and suddenly it hurt like bee stings. The sheets felt like six-hundred pounds weighing heavily on her. She hated taking medicine, and now she had to take multiple medications six times a day to treat all the issues. She dreamt about food, only to get sick every time she tried to eat. She had been losing a lot of weight each week

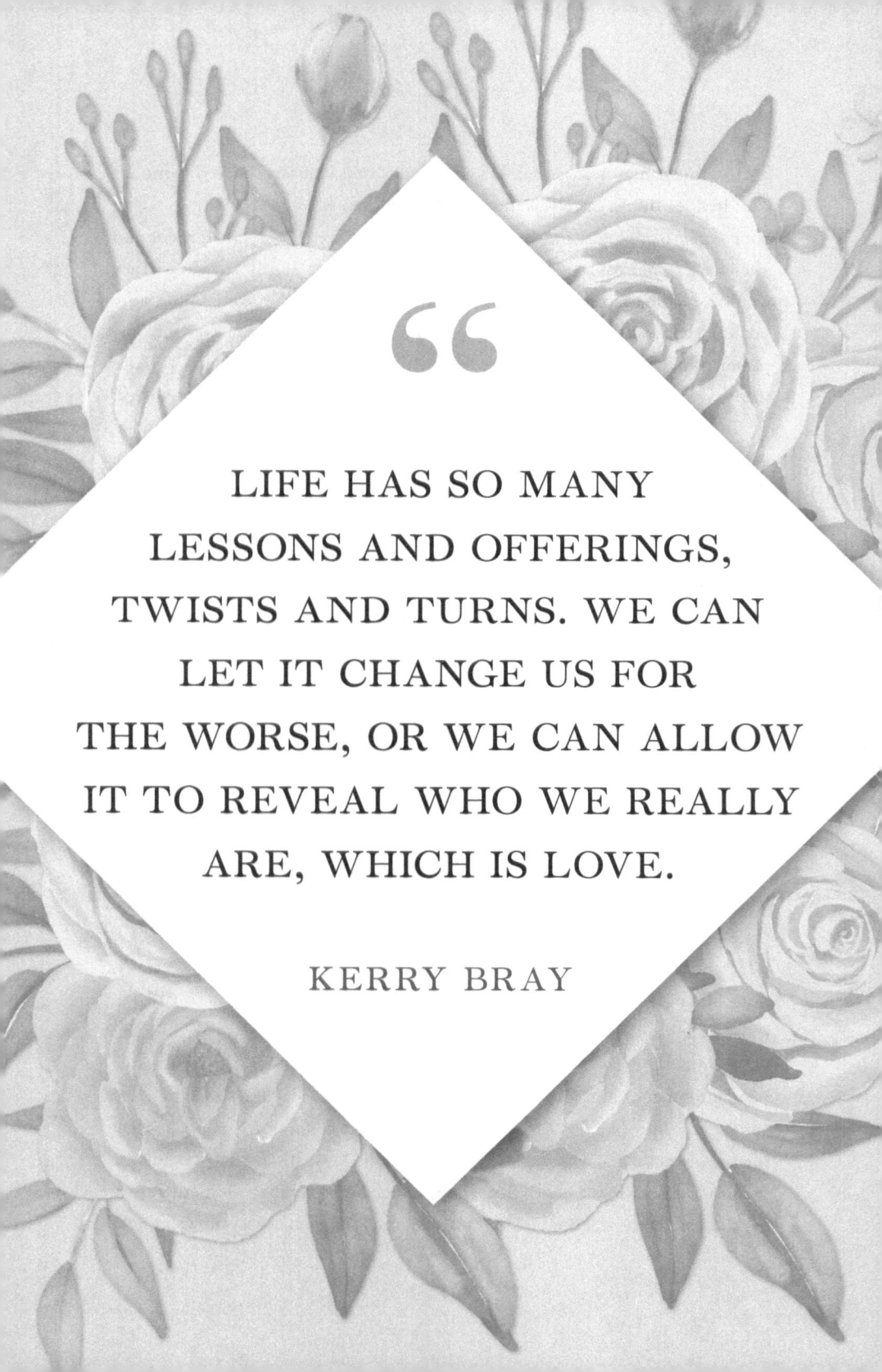

"

LIFE HAS SO MANY LESSONS AND OFFERINGS, TWISTS AND TURNS. WE CAN LET IT CHANGE US FOR THE WORSE, OR WE CAN ALLOW IT TO REVEAL WHO WE REALLY ARE, WHICH IS LOVE.

KERRY BRAY

and stopped eating meals in January. She would have a few nibbles here and there or drink Ensure. Everything tasted awful to her.

The doctors started saying phrases like "failure to thrive" and told me she was beginning to decline rapidly—both signs for a hospice call. The first time hospice came out, she was uncooperative. She didn't want the service; she didn't want any help. She was uncooperative with everything and everyone. She was also refusing her medicine. Within the next two days, her whole demeanor changed. She became more unresponsive and took a turn for the worse. Hospice came back out, and it was obvious she was ready for it. She was officially one-hundred pounds.

She really wasn't herself anymore in that she had become unreasonable. She wasn't able to make her own decisions. She had become paranoid and felt everyone was against her. She didn't think I belonged at home with my family taking care of my four children while she was so sick. She wanted me to leave them and move in with her and told me I should be there all the time. I was with her as often as I could be, not knowing how much time we would have together. Sadly, that time spent together was filled with so much conflict. Loving her though at times feeling she did not love me, I still ensured she was being cared for properly by her medical team. She chose me to be the one, and as hard as it was, I knew what I had to do. I would have to flip the switch between holding a sacred space for her to transition with ease and peace to literally fighting with the staff to get her meds on time and whether the nurse on duty felt she needed them even though they were doctor's orders! It was such a mind-fuck, this whole process. I was trying to help, yet nothing I did could improve or fix it. I did everything I could to make her happy, but nothing worked. She wanted me there but was annoyed with everything I was saying and doing. She was just so tortured.

The final days started on Monday, March 28—hospice said she waited for me. She looked different; it was as if she had left us already, and her transition was beginning. I just returned from a family trip, which I had tremendous guilt about going on. Guilt is like that; it can be irrational even when you have good intentions. My family had a special trip planned. I had already rearranged so many things over the past few years. We canceled two other trips prior to this year because my mom was sick. The kids didn't understand. From their perspective, we kept canceling and changing things around for her, and she was just so angry with me all the time. They didn't fully grasp our relationship or how love can run as deep as hurt. We were supposed to be gone for fourteen days, but I shortened the trip to ten, which still felt so long. I am a mother to my own children and had to focus on them and our situation. Leaving at all made me feel terrible inside. I was so conflicted.

In the weeks leading up to the stress of leaving for the family trip, she was confused and not making sense. But miraculously, we had a great visit a week or so before the trip! She even apologized and told me how much she loved me, appreciated all I had done for her, and that no one could have done half of what I did.

Boom, there it was, validation! And I felt all the love I had needed my entire life in that one single moment. All I ever wanted from her was to be seen, loved, and appreciated just as I am. Sadly, the next day she returned to not making sense again. I am so grateful for the gift of that single moment.

I remember talking to the hospice nurse, who said I needed to enjoy the trip with my family. I had been burning both ends of the candle: trying to be there fully for my mom and then be fully a mom to my own children. It was an impossible situation. I was so drained. At some point, I had to trust I was doing the best I could. I made sure my mom had round-the-clock private duty care. I spoke to hospice, the nurses, and the private care multiple times daily. I also had a senior care company overseeing everything. Also, my uncle went there a few times a week and gave the nurses a break.

When I returned, I took the next two weeks off from everything. I wasn't sure how much time she had, but I wanted to be there with her as much as possible. We couldn't spend time like this together before because all she wanted to do was fight with me or criticize me. I knew I was appointed to be her caretaker. As hard as this was, we would experience a closeness that would bridge us together.

I felt that being loving and doing my part, being kind (even when kindness wasn't coming back to me), was important. It was difficult because, over the years, she became envious of me, my life, my experiences, my marriage, and my relationships with my children and friends.

I am a free spirit, and she didn't support my decisions and my choices, especially traveling.

"When you have children, you don't do that anymore; it is all about them now." She would often scold me about my choices and make me question myself. She made snide remarks and critical comments on every aspect of my life. It was exhausting. I was rewarded when I met her standards, from my clothes to meals, decorating, and even haircuts. I could never really be "me" when I was with her. She was bitter that I had so many people and experiences. And she felt she should be the priority. Everything was about her, and she only focused internally.

Being an empath, her pain was mine. I held it like a weight for so many years. I also struggled with boundaries; being able to be myself and share myself without consequence was not an option. Even before she got sick, and especially after, I would visit with her often. Still, it was hard because she never left me feeling like she liked me or enjoyed my company. She didn't want to be alone. She was so lonely. I wondered what happened to her over the years. She was very loving when I was younger and very loving to my children. She encouraged me to be independent and supported me when I became a flight attendant—especially on September 11, 2001, when I was unsure if I should quit. She said, "No way are those terrorists going to take this from you!" And now we've come full circle back to that closeness because, in the end, she trusted me to take care of her, all her affairs, and her wishes.

I am grateful for her love and support over the years, yet sad that I felt I would never be good enough for her, even when she was loving toward me. Love can be messy like this. Not all relationships are easy. Something so strange to me is that she was the kind of mother who put herself first, yet when I became a mother, judged me if she felt I was not putting my kids first—what a confusing message. And then, when she became sick, she wanted me to put her first instead of my children. I had to learn from my own spiritual practices how to love myself and put myself first so I could give the BEST of me and not what was left of me. Learning that I was a priority was strange, and I still need to be reminded sometimes. I am continually a student of myself, and my spirituality is everything to me. It is my internal guide and my discernment system. It helps me to always strive to choose love and kindness overall and to keep looking for the good in everything, knowing we are all beings full of love and light.

And maybe by keeping my healthy boundaries with her, I was really offering her a way to shift her karma and reconcile with God as she transitioned. Maybe I was showing her how to love and what real love is by giving her an example of how to do it.

People who knew her, knew her to be tough, strong, and independent. They say that you always hurt the ones you love the most, and I have also heard it said, "Hurt people hurt people." And that is very much how she lived her life. It wasn't always intentional or conscious on her part. She had a lot of hurt in her. She seemed to find fault with others. She always seemed more interested in being right than working through a problem. And somehow, she was always the victim. The ultimate betrayal was that her own body betrayed her with this disease.

She really taught me what unconditional love was, inadvertently. It seemed she felt love by being able to control and manipulate to regain control, and I am the opposite. I feel it by freedom. The more conditions that were placed made it more difficult to please her. She really helped me understand and shape my own mothering. I want my children to know that they are worthy of my love without condition. In this, she was my teacher; in the end, I was hers.

Every day her suffering continued, I prayed that this was the day that all lessons be learned, that her suffering was coming to an end, and she would have peace. And every day, I would think, I guess this was not the day. Every day, it felt like I was having my heart ripped out, witnessing her pain because I knew that she, in all her own hurt, was a beautiful soul being called home. I was crushed, tears rolling down my cheeks endlessly. And when I thought I was all cried out, more would release because it was just too damn painful to watch her suffer another day again at another level. All I could do was be there for her to work it out with her God. I was her partner in this—bathing her, ensuring she got her ice and didn't choke, getting medicine as needed, fighting for her to be treated with dignity, yet making the environment as peaceful as possible and letting nature and God do their part.

Everything was so complicated. I felt a strong need to protect her. Nothing seemed like it was going smoothly for her. She was so fragile in and out of this world. The days went on, and relatives came to see her. I like to believe she made peace with her birth daughter when she visited.

Then, things changed with her breathing, and it was difficult for her to breathe. She had what I now know is called terminal restlessness. She was given morphine every hour, yet she was still uncomfortable. Around midnight, I had to call hospice back at one point because she had a full-blown panic attack. She was in despair; she was begging to get out of bed and asking me to help her. She was having seizures every five minutes. Her whole body would get stiff and then shake. She finally started to get some comfort. The hospice nurse came right over, like a little angel with her tinctures, put together a medication plan, and over a few hours, we got her settled. We bathed her and got her into comfortable clothes and brushed her hair and talked to her about beautiful flower gardens. It was a loving ritual. The hospice nurse said everyone likes to feel fresh, and my mom knew what we were preparing her for. I just felt like I wanted to do any loving things for my mom to make her comfortable.

Only now can I see how important that was.

At some point, she said she loved me.

This is not what you want for someone you love. It is hard to watch, and there is such a feeling of helplessness. She always said she didn't want to get sick or end up in a home. She just wanted to go to bed one night and leave peacefully in her sleep. I prayed for all of those things. Sadly, that was not how it would go for her.

In the morning, the hospice aide came back to help. She suggested I get a coffee just in case, "Sometimes they like you to go so that they can go," she said. I went out entirely, knowing she would not go because she wanted me there. I cried again and threw up. It was all just so much. When I returned, the head hospice nurse came to assess. She said it would be just a few hours. I had the recliner up against the bed; I grabbed her hand and held it. I smiled, saying to her, "We are finally alone and having our sleepover!" as she always wanted. She squeezed my hand, and we listened to a beautiful meditation about transitioning. We had lavender in the diffuser, and she took her last breath within forty-five minutes. I told her how much I loved her and looked her in the eyes as I cried. I could feel her spirit leave her body, but it stayed in the room with us.

About ten minutes later, the nurse came in to check on us and told me she was gone. I said, "I still feel her here; I am not ready to leave her."

The nurse responded, "Stay for as long as you want. She is not ready for you to let go of her hand." And she was right; that hand was not letting go. The other one you could move, but not the one holding mine. I played some yoga music and stayed with her until hospice returned to pronounce her dead. The funeral home arrived to take her body. The hardest part of all turned out to be when I had to leave her, knowing that was the last time we would be together.

The following two weeks, I felt showered with love between food, flowers, visits, and check-ins. Yet, I still needed time to let this all "land" and time to process it.

It felt so heavy, like a haunting. I prayed for signs but never got any, which made it worse. I decided to book a trip to Miraval in the Berkshires. Some essential self-care tools I use are spiritual practices, meditation, and yoga. There is also healing in travel. It promotes health and well-being through connection with others and community. I have always had a wanderlust for as long as I can remember. Travel always brings me peace and joy in my soul. I needed time to let all this land and process what I had just experienced. My sensitive heart was hurting and questioning if I had "done it right."

I arrived, settled, and walked all around the property. I experienced chakra cleansing sound baths, read a book, had a sweet slumber massage, and went to bed early. I enjoyed green juice, quinoa oatmeal, and a stretch class the next day. I did a yoga nidra meditation, reiki session, and rituals to release and restore. I took an insightful writing class complete with angel cards. I explored our relationship through reflection, and what came up in the cards unearthed the hurt I needed to acknowledge.

Then, when I finally had a quiet moment, I received my sign. I had spent four whole days immersed in spiritual nourishment. I was having lunch alone, and amidst the entire place, a family sat together. Now, this is the kind of place where people are reading a book, talking with a friend, or journaling. I would never expect to see anyone playing games. YET here they were breaking out a game of Rummikub®!!! Her favorite game! I broke down into tears and thanked her for letting me know she was okay. I felt a warm feeling of love and relief wash over me. I am unsure what she and God were working out for the past two weeks, but her sign finally came to me. The following day was her birthday, and we celebrated at her favorite diner when I returned home.

Why does it hurt so much when someone who isn't kind to us passes away?

What am I mourning when I really didn't feel love from her?

Why am I so shaken when we didn't really have a good relationship for most of my life?

Why does it feel like I am motherless, yet I felt like I had to be my own mother my whole life?

I have discovered a newfound freedom in being myself. There is a way to mourn her loss and feel relief from the dysfunction, and to be able to love still even when I didn't always feel it toward me. I realize now that she loved me the only way she knew how, and I cannot hold on to bitterness. I have become a better daughter, mother, wife, and friend because I have the desire to choose the path that wasn't always shown to me, and for this, I thank her.

Life has so many lessons and offerings, twists and turns. We can let it change us for the worse, or we can allow it to reveal who we really are, which is love. We are so much more than our bodies, and we are all connected. We are all energy at our core. We are spirits housed in this temporary shell for whatever time we are afforded. We are infinite possibilities beyond what our conscious minds tell us. I don't believe we started as a body, and I don't think we end as a body. Our spirits animate us. We are all made of stardust, and we are all beyond what we can imagine. We have levels of awareness and depth. And we are all just walking each other home.

It has been difficult to share this inner and outer conflict. I know others go through this; ultimately, I learned to appreciate my mother and my life more. Being honest and open with my struggles and yet still choosing love is my yoga. As a teacher, sometimes there is this illusion that we are perfect and no longer face hardships. Or we feel we must be perfect in every way. I walk this path, not as perfect but the opposite. I am having an authentic human experience. It's messy, and I don't always hold it together as I would like. I try to offer myself and others grace and compassion. Through all these ups and downs, I still sought the loving path because that is who I am—showing up for her the way I wanted to be shown up for. Giving more of what it is that I really seek and desire.

We are all the embodiment of love, part of this cosmic universe, and our home is the place of infinite possibilities. Our human experience here on earth is a temporary one. Our lives are a sacred journey. And out of all my travel, the most powerful and unexpected journey was the one I took to walk her home.

ABOUT THE CONTRIBUTOR

Kerry Bray is the founder of Wander Travel Company. She has been a Luxury Travel Advisor since 2005 specializing in custom luxury and wellness travel experiences and retreats. Kerry is known for curating and planning bespoke journeys with unlimited personalization and unique adventures that allow her clients the unprecedented opportunity to truly connect with every aspect of their chosen destinations. Kerry understands what a truly soulful vacation entails and, unlike anyone else in her field, she can seamlessly link luxury with mindfulness, health, wellness, and spiritual exploration. Kerry recently added another business to her growing portfolio of luxury brands, Down to Basics—a luxury bedding boutique.

As a mother, wife, yoga teacher, spiritual guide, mindfulness leader, and free spirit with a wandering soul, her loves at work mirror her loves in general—the water, reading, nature, and traveling. She lives near the beach in New Jersey with her husband, her four children, and their two dogs, and enjoys volunteering in her community along with teaching and participating in local wellness classes.

Bits of Her Heart...

Kerry Bray

Simple luxuries in life go a long way.

FUN FACT...

Kerry was born on the 4th of July! Relaxing to her is reading a book on the porch in the rain or at the beach. Her guilty pleasure is attending an exclusive and elegant tequila tasting!

12

WHAT I DIDN'T KNOW HAVE BEEN MY GREATEST LESSONS

BY MAUREEN SPATARO

To every person who has ever had the privilege of being a parents' escort as they travel toward their life's final sunset, I dedicate this chapter to you.

"I don't want a call. I don't want any call. Someone has to come and tell me." I was sitting at my brother Christopher's kitchen table.

"What? You don't want a phone call?" Chris looked confused.

"If I'm not there when the time comes, I don't want a call. I could be driving, or shopping. I could be in the house by myself. You have MaryAnn and the kids. Bobby has Jeanmarie and the kids. Who do I have? I live alone. I don't have anyone at the house with me or to go home to. I don't want a phone call. If I am not with Mom when the time comes, call a friend of mine—Carla or Sue—and tell them to find me or to come to the house. If I'm at work, call my boss. Just make sure I'm not told over the phone."

Years ago, when my grandmother died, I was home with my then-husband when my brother Bobby called.

"Maureen, Grandma is gone."

"Did you check by the bank?" My grandmother was a wanderer. She would walk her Brooklyn neighborhood streets for hours each day, stopping in coffee shops, sitting by the bank chatting with friends, and feeding the pigeons. The first thing that popped into my mind was that she could be anywhere.

"No, Maureen, Grandma is gone."

"Bobby, she's not gone." He was only seventeen, so I figured he probably wasn't aware of how long and how far our grandmother's daily walks would take her throughout the neighborhood. "Did you check the coffee shop across from Lenny's pizzeria? That's where she goes for coffee."

"Maureen, you don't understand. Grandma died. She is gone." He went on to explain that he and my mother went to my grandmother's apartment when she wasn't answering her phone. She was late for dinner, and my mother took a walk over with my brother to see what was going on. They found her in her chair. She had been gone a few days.

My husband told me that I screamed "NO! NO! NO! NO!" as I dropped the phone, crying and howling. As the meaning of what my brother said hit me, the pain was soul shattering. I finally understood. She was gone. My sweet grandmother was gone forever. There was no goodbye. There was no time to tell her how much I loved her and what she meant to me. There was just two words, "She's gone."

Thirty years later, the shock of my brother's words remains seared into my brain.

Thirty years later, I am sitting at my other brother's table making sure he understands I do not want to be told about our mother's passing with a phone call.

"Promise me, Chris. Make sure MaryAnn knows, too. I never want a call like that again."

Our mother has been fighting Stage 4 metastatic kidney cancer for six and a half years. She was one of the ghosts of 9/11. She worked three blocks away from the Towers, and seconds after evacuating her office she stepped into a plume of ash, smoke, debris, pulverized bones, and burnt flesh that covered her from head to toe. Her building stood unscathed, but the effects of that moment remain a daily reminder. Fifteen years after surviving the unimaginable, what my mother thought was her sciatica acting up "from being a woman of a mature age" was

What I Didn't Know Have Been My Greatest Lessons

actually diagnosed as a cancerous tumor in her kidney. Several years later, my mother's cancer would be directly linked to 9/11.

Her kidney and the cancerous tumor were immediately removed, and she was declared cancer-free. A year later, we were told that some residual cancer cells that hadn't been detected and removed metastasized to Mom's lungs and bones, and a cancerous tumor had developed at the base of her spine.

After her initial treatment left her sicker, weaker, and declining at a rapid rate, the treatment her oncologist settled on was miraculous. Within two weeks, Mom was regaining her strength and her appetite, and she vowed to live life out loud. For the next five years she would travel, start a food pantry at her parish, join a local church group, continue her weekend waitressing job, and celebrate all the milestones her grandchildren would reach.

But, cancer is a relentless opponent. And, as it progresses—as the miraculous treatment reaches its peak—a determined spirit cannot stop the physical effects on the body in which it resides. Cancer cannot simply be loved away. Although grateful and blessed for the time my mother's treatment has given all of us with her, it has also presented moments for which I wasn't prepared.

I didn't know grieving started before your loved one passes away. I started by grieving the loss of my mother's independence. Since her cancer has progressed, mom can no longer go to church because the swelling in her legs and feet makes it too difficult. She also stopped going to her senior citizens' group meetings for the same reason. As time passed, Mom had to stop driving, which means she can no longer just pick up and drive to her kids' homes for a day or weekend stay. I remember the day she got her license. She was in her forties. My father wouldn't allow her to drive, but she got her license anyway. It wouldn't be until they divorced that she would buy her first car. How proud she was to have saved for it! It was like her chariot. It was her independence. Thirty years later, cancer has taken that from her.

Mom's progressing cancer means difficult conversations must be had. As her executrix I have had to sit with her and go through all of her papers, her accounts, and her wishes. The paperwork includes letters in unopened envelopes addressed to me and my brothers and little notes she wrote to us on some of the documents I unexpectedly came across starting with, "Even though I'm gone..." Watching her try to remain strong and unyielding until she has to excuse herself for a

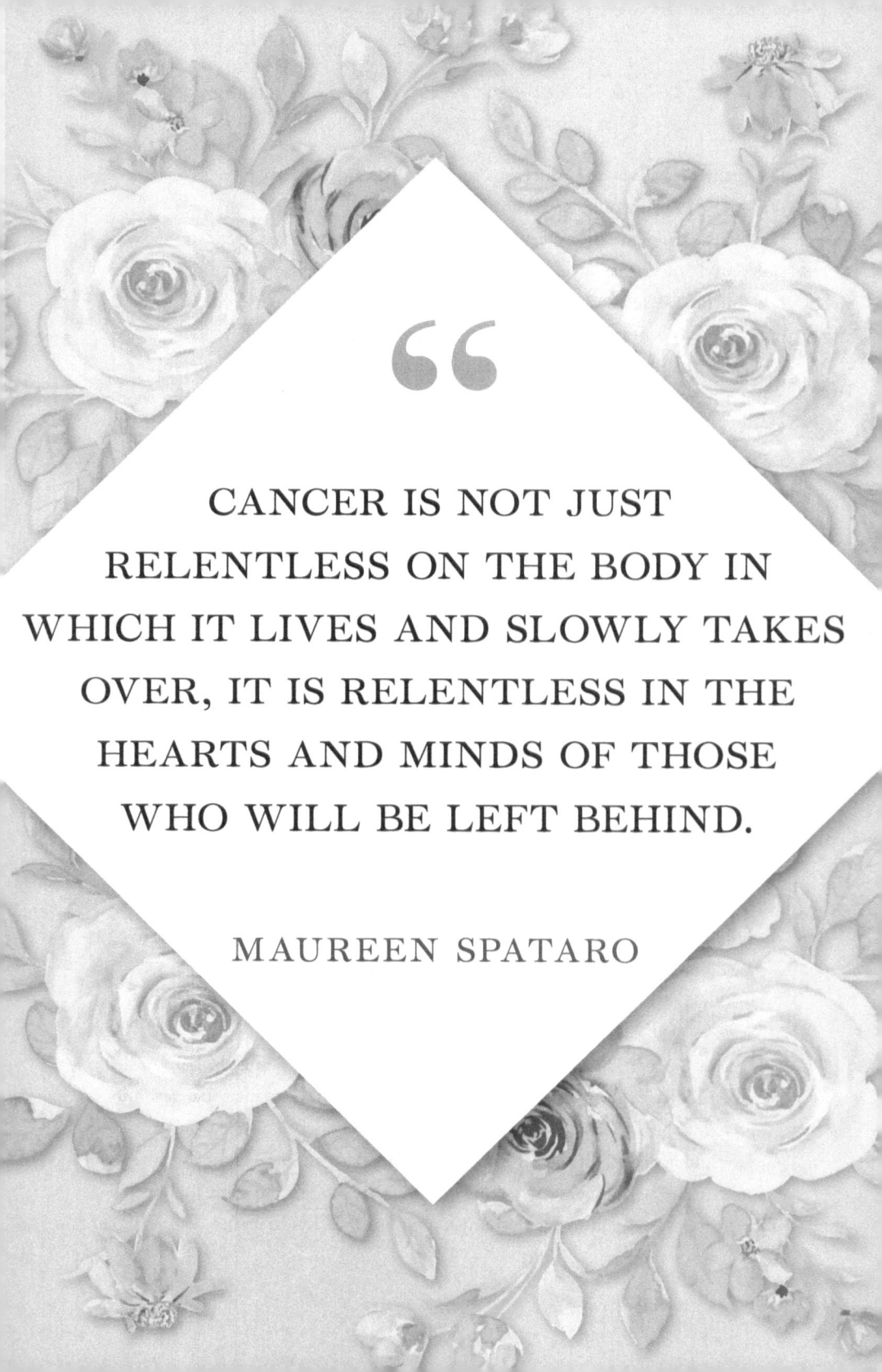

> CANCER IS NOT JUST RELENTLESS ON THE BODY IN WHICH IT LIVES AND SLOWLY TAKES OVER, IT IS RELENTLESS IN THE HEARTS AND MINDS OF THOSE WHO WILL BE LEFT BEHIND.

MAUREEN SPATARO

What I Didn't Know Have Been My Greatest Lessons

moment wasn't something I was prepared for. Allowing some tears to fall quickly, then pulling them back, was something I never thought I could do.

I didn't know I would watch my mother slowly shrink away as her cancer advanced. She was never a tall woman, but her frame is much smaller now. The bruises and rashes I see on her skin with no explanation quietly take my breath away. Her pants that began to fall off because they are too big, her little toes that look like plump mini hot dogs, and her ankles that look like bricks from the swelling are all the visuals to what her illness is doing to her.

My beautiful mother was such a modest woman. A lady in every sense of the word. I didn't know that the first time I had to help her undress and take a shower I wouldn't be fully prepared. *I'll warm up the towels in the dryer and bring them in for when she is finished so she is nice and warm.* That was my plan. I was proud I thought to bring her warm towels. But I didn't think about before she got into the shower. Seeing her try to hide her frail, naked body with a small hand towel to save some of her dignity made me choke on my stupidity. Why hadn't I brought the towels in beforehand?! What was I thinking?! She was cold from the toilet seat she needed to sit on to undress, and she was embarrassed that I had to remove her undergarments. I didn't know. I helped her into the shower, sat her on the shower seat, pulled the curtain as she thanked me, closed the door behind me, and smothered my tears with that hand towel. When it became uncontrollable, I went down into the basement and screamed. I didn't know; I wasn't prepared.

I didn't know that each day before I fully woke up, I would wait before getting out of bed and listen to hear if she got up to go to the bathroom. And, if she didn't, I would quietly walk into her room to see if she was breathing.

I didn't know how hard I would pray as I pulled into the driveway. I didn't know how frightened I would feel when I put the key in the door and quietly prayed as I walked in that I would hear, "Hey Sweetie!" On the days she didn't hear the door open and close, I would hold my breath as I entered the kitchen, praying I would see her little body on the big red chair she always sat in. When I walked in and said, "Hey there!" I could breathe again when met with her beautiful smile. I could thank God once again for giving me another night of dinner, chatter, Jeopardy, and Wheel of Fortune.

I didn't know that hospitals either treat you with dignity or they take it away. I didn't know that most of the doctors that came in with their cavalcade of interns would speak about my mother as if she wasn't lying in the bed in front of them. That they would speak too fast for her to follow what they were saying, and that I would have to tell them to slow down. I didn't know they would sigh in frustration.

Long-term plans were my mother's goals. Early on in her illness she would make plans six months out. "Having goals to reach makes me stop thinking about cancer. I have something to look forward to. I let cancer know it's my choice. I will let cancer know when I can't."

Now, making plans has taken on a whole new mindset. When I ask my mother what she would like to do for her birthday, or Mother's Day, or even the holidays, her response isn't "Let's have it by your house," or "Let's go out to dinner." Her response is, "Let's see where we are when the time comes. Let's see how I'm feeling." There are no long-term goals. There is only today and the moment we are in.

I never knew what creatinine levels were, but now I do. And I understand what increasing creatinine levels means.

I wasn't prepared when the priest came in to give my mother communion during her last hospital stay. Her tears were endless, as was her gratitude.

We are told as our parents get older that we switch roles and we become the caretakers. I didn't know what that entailed and that it meant I would see fear and uncertainty replace the confidence and self-assuredness I used to seek in her eyes, in her voice. Now she looks for it in my eyes and my voice. She needs me to remain calm and speak slowly when I explain what the doctors are saying. She looks for the smile and pat on her hand to tell her, "We're still good." And, when she doesn't think she sees it, she simply says, "This is just another bump in the road."

I didn't know I would make sure I saved and resaved as many voicemail messages from my mother as I could so I can hear her voice when she is gone.

I didn't know I would actually try to plan the days following my mother's death beforehand and prepare myself for how I would act at her wake. Make sure I had the right clothes—dresses. I know she would want me to wear dresses and look like a lady. I have told myself over and over, as if to ingrain it into my psyche so when the time comes it will be second nature, "Make sure you stand to greet everyone after they pay their respects. Don't sit in the front chairs. Thank everyone." I wonder if we have enough pictures to put up at her wake and if I should start putting them aside now, and what music should be picked for her mass.

I didn't know I would already be writing her eulogy, or deciding that when

What I Didn't Know Have Been My Greatest Lessons

the time comes, I will sit at the end of the pew so I can keep my hand on her casket. I want to reassure her I won't let go until I have to—that I will escort her right up to the end.

I didn't know I would keep telling myself to get my daughter's friends' numbers, so she won't be alone when she gets the call.

I didn't know how angry I could get at friends or family.

"Stop thinking what if..."

"Enjoy her while you have her..."

"I understand. I lost my mother when I was young, and I had to live my whole life without her. Be grateful you've had her this long."

I didn't know I would want to scream "WHO SAID I WASN'T GRATEFUL? DID YOU EVER THINK HOW HARD IT WILL BE BECAUSE I *HAVE* HAD HER SO LONG? DID YOU EVER THINK ABOUT HOW I HAVEN'T KNOWN A DAY WITHOUT HER FOR OVER FIFTY YEARS? HAVE YOU EVER CONSIDERED THAT?"

I didn't know people would want to play the "Whose Grief Is Worse?" game with me when I was trying to talk about the feelings they assured me I could talk about.

I didn't know my life would change before she was gone in so many profound ways.

I never imagined I would pray God takes her before the pain becomes intolerable. I never knew how guilty I would feel or how desperately I would try to make God understand that it's not that I want her to go, but that I just don't want her to suffer. Because what I do know is being in pain is her biggest fear.

On the days Mom's pain or exhaustion is taking over, I often think of a line in *Terms of Endearment*. Debra Winger's character passes, and Shirley MacLaine says to her son-in-law "I'm so stupid. Somehow, I thought once she was gone it would be a relief."

I quietly pray, "Please don't prolong her passing if all she is going to be is in pain. Please let her go peacefully, in her sleep." I hear those words Shirley MacLaine speaks, and I understand that what I haven't known all this time is nothing compared to what I will have to learn.

I know I will one day have to learn to live in a world without my mother. A world where there are no more phone calls, no more visits, no more birthdays, hugs, kisses, or reassurances that things will work out. There are some days I can't breathe through the tears I cry. Cancer is not just relentless on the body in which it lives and slowly takes over, it is relentless in the hearts and minds of those who will be left behind.

My beautiful mother—Veronica Alice Richards. My mentor. My heroine. My go-to. The mender of my broken hearts. My personal Dear Abby. My biggest cheerleader, and the one person who has been the constant throughout my life. The person who helped me pick up the pieces of my life every time it fell apart.

What will I do without you? How will I ever be truly happy once you are gone? Do you hear me when I softly say, "Please don't go" as I watch you sleep? There could never be enough time to thank you, hold your hand, or just sit with you.

The hardest realization is there will never be enough time to show you and tell you how much I love you.

So many things I didn't know. So many more things I will learn, and decisions that will have to be made at what will surely be the worst moment any child must face. The one thing that brings me comfort is if I am not there when my mother passes, a person I trust will be there for me to grab on to, to hold me, and to bring me to her. At a time of so many unknowns, it's the only thing I do know.

What I Didn't Know Have Been My Greatest Lessons

A NOTE FROM THE CONTRIBUTOR:

As of this date, September 10, 2023, my mother has surpassed her last prognosis of 6 to 8 weeks to 13 months. She continues to show us that living in faith and keeping a positive mindset is far more powerful than a limited prognosis, and provides her everything needed to simply live in the joy and gratitude of every moment. I have learned so much from her.

My message as a surthriver is that hope always floats. The single most important ingredient to help you move past trauma is willingness. The willingness to face the pain and shame that weighs you down, develop skills that help you work through it, and release it. Once you release it, there is a wide-open space within for joy to reside—the joy of knowing you must put yourself first, you can make choices that are best for you, and you will only surround yourself with people who love you and have your best interest in mind. Your world goes from black and white to color, and you build on that as you create your life after trauma.

ABOUT THE CONTRIBUTOR

Born and raised in Brooklyn, Maureen is first and foremost the proud mom of her daughter Kayla, a Captain in the U.S. Army JAG Corp. A peer group leader, advocate, speaker, and survivor who endured abuse starting at the age of six and through her adult years, Maureen's experience and expertise has been featured on *Wake up With Marcy*, *Sonstein Sundays Podcast*, *Women in the Loop on iHeart Radio*, *This is It TV*, and *Wheelhouse: Women Changing the World and B*Inspired*.

In addition, Maureen has shared her message of *surthrival* and hope as a speaker at Georgian Court University, Monmouth University, Stockton University, high schools throughout New Jersey, The Stephanie Nicole Parze Foundation, the Attachment and Trauma Network Conference in Washington D.C., and *What's Your Story USA* in Garwood, New Jersey. Maureen is also the author of *Press Pause* available wherever books are sold. In 2022, Maureen became a member of the Stephanie Nicole Parze Foundation, leading the foundation's C.A.P (Circle of Angels Program), which will provide peer-led support groups to survivors of sexual and domestic violence, and a supporter of B.A.C.A (Biker's Against Child Abuse).

Bits of Her Heart...
Maureen Spataro

I am not braver, stronger, or more courageous than anyone. I am simply willing.

FUN FACT...

Maureen's nickname is Moprah and the song that best mirrors her life is "I'm Still Standing" by Elton John.

SECTION 5

WE ARE THE EPITOME OF LOVE AND GRACE PERSONIFIED

BEAUTY FOR ASHES
by Wendy Laffey

LIVING LIFE INTENTIONALLY
by Brenda Karinja

THE LOVE MODEL
by Jazimin Garrett

> LOVE AS IF THERE IS NO OTHER CHOICE; LOVE AS IF WE HAVE THE ABILITY AND POWER TO HEAL ALL IN THE WORLD THAT IS BROKEN AND LOVE IT BACK TO LIFE.

13

BEAUTY FOR ASHES

BY WENDY LAFFEY

This chapter is dedicated to the brokenhearted, the crushed in spirit, the abused, the abandoned, the suffering addict, the one stuck in a pattern not serving themselves or others, the one feeling unworthy. This chapter is written in love to you.

I believe in my heart that my story is common to so many others that suffer abuse, addiction, and trauma. By sharing my story, it is my hope to help someone overcome, heal, forgive, and live a full and meaningful life. And if you are not personally struggling, but know someone who is, please keep this story in your heart and give them grace. I want to give all the glory to its rightful owner, Jesus.

While most stories start at the beginning, this story starts toward the end. This particular night I found I was dealing with the strong desire to use drugs. I was in a period of severe depression, and I so often escaped to the temporary comfort of drugs and alcohol. I found a friend that sold ecstasy, and its namesake is the response your body feels after swallowing the little magic pill. However, on this night, that's not what happened once I took it. In fact, just the opposite occurred. After just a few minutes, my body responded like never before. I immediately lost all my motor skills and the ability to speak. I was stricken with fear and could barely breathe. I felt like I was stuck in a prison, which was my body, infiltrated by demons who were tormenting me. I recall being on the floor in such severe pain, completely alone, and so close to death.

In my solitude and desperation, I cried out to Jesus. I begged Him to save me! Over and over again, I just cried out and repeated the name of Jesus. He heard my prayer, and He was faithful. As I was writhing in pain, I was given a vision of a physical map that was laid out in front of me. I could see many destinations on the map, and each one represented a relationship in my life. In my vision, I was being escorted from one relationship to the next. At each new location, I experienced an interaction with myself from the perspective of my loved one. I could physically feel the pain I was causing each person through their perspective as a direct result of my addiction. It was the most emotionally painful experience I've ever had.

Quite frankly, it was more than I could bear.

Addiction is such a selfish disease; I was so fixated on feeding the addiction and escaping from pain that I didn't see anything beyond the immediate satisfaction. It was at this point that I experienced what could only be described as a stab in my heart as I heard words that would forever change me, "You're ineffective!"

I knew in the depths of my heart the meaning of these words.

This was a direct message from God to me. He was telling me that in my lower vibration state of mind, I was ineffective to the people He had entrusted to me. God planted the seeds of my heart's desires into my soul when He created me. He designed a purpose for my life, and I was totally ineffective to Him because of addiction. God is so good that He used this lowest point in my life to speak to me in a way that I would finally understand. He made it clear to me that I had to stop living in fear and running from my past. I had to finally listen to Him. He was calling me and compelling me to finally be effective; effective for Him.

I responded to His loving call.

That night, I promised Him and myself that I would never allow this to happen again. That night, because of the loving call of Jesus, marked the beginning of the end of my addiction to drugs. This is not the end of my story, for I continue to be a work in progress. Philippians 1:6 tells us, "Being confident in this, that he who began a good work in you will carry it on to completion until the day of Christ Jesus."

Beauty for Ashes

To help you understand where I am now in my Christian journey, let me tell you where the story begins.

Growing up in a broken home, I faced many difficulties and challenges living in a toxic and volatile environment. It wasn't easy, but I learned some valuable lessons that lead me to the Lord. Even in this brokenness, God was with me from the very beginning. As we read in Jeremiah 1:5 "Before I formed you in the womb, I knew you. Before you were born, I set you apart."

As a young child, I was forced to fend for myself and be on my own. I started working with a family at twelve years old. I babysat their children while my sisters worked in a different section of their family business. I would take taxis from school to work every single day after school. At that time, I was enjoying playing sports, but I knew working would provide me with the ability to provide for myself some of the basic needs I was lacking at the time.

Soon after I started working, my boss began flirting and speaking to me sexually. Things escalated from words to physical touch quickly. He would walk by me and brush my skin by touching me or bumping into me. One night we were all walking out of the main entrance of the business. All the lights were shut off, and I felt a pinch on my back side. I was stricken with fear. His wife was in front of me and his children (who I grew to love dearly) were in front of her. I had no idea what to do next, so I did nothing. I was so young.

From there, things continued to get worse, and the touching turned sexual. He would do anything to get me alone. One time he shoved me in a closet, and another time he had me cornered in the back of a truck. I felt as though I had no one to help me. My father was oblivious to it, my sisters were too, and my boss would threaten me and tell me that if I told anyone what he did, it would ruin his marriage. He also said that he would lose his family and my sisters would blame me. I felt like I was stuck in a web. I was being abused but I confused the abuse with love, as if he was afraid for being discovered having an affair, as if this was an actual relationship. Clearly it could not be. He was an adult and I was a young girl.

Not knowing what to do, I ran to drugs to escape. It started with marijuana and soon moved to ecstasy. Later cocaine and alcohol became my drugs of choice. I never learned how to cope with my trauma. Running away and numbing the pain was all I knew how to do.

When I was fifteen, I became pregnant. I was treated like cattle by him, and I was told to "take care of it." Being so young, I truly believed abortion was a viable option. I couldn't imagine keeping his child, and I was just a kid myself. The experience was traumatizing. My best friend at the time was the only person I confided in, and she agreed to go with me.

Even though I chose abortion, God loves my child, just like He loves me. I have peace in knowing my child is safe in Jesus' loving arms. Because of God's love, forgiveness, and amazing grace, I will one day be holding my child in my arms too. Forgiveness is one of the miracles of God's grace. Its healing power is magnificent!

At age sixteen I lived on my own. That's where my story continues.

I had developed a close friendship with a boy named John. One of the things I loved the most was his sense of humor. No one could make me laugh as hard as he did. I confided in him and explained the details of what was happening with my boss at the time. He and I were both trying to run away from our lives. He was confused about the direction of his life, and I was trying to break free from the web of lies and abuse I was dealing with on a regular basis. We ultimately sought refuge in each other and began to date. He was the first male I ever felt I could truly trust. This gave me the strength to finally break free once and for all from my situation. I abruptly quit my job and explained to my sisters, my boss, and his wife that I was moving on, and I never looked back.

One night when I was nineteen years old, John came over and told me he had something very important to tell me. He sat me down and told me he was diagnosed with HIV. I knew he was so scared, but a piece of me believed he was telling me I had HIV too. It was like he was hoping he could have someone else in this life to deal with the pain and stigma of having this disease. In my mind there was no way I didn't have it too, but once again God was watching over me.

I went an entire year believing I was HIV positive. At the time, HIV was still perceived as a death sentence, and I lived that year in total fear and recklessness. I remember moving from one apartment to another and never unpacking the boxes. I was not motivated to do it. I just ran to whatever would numb the pain. I was caught in a vicious cycle of numbing the pain, going to work, remembering the death sentence, waking up, and trying to survive all over again. At this point John and I split up but remained friends.

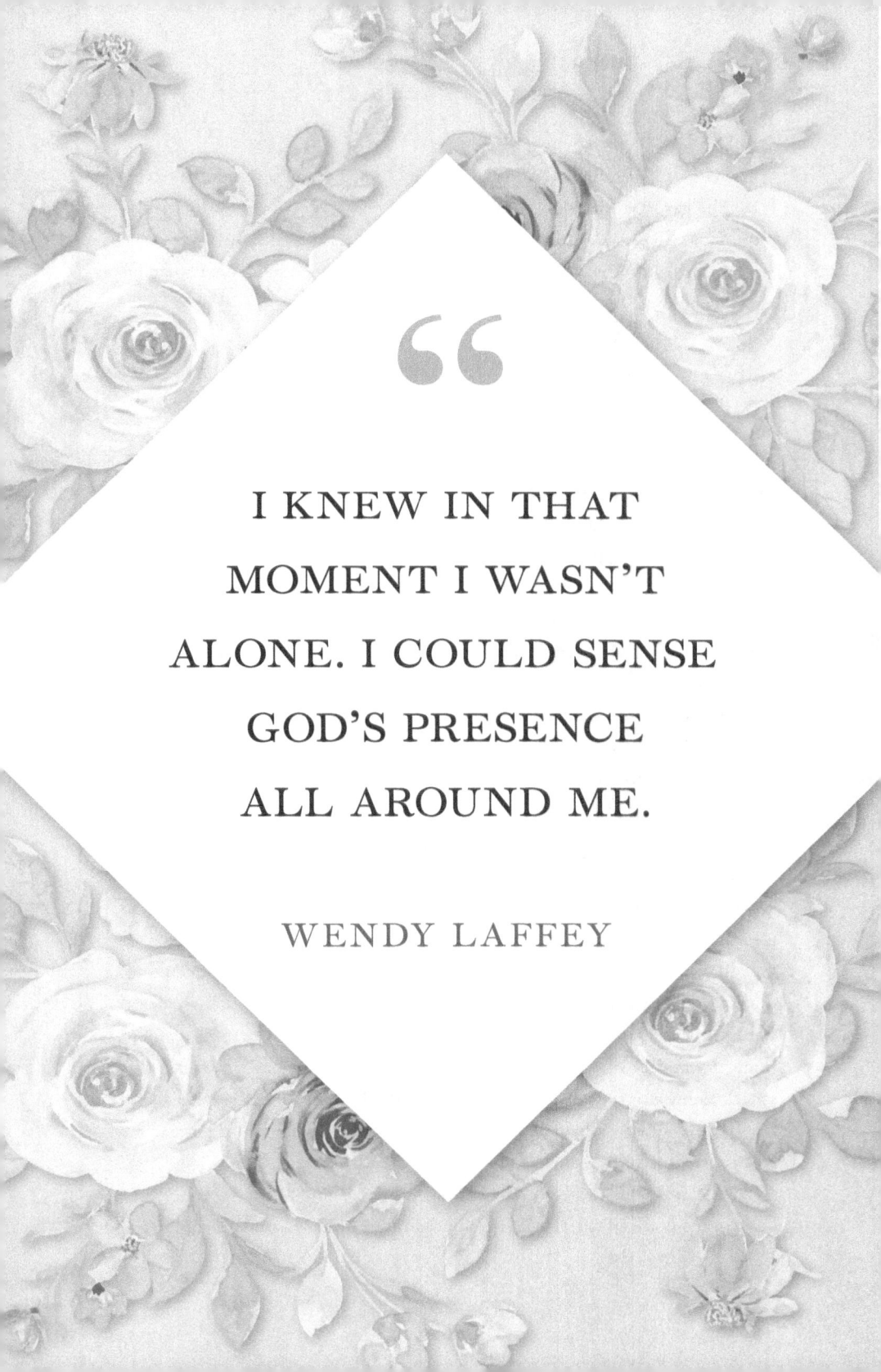

> I KNEW IN THAT MOMENT I WASN'T ALONE. I COULD SENSE GOD'S PRESENCE ALL AROUND ME.
>
> WENDY LAFFEY

After a year of suffering, I finally confided in one of my sisters about having HIV. She gave me the courage to schedule an HIV test with my primary care physician. I finally agreed to do it and made the decision to face this on my own.

I was sitting in the waiting room in complete fear when suddenly I heard my name being sung out of the speakers:

Who's bending down to give me a rainbow?

Everyone knows it's Wendy...

I had chills up and down my spine, and I scanned the room to see if anyone else was hearing what I was hearing, but no one was there but me. I knew in that moment I wasn't alone. I could sense God's presence all around me. The song by The Association is actually called "Windy," but all I heard was God calling my name, "Wendy."

A few days later I received a call from the doctor himself, and he said, "Wendy, I have the results from your HIV test. It's negative!" He sounded so genuinely happy for me. He said, "Wendy, go and enjoy your life." I remember running out of the back doors of my office at the time, and it was a beautiful sunny day! I felt a weight of bricks lifted from me. I immediately looked up in the sky and thanked God for the second chance at life! It was God's protection once again, as God promises in Jeremiah 29:11, "For I know the plans I have for you, declares the Lord. Plans to prosper you and not to harm you, plans to give you a hope and future."

My father became very ill soon thereafter. This was very difficult for me because my father always tried his best under difficult circumstances to provide for us. We didn't have a great relationship until I moved out on my own, but once I did, it seemed like he and I were finally understanding one another. I knew he loved me. That was never a question. After a year or so of being sick and in and out of the hospital, he passed away. When I walked up to give the eulogy, straight ahead staring at me was my former boss and his wife. At this point, I was so far removed from him that I understood the severity of what he did to me for years. I was so sick to my stomach, angry, and immediately filled with the desire for justice. How dare he smugly attend my father's funeral knowing what he had done to my father's daughter! My resolve only grew stronger with time passing.

While mourning the loss of my father one late evening, I told my sister everything over a bottle of wine. We were alone, and the details just poured out of me.

I could no longer contain the burden of carrying them. She woke up the next morning enraged. She encouraged me to tell my other sister right away in an effort to rally support around me and begin the process of healing.

My former boss happened to be on a cruise at the time with little to no access to communication on land. This gave us the necessary time to figure out the first step and the best way to reveal the truth to his wife. We decided it was best for me to write a letter to her and provide proof in the form of cards and gifts he used to sexually groom me. Grooming is a preparatory process in which a perpetrator gradually gains a person's trust with the intent to be sexually abusive.

I never prayed so much in my life. I remember just praying the Our Father over and over because that's all I really knew. The day she got back from the cruise she received the letter. She called me immediately, and I was so scared to pick up the phone. Her first words were, "Wendy? I'm so sorry that happened to you!" She was in tears. She said, "No one should ever be treated the way you were treated." Her next words were not what I ever expected. She said "Wendy, I'm only going to ask you to do one thing. You have to go to the police, and you have to go right now!" I literally felt like someone was physically carrying me the entire time. Which reminds me of another wonderful promise from God in Isaiah 43:1-2, "Fear not for I have redeemed you; I have called you by name, you are mine. When you pass through the waters, I will be with you; and through the rivers, they shall not overwhelm you; When you walk through the fire, you shall not be burned; and the flames shall not consume you."

He was arrested immediately and charged with twelve counts of endangering the welfare of a minor in a supervisory position amongst other charges. He was strip-searched and let out on bail. Bail was set in the hundreds of thousands. I was summoned to go before a grand jury and share the nightmare in front of so many strangers. This required me to expose the details of my nightmare, once again leaving me feeling completely violated.

The case dragged on for about two years. It was so difficult to function normally while being drawn through this painstaking process for this long, but this was the only alternative. One day the prosecutors called me and explained a recent situation with another high visibility case similar to mine they had just lost and were devastated. They used that as leverage to encourage me to accept a plea. I honestly was so tired and drained. I was ready to put this chapter of my life behind me. I agreed to a deal that sentenced him to a large fine, probation for five years, and mandatory registry as a sex offender under Megan's Law, as well as maintaining and updating the registry annually. I also fought for and succeeded in having the ability to testify against him if he ever hurt anyone in the future. He also lost his family and fortune through this process. I would have preferred to see him behind bars, but I was over the daily stress and the toll the process was taking on my health and well-being.

Three months before the sentencing, a girlfriend of mine kept urging me to meet this guy named Billy, saying that she thought he was perfect for me. Truth be told, I didn't want to see any guy; I just wanted to be alone for a while. But she was persistent, and I finally agreed to meet him. I can remember the first time I saw Billy. He looked exactly like who I envisioned I would be with and eerily like my dad, which I found comforting. I had an immediate sense that there was something special about this man. We met just a couple of times before I knew he was the one God planned for me. We fell in love quickly. Billy accepted me for who I was. He was so very compassionate about my past. Over and over, he would tell me that things would be all right, and he was right.

Billy and I grew in love and in faith together. We now have three beautiful daughters and are raising them to live in faith, putting Jesus at the center of our lives. I've learned so many valuable lessons through my walk in faith. One of the greatest lessons is my desire to forgive everyone. I told you before how I would pray the Our Father because that was the only prayer I knew at the time. In that prayer, we pray, "Forgive us our trespasses as we forgive those who trespass against us." Jesus himself said from the cross, "Father, forgive them, for they know not what they do." Forgiveness is at the very heart of Christianity.

I was put to the test with forgiveness, not just in theory but in actuality a few years ago. I was walking with Billy and our girls in Asbury Park. We entered the Convention Hall promenade, and I heard Billy scream "Laffey!" I instinctually knew somehow that he wanted me to follow him fast because there was danger. The place was packed. When we got to an area clear of people to regroup, he told me that my former boss was sitting at the coffee shop right when I walked in. I expressed to Billy that for some reason I needed to see him for myself. Billy understood and immediately said, "Yes, go ahead." There was a band playing in the middle of convention hall, and I fought my way to the one side of the open circle where a few kids and people were dancing in the center. Straight ahead in front of me on the other side of the open circle was my perpetrator, sitting in a wheelchair. He and I locked eyes, and I stared at him out of sheer curiosity. I wanted to know how I would feel after all these years and after all that happened to me. Time went by so slowly, and I literally felt nothing but the peace that surpasses all understanding. I had no anger inside of me, and I know it was this boomerang of God's goodness. Here I was with my beautiful family enjoying the fruits of life, and now with years having passed by, he was this complete stranger. I had forgiven him. I no longer carried the burden of what he did to me. I found myself realizing in that moment that Jesus died for him too, so I prayed for him. It was the true power of forgiveness. Then I turned around and went shopping with my family.

I often think about that little girl within me and what I would say to her if I had the chance to speak to her before all of this happened. As I tell you what I would say to that little girl inside of me, I encourage you to think about the little child inside you. We all have a story and have been through experiences in our lives that have caused us pain and sadness.

Here is what I would say to the little girl inside of me:

Beautiful Wendy, you are magnificently made! You're going to go through some terrible things. I'm so sorry you have to go through this stuff. You're going to feel like it's all your fault, but I promise you that it was never your fault. You did nothing to deserve what's to come. God will be with you through it all. He loves you more than you could ever imagine! When Mom leaves, God will be wiping those tears from your face. When Dad dies and you will lose his giant bear hugs, God will be hugging you. When you're being abused, God will be crying with you. Through all the trials and tests, God will be with you. He'll never abandon you! He will give you the strength you need to survive, and he will love you through each and every moment.

Wendy, God has an awesome plan for your life. One day God is going to bless you with an amazing man who will become your husband. He's going to love you through all the pain you've gone through. You're going to learn so many valuable lessons through your marriage that will strengthen your faith in Jesus.

Gods going to give you the greatest gift and her name will be Grace! She'll love sports, dancing, and school. She'll look just like her Daddy but she's sensitive, affectionate, and strong-willed just like you.

He's going to bless you with a second daughter Claire who will remind you so much of your Daddy. She'll have the most beautiful shade of red hair just like him. Claire is so silly and easygoing. She'll love when you hug her and spend time with her, and she will show you unconditional love so much so that you'll almost feel like you don't deserve it.

The Lord will give you a third daughter you'll name Pearl after the parable of the pearl of great price in Matthew 13:45-46 in the Bible. A pearl is produced by an oyster's discomfort and irritation. You might say a pearl grows out of hurt or pain. Every moment spent with precious Pearl will remind you of God's Goodness. She has the heart of pure gold, and she'll be a miniature version of you.

He plans on giving you a wonderful job that you'll use to pray for people and help them into homes. You'll get to know and be allowed to touch so many lives through your work. This is something that you will find very gratifying and fulfilling.

God will bless you with a renewed relationship with your mother and siblings, and lots of great friends and a church that will treat you like family.

One day God will call you to speak to other women about what you went through, and he will give you the strength to do this so that you can help others. He'll allow you to use your pain to show his precious children how awesome God is and that your trials don't define who you are. You'll show them that with God, all things are possible!

One last thing, I am so proud of the girl you are and the woman you'll become! Your heart is big, and you won't ever lose that part of yourself. After years of abuse, you never allowed anyone to take that part of you away.

Perhaps my purpose is to encourage those who are going through what I went through or who have a past similar to mine to talk to their own "little selves" inside of them. I want you all to realize that throughout your struggles, God was with you. He will never forsake you or leave you alone. Jesus himself tells us, "In this world you will have trouble, but take heart, for I have overcome the World."

In light of all the troubles I faced in life, I overcame them with the help of Jesus. He loves me and he loves you as well. He has a wonderful plan for each of our lives. He will take all the bad that has happened and work it for good. All you have to do is love him and surrender to his plan and purposes for you.

I can honestly say that I love the imperfect woman I am today. I am a wife, a mother, a daughter, a sister, a friend... but most of all, I am the daughter of the most high King, who is not moved by this world. For my God is with me and goes before me. I do not fear because I am His.

In 2 Corinthians 5:17 it says, "Therefore, if anyone is in Christ, he is a new creation. The old has passed away, behold, all things have become new!"

We've all done things in our past we're not proud of. After years of abuse, afflictions, and addiction I realized running away from my problems in the form of drugs or alcohol only compounded the pain. They're ineffective. I was ineffective. The only way I found true healing is by facing the things I feared most head-on. One step at a time and one foot in front of the other. Little by little and day by day I began to seek The Lord and his Word, and my life began to change for the better. I was completely broken, but God literally put me back together right in front of the people who broke me. We are promised beauty for ashes, and I can say that is what I was delivered: more beauty from all of this pain than I could ever have imagined.

If after you read my story, you're feeling a strong sensation or hearing a still small voice to seek God and his will for your life, I would like to encourage you to read this simple prayer in faith. "Lord Jesus, please forgive my sins. Thank you for loving me and dying on the cross to save me. Come into my heart and be my Lord and Savior. Help me become the person that you created me to be in every area of my life. In Jesus's name, Amen!"

ABOUT THE CONTRIBUTOR

Wendy Laffey is a Christian, a wife, a mother of three beautiful girls—Grace, Claire, and Pearl —and a devoted mortgage loan officer for twenty-one years helping hundreds of people achieve the dream of home ownership! Wendy has lived on her own since she was sixteen years old and began her career fresh out of high school as an assistant to a top producer in the mortgage industry. She worked her way up to becoming a loan officer herself in just a couple of years and has been growing her successful reputation in the industry ever since. Wendy is looking forward to sharing her personal testimony of humble beginnings, tragedy, and abuse and how she's overcome through her relationship with Jesus, His healing, and the divine plan he had for her life and future.

NOTE FROM THE CONTRIBUTOR

We would like to offer our deepest condolences and heartfelt prayers to the children, family, and loved ones of the man in the wheelchair who lost his battle to cancer in 2022. May they feel the peace, protection, comfort, and love from our Heavenly Father all the days of their lives.

Bits of Her Heart...

Wendy Laffey

Whatever you do, do it for the glory of God.

FUN FACT...

Wendy loves to dance more than just about any other activity, and someday soon she wants to learn to shuffle dance with her daughters. Her guilty pleasure is turning the volume all the way up to sing and dance in her car alone!

LIVING LIFE INTENTIONALLY

BY BRENDA KARINJA

My chapter is dedicated to someone who has just suffered a loss in their life. This is a story of darkness and how I chose to see the light within and shine it in a way to help me move forward and live with brightness. I hope you find a small piece of my story that will help you with your chapter.

I drove home from the hospital in a total fog. I got home, laid on my couch, and I looked out at the trees that seemed to be blowing back and forth. It was a windy night. I remember just staring at the trees wondering how I was going to wake up the next day without my mom? I remember thinking how was I going to be a mom without a mom? How was I going to mother my children and be present for them when I was hurting so deeply?

The days immediately following my mom's unexpected passing, I felt lost. I just laid in bed, disconnected from the world around me. I just didn't have the energy for anything. I was in a depression, and some days I could barely shower. I remember that one day one of my best friends came over with a tray of food to feed my family. She told me to get up, get out of bed, and brush my hair. I guess she could see I hadn't really left my room.

I'm so grateful for the support of my husband, friends, and family because

I don't know how I survived those early days after her passing. I often can compare myself to being on autopilot because I was there, but I really wasn't there. My mind was just questioning and replaying the moments over and over in my head. I wore her clothes every day to feel close to her. I put on her perfume and even used her hairbrush. I know now that God must have had me in the palm of His hands because I don't know how else I got through those days.

We did not expect my mom to pass as suddenly as she did. I felt like I blinked, and she was gone. That can happen at any moment to any one of us, and so I decided I just couldn't waste another moment of my life. It is precious. Eventually, I made the decision to live my life in a different way, with more intention. Thinking about how my mom lived her life inspired me to reexamine my own, beginning with my birthday.

My birthday, which is actually on Valentine's Day, to me is like my New Year's. It's a day of renewal, it's a day of reflection, and it's a day that is a blessing. Growing older is a gift, and since my mom's passing, each year I try to find little ways to celebrate that will enrich my life in the year ahead even more, so I buy myself five special gifts.

As a mom, you tend to not do things for yourself and at times you might put yourself on the back burner. At least I often do! But when it's my birthday, I am intentional with myself and really think hard about things to gift myself that will make me a little happier, things that will make my life easier, and things that will just bring a smile to my face. For example, this past birthday one of the five gifts that I purchased for myself was a pair of running sneakers. The sneakers to me symbolized being closer to the earth and remind me that I am capable of more— that I am capable of putting my feet to the pavement, hitting the ground running, and achieving my goals.

I began this tradition of giving gifts to myself the year after my mom passed. I was struggling and missing her so much. So, I bought myself a pair of earrings. I just felt like getting those earrings for myself would make me feel pretty on days when I didn't feel like getting dressed or doing much of anything. I knew that looking at these earrings would make me feel like I was put together. Plus, wearing large earrings helps me to feel powerful.

The gifts don't have to be expensive. They don't have to cost anything at all! These gifts are just intentional ways to honor myself, whether it's with materialistic things like earrings and sneakers or it's writing a letter to a friend or writing special words to myself or even just picking fresh flowers. Celebrating my birthday in this way keeps my mom close to my heart. She loved honoring people so much. My mother had a never-ending heart and a welcoming soul, and she was a giver to everyone. I picked up on it when I was a child and appreciate her giving heart even more so now as an adult and mother.

I'll never forget the time I came home from school, just getting off the school bus in fourth grade, and I opened the door to see a family I didn't know at the dining room table. I remember asking my mother, "Mom who are these people?"

She replied, "I met them at the store and found out they are living in their car. They have no food, so I wanted to make them dinner." See—how can you not love my mom? Heart of pure gold. She was always looking for ways to help people.

I remember another time when my neighbor across the street told my mom that she liked her shoes. My mother took her shoes straight off of her feet and gave them to her! Even after my mom passed, my neighbor was still wearing the shoes, and every time I saw those shoes I thought of my mom. My neighbor was a dear friend to me. She recently passed, but I could always see how happy she was in my mom's shoes.

My mom loved connecting with people. There was always a pot of coffee on at my mom's home to share. Mom would invite people over to sit around her table and talk. And if nobody was over in person, you would find her on the phone. She was always talking to someone! I wish I could sit at the table with her now and have coffee with her again.

Reading these stories about my mom, I am sure you are getting a sense of who she was. I was blessed to have such a loving presence in my life. She inspires me with everything I do. I do it in my own way, and now with such intention. If someone needs something, or even just likes something, I try to give it to them. If someone is down, I try in little ways to lift them up. Like one day when I was at the dollar store, I could see the woman working there was in emotional pain. We had a brief interaction, and my heart knew exactly what to do. I went and bought her flowers. When I showed back up at the store just a short while later, flowers in hand, we both got teary eyed. Being intentional with my life offers me so many more opportunities to connect and be present with people, just like my mom always was.

> NOTHING ELSE MATTERS BUT THE LOVE WE HAVE, THE LOVE WE GIVE, AND THE LOVE WE LEAVE BEHIND.
>
> BRENDA KARINJA

Living Life Intentionally

My mom inspires our traditions, too. Like Sunday dinners. Growing up with an Italian mom, we always had big Sunday dinners together at the table. I remember when my grandmother was alive, all of my aunts and uncles and cousins would come over. Then, when my grandmother passed away, my mom still continued that tradition. She would cook big pots of sauce and meatballs with the intention of family around our table and the feeling of togetherness! Whatever she did, it was always done big. I love to continue this tradition with my children with my own special touches. Instead of always making Italian dinner, we will often take turns picking a theme, like Mexican food! I want everyone to be happy and together, enjoying our favorite foods and making a big meal from appetizers to desserts! They know just how important it is to me to be there for Sunday dinner. It gives the family time to connect and appreciate one another.

Not just traditions, but the little things my mom did have also carried over into my parenting. My mom was a huge note writer. I really cherish those notes and cards now that she has passed. Today, as a mom, I parent a little differently than I did before she passed away. I always told my children I loved them and wrote notes, but now I'm even more intentional with them. I try to create ways that they will remember me when I'm no longer here. I make leaving the notes more of a surprise, rather than just a quick note on the counter. When my daughter returns from college, she always brings clothes and her book bag. Before she returns back to school, I like to hide little notes within her belongings so that she can get a special treat from me to let her know that I'm thinking of her. I'll leave her notes in jean pockets, coat pockets, and in her pencil bag! I especially love to leave notes inside her mac and cheese boxes or in her laptop telling her how beautiful she is and that I'm proud of her, that I love her, and that I always support her. The best part is she always texts me a pic of the note signaling she got it! I can only imagine how she must feel seeing those little notes. It's nothing fancy, just words on an index card. But they are from my heart with intention so she will always think of me and this tradition. I hope one day she makes those notes into a book!

Intentionally, I try to do these small things and treasure every moment I can connect with my children, with family, with friends, even with strangers the way my mom did because our physical lives are not promised. We do not know when our last moment will be, as I learned through my mom's unexpected passing.

I was in deep water in the days and months after my mom's passing. I learned to take life one day at a time, just like she did, and I knew that my children still needed me to show up for them, even on days when I was hurting. Some days I would feel okay in one moment, and then out of nowhere I'd be hysterically crying. There were other days that I would feel guilty if I didn't think about my mom for a portion of the day. I kind of felt like I was moving on, and I was forgetting her, but of course I wasn't. What I have learned was that I was living life moving forward, bringing with me the things that I missed the most about my mom. I would make her recipes and have family over because I knew that's what mom loved. And on other days, it was just one emotion after another of really missing her, and the reality was setting in that my mom was no longer here. I wasn't going to get a phone call that she was just calling to check in. She wasn't just going to pop over and see my children and bring them snacks or see them off the school bus. And when I got myself thinking of all of the things that I wasn't going to be celebrating with my mom on a daily basis, those feelings felt like waves were just crashing over my head. I felt like I couldn't breathe, and I felt like I couldn't pick myself up on those dark days. I would just sit on the couch, and I would barely get my children off to school. Going through my mom's things sent more tidal waves crashing down on me. I couldn't see how I would ever make it through. As time went on, those days became less and less. I remember intentionally choosing to listen to music from when I was younger and that reminded me of my mother—Stevie Wonder and Gladys Knight and the music of the '70s and '80s. On those dark days, that music comforted me, and it gave me what I needed to move forward and to live life without my mom.

Finding clarity through all of this loss and pain and love really didn't come from one specific situation. I think clarity came from a collection of everyday actions; taking one day at a time realizing the strength I had within was born of my mother's strength, and now it was up to me to live a life of purpose and intention for myself and my family. I think since my mom's passing in 2014, I feel love more deeply. I feel even more so that my children are gifts, and how I make them feel is so important. If I let them know how loved they are, they will be blessed forever as I am blessed forever by the feeling of love my mom gave me. I also find peace in still looking at those trees—the same trees I looked at the night that she passed. Whenever I need clarity, looking at the trees always reconnects me back to the night my mom passed; knowing how comforting they were to me really comes back tenfold.

I think the shift from total despair to living so intentionally happened through a "one day at a time" mindset. Living a life with purpose and intention happened gradually over the years since she passed. The shift to me was recognizing that this story of mine is a gift to share, knowing that I can take this pain and sadness and turn it into good to help others heal is an amazing feeling. From the point of my mom's passing to now and forward, I live my life in a way so that I am what I miss the most about my mom. I think that really missing my mom's heart and how she made me and everyone around her feel impacted me so much. She inspired me to live my life with meaning for myself and for my family and those around me. I live more purposefully from how I speak to my children to preparing what I'll leave behind for them that one day they will cherish and hold in their hearts. I live with intention for myself and my health and celebrate my soul as a person, as a mother, as a wife, as a friend, and as a sister!

We can all only hope that our lives will ripple out and impact others the way my mom's has, with future generations carrying on traditions and creating their own traditions with our lasting imprints woven into them. We can take the inspiration from generations before us and use it as a catalyst to create the lives we want to live, purposefully with intention. Nothing else matters in this world but the love we have, the love we give, and the love we leave behind. How will you live more intentionally today?

A NOTE FROM THE CONTRIBUTOR:

I want to thank my family for their support especially my daughter Haley who said, "You have to say yes and do this project!" even if it was out of my comfort zone. I would love to thank Jenn and Jess for their belief in me to include me in this beautiful anthology, and I want to thank my beautiful Mom for creating the blueprint of my being.

ABOUT THE CONTRIBUTOR

Brenda Karinja is a long-time resident of Ocean Township, married to her high school sweetheart. She is the momma of three teens, and just added a pup to the mix to help her adjust as her firstborn flew the nest to pursue her dreams in college!!

Brenda has a big heart and enjoys helping others. She loves to listen and lend a hand where needed. She works from home around the chaos of her family and life helping others feel good about the skin they're in... literally! She loves to make people laugh and smile.

Her family is her whole world, and she feels she's here to share her gifts of intuition, and sensitivity to help others.

"A ship is safe in harbor, but that's not what ships are for."
William G.T. Shedd

Bits of Her Heart...

Brenda Karinja

Be the energy you want to receive.

FUN FACT...

Brenda was super shy growing up and now she loves to sing with a microphone! She is afraid of heights. The first time she went on an airplane was on her honeymoon. She loves hugs and making homemade soup.

15

THE LOVE MODEL

BY JAZIMIN GARRETT

Dear Reader, I'd like to take you on a mini journey of resilience through love. The love others have had for me and the love that I have built in myself. I don't claim to know it all but what I do know is that I have come so very far, and you can too!

"Be soulful. Be kind. Be in Love. Be foolishly in love for love is all there is."

Rumi

Have you ever had a series of events or even one life-altering event caused by outside circumstances that left you feeling helpless, robbed, confused, and completely shattered? Have you ever then thought, *How am I going to ever get out of this sadness, pain, and grief?* or *Why is this happening to me?*

The "why is this happening to me?" is a hard one to grasp. In fact, there are many situations that have happened to me, and I still wonder why. I've often wondered so much that I decided I needed to leave the why on the shelf and focus on the how. Leaving the why on the shelf is NOT easy. I still struggle with that one as it's natural to question why things happen to us, and if there was any part in it that we played a role in. Oftentimes there is not, and that's when we need to learn that the "why" question, or confusion, isn't serving us. The better question I have had to ask myself is how.

How will I navigate this?

How will I get through?

How will I move forward in order to thrive and enjoy the beauty that is life set before me?

I do feel certain that there is a powerful feeling, being, element, action, and reaction... that encompasses everything that has gotten me through: Love.

I was just off the plane from a trip to Denmark with friends, and I reached for the phone to call my dad and mom to let them know I was home safe and sound. My mom answered the phone, and I knew in her voice something was wrong. You see, my dad had already suffered from five strokes, and he wasn't in the best shape. I had been to see him just before I went to Denmark, and we had the most special time together. I live in California, but I happened to be on the east coast in North Carolina for work when my mom called that day to let me know my dad was in the hospital. I didn't hesitate; I went directly up to New York, and when I arrived, to my surprise, they were releasing him. I was delighted to be able to spend the day with him. He didn't want to go straight home; he wanted to go get cheeseburgers at *Five Guys,* so we did that instead.

We had a lovely lunch and, despite my dad's condition, he was pretty lively. After lunch we went on a couple errands and then to my grandmother's house. My dad was again super lively for his condition, and he insisted that he just wanted to hang out and not go home. I was able to laugh with him, hold his hand, and just be around his infectious smile. We had so many beautiful moments that day, and every moment I was praying for him to be better. There wasn't a second that I wasn't in prayer in my head hoping for the best for my dad. Later that evening as I held my dad's hand, I asked him if he had anything to tell me. I asked him about life and how I was doing and if he had any advice for me. He simply said that I was doing amazing and that I had to keep on going and being me, which was a part of him.

Throughout the night my dad laughed, made jokes, and just beamed with happiness. I knew that happiness came from being with me. My dad and I had the most special relationship. He was the kind of dad that dreams are made of: he loved big, was always there, and helped anyone, even strangers. I could never envision a life without my dad. My dad has been my rock, my hero, and my everything my entire life. When I was a little girl, he divorced my birth mom and fought for custody of me and my two brothers. She was unfit to parent us as an addict, choosing a life of drugs and alcohol over her children. Being raised in the early part of my life by a mother who fell far short, I experienced many things at a very young age that were awful, from abuse in every way, to abandonment. My dad was the complete opposite; he was a man to look up to. My dad was in the United States Navy and spent years traveling the world on military ships. He was a chef, and in his spare time he enjoyed photography. He always had a camera around his neck and had endless albums of photos of his travels. He literally took every opportunity while he was in the Navy to travel. That's where he met my stepmom, (now Mom), Jenny.

Larry & Jenny, Jenny & Larry. True Love.

Jenny was and is an incredible woman. She, alongside my dad, fought for me and my two brothers. She worked tirelessly with my dad to get custody of us. You may think that would and should have been easy with my mom being on drugs and all, but it wasn't. We were fighting something even bigger than drugs; we were fighting racism. In the 1980s, it was UNHEARD of for a black man to get custody of three children from a white woman. After many roadblocks, hearings, letters, and lawyers, the courts finally deemed my father "fit for custody." How they could have even thought for a second that my birth mom was the better parent just because of the color of her skin is disgusting. The fact that a court of law was considering the welfare of three children was better with a drunk, drug addict, rather than my black dad, is absolutely horrific. I will say, the court did its due diligence and investigated both parties. The best thing that ever happened to me was my dad getting custody of us. I can't even imagine the life I would have had in my birth mom's care. I am beyond grateful that Jenny was there to help my dad and the court see what was right.

Actually, gratitude doesn't even begin to cover it, and now you might understand a bit better why when Jenny called to say my dad was in the hospital, I didn't hesitate. Spending the day with him was a gift; I know now that that day with my dad was made special for me. The following evening when my parents dropped me off at the airport my dad gave me the biggest hug. This might seem normal to most, but in my dad's condition I couldn't believe the strength behind

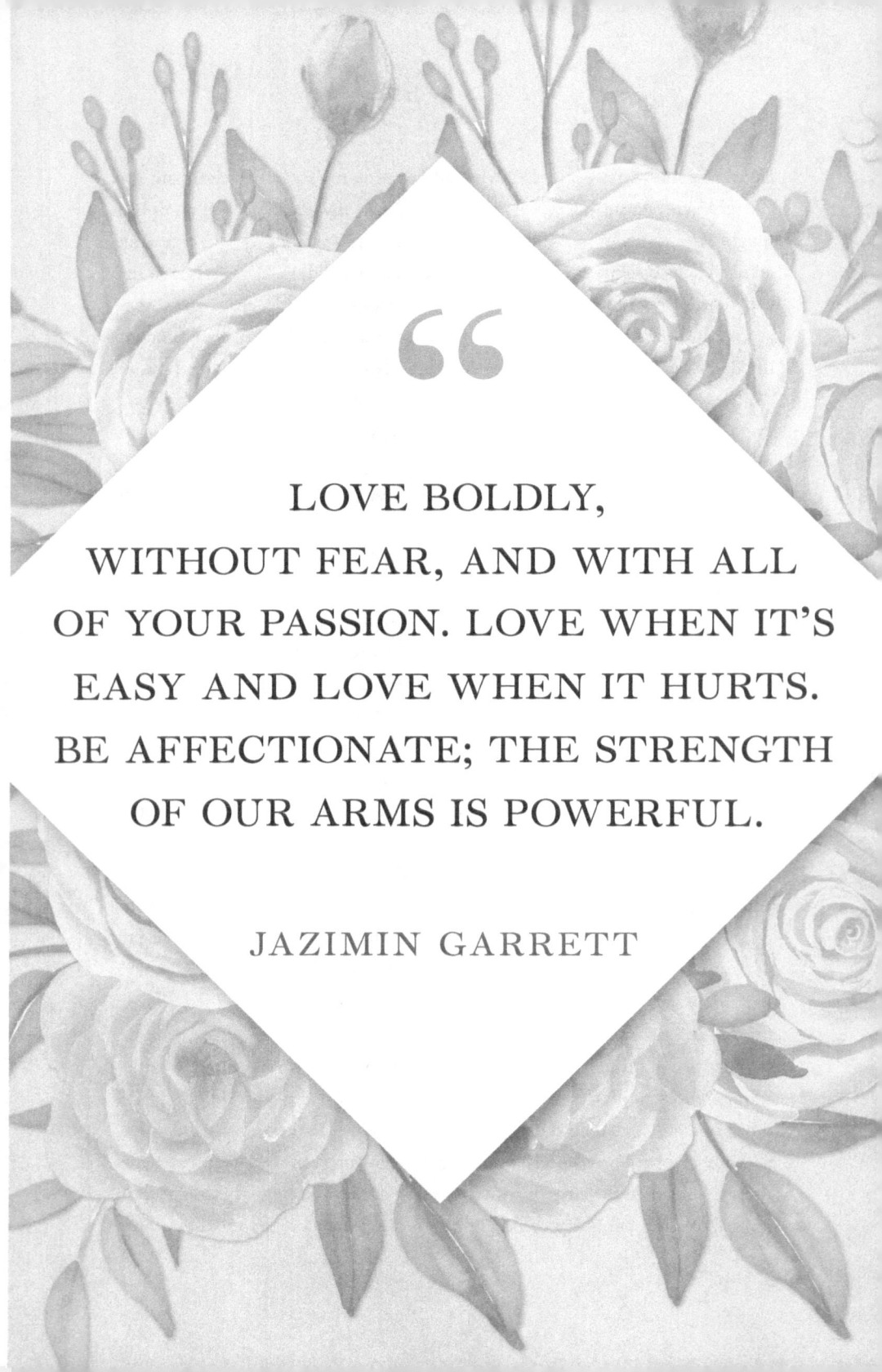

> "
>
> LOVE BOLDLY, WITHOUT FEAR, AND WITH ALL OF YOUR PASSION. LOVE WHEN IT'S EASY AND LOVE WHEN IT HURTS. BE AFFECTIONATE; THE STRENGTH OF OUR ARMS IS POWERFUL.
>
> JAZIMIN GARRETT

it. As I hugged him back, I told him that I needed him to stay alive, that we had so much more to do together. He said he loved me so much, that was happy to see me, that he was proud of me, and that I was doing great. I fought back my tears to stay strong and kept a big smile as I waved to my dad.

When I heard the tone of my mom's voice on the phone that day when I was getting home from Denmark, my chest hurt. Funny how when you are really connected to someone, pain manifests itself square in the heart. She went on to say that she didn't think my dad had much longer to live. I was heartbroken. It was the day before Thanksgiving, and flights were terrible! I booked a flight, but it wouldn't get me to New York until the morning after Thanksgiving. On Thanksgiving morning, I had signed up to run the Oakland Turkey Trot. This is a 5K and festival in Oakland, California, and something my company encourages us to do to give back, give thanks, and have fun together. Since I moved across the country, some of my coworkers are more than colleagues; they are my friends and family. I don't know how I had the energy, but I was up and at my coworker Jessamyn's house. We had coffee and walked to the lake to meet up with our CEO Adam who was also running the race.

It was a BEAUTIFUL DAY! The sun was shining, and I felt an uncanny magnificent presence all around me. I immediately knew it was the presence of my dad and I soaked it all in. I began the race and felt an immense amount of joy and love radiating around me. I ran effortlessly around the lake, taking in the sun rays on my face and feeling the words of my dad. I felt a lifetime of love enveloping me. I felt hopeful and that my dad was showing me that no matter what he was always there with me. Following the race, we were all feeling good on that "runner's high." My CEO Adam had invited me to his house for Thanksgiving dinner with his family, and that morning I grabbed a bite with Jessamyn at a diner then went home to pack and relax. I was just putting on my jacket and grabbing a bottle of wine from my stock to head to dinner when the phone rang. It was my brother telling me that my dad had died.

My North star was gone.

Losing a parent is indescribable, especially one that was the epitome of love. Love is what gets me through even the most challenging of times. The love my dad had for me holds me up. The love he showed me taught me to give that love to others. You see, no matter what we are going through it's the love that we either get from others or the love we have stored in ourselves that will push us to the other side. In my world, I choose to lead with love. I love deeply and intentionally whether in my life it is a lover, friend, coworker, stranger, or anyone. I always want people to feel loved by me and to feel cared for and thought of. I truly believe love makes the world go around. My dad exemplified this. When I learned of his passing, I felt an even greater responsibility to live as he lived and carry on all the things he taught me, and "be" the love the world so desperately needs.

I have been through some of the toughest times, and it has been the love of parents, friends, co-workers, and strangers that has kept me afloat. Things are always going to happen to us; it's the way we choose to deal with them that is most important. I'm not saying to just get over it. What I am saying is to find your people and build love and strength within yourself for those times you find yourself alone. I have had to call on this love more times than any human should.

For instance, when I was twenty-five years old, I lost another North Star in my life, my brother Marcus. I didn't lose him to death. Marcus is still alive, but he is incarcerated for the rest of his life. The hopes and dreams that we had as brother and sister were destroyed (this story is a whole book in itself). He, in a moment, made a decision that would shatter the lives of so many, literally and figuratively. He took the life of his significant other and two other innocent bystanders. When I got that call, my life was forever altered.

My brother was my best friend. Before my dad got custody of us, he protected me from the vile and unimaginable things that happened while in my mother's care. We bonded deeply because we experienced so much chaos together, and we got through it together. Love is beautiful and complicated like that. Love bonds us through shared experiences. And when we love a person unconditionally, that means loving them even when we don't love or understand their choices. I can never fully grasp what happened in that moment when my brother did what he did, but I do know my love for him transcends his mistakes. We had the wildest hopes and dreams for our lives and future families. Oftentimes in life I would tell myself I didn't need anyone because I had him, and then he was gone—not gone but still here to live the worst life imaginable. Losing him to incarceration was like a death. I grieve him every day as he is locked away for twenty-three hours a day, stripped of his dignity and rights.

The trial was so painful, as nobody won. We all lost. I lost a brother and sister in Rachel, and Rachel's parents lost a child. My parents lost a child. Worst of all Marcus and Rachel have a child, Shaylyn, who now lost both of her parents.

How was I ever going to get through this?

Again, with love.

My friends loved me through this, as I loved my parents and Shaylyn through it. My friends sacrificed their own time with family to go on visits with me to see my brother in prison. They held me as I wept for years, and still until this day I break down at times. This grieving isn't something that just goes away; it requires constant love to get me through. Sometimes it's the love from my friends or lover. Other times I find myself alone, and it is then that I can reflect on the love and memories I have stored to move my spirits to a happier place. It's the love of Deity showing me that while Marcus made a mistake, he is still worthy of my love and His. The amount of people who have helped me through this situation is countless, and the amount of love I have been freely given is infinite, as I will forever be navigating this pain. Just as I will forever be navigating the pain of losing my dad. If you've ever lost anyone who stood for you when the world was harsh and cruel, or if you've ever lost anyone you've loved so deeply, I'm certain you can relate to the hole in my heart and have one of your own. And if you can't relate, please consider yourself lucky. For it's an ache that doesn't subside with time.

Throughout my life, while I have had so many heavy things happen to me, I have also been fortunate enough to have some really beautiful moments as well. Those beautiful moments are the ones I choose to hold onto and with which I press forward. The lesson that I have learned is that I have to keep going. I have to keep loving and being loved. My life is good, and I deserve a happy life too. I can't let these things wipe me out or drain me dry. My life has too much value to give up. The lives of others have too much value for me to not be here to pour into them as well.

There's so much more to the story of my life and the stories of these two incredible men in my life, and I know one day I will share the full versions with the world and you; it is my hope you will see the great magnitude of what I have pulled myself out of with the power of love. And if I can do that, so can you. Until then, I will leave you with this:

Never underestimate the power of kindness, of giving your time to others, and of pouring into yourself and those around you. Love boldly, without fear, and with all of your passion. Love when it's easy and love when it hurts. Be affectionate; the strength of our arms is powerful. Be light and love.

I wrote this three times and, as they say, the third time's a charm. I wanted to share that while I wrote these last few paragraphs, I had a song on repeat the whole time—"Lift Me Up" by Rihanna.

This song encapsulates what I am trying to say. Music is a huge part of my life; it can take me from dancing to that ugly cry real quick. Sometimes we all need that ugly cry. I've had that cry thousands of times, alone, in the arms of a lover and in the arms of friends and women I call sisters. I'm not saying all you need is love and then it's easy; I'm saying you need love, in a circular never-ending, infinite form, to both give and receive, because it's hard, but you're worth it.

> *Three things will last forever—faith, hope, and love—*
> *and the greatest of these is love.*
> **1 Corinthians 13:13**

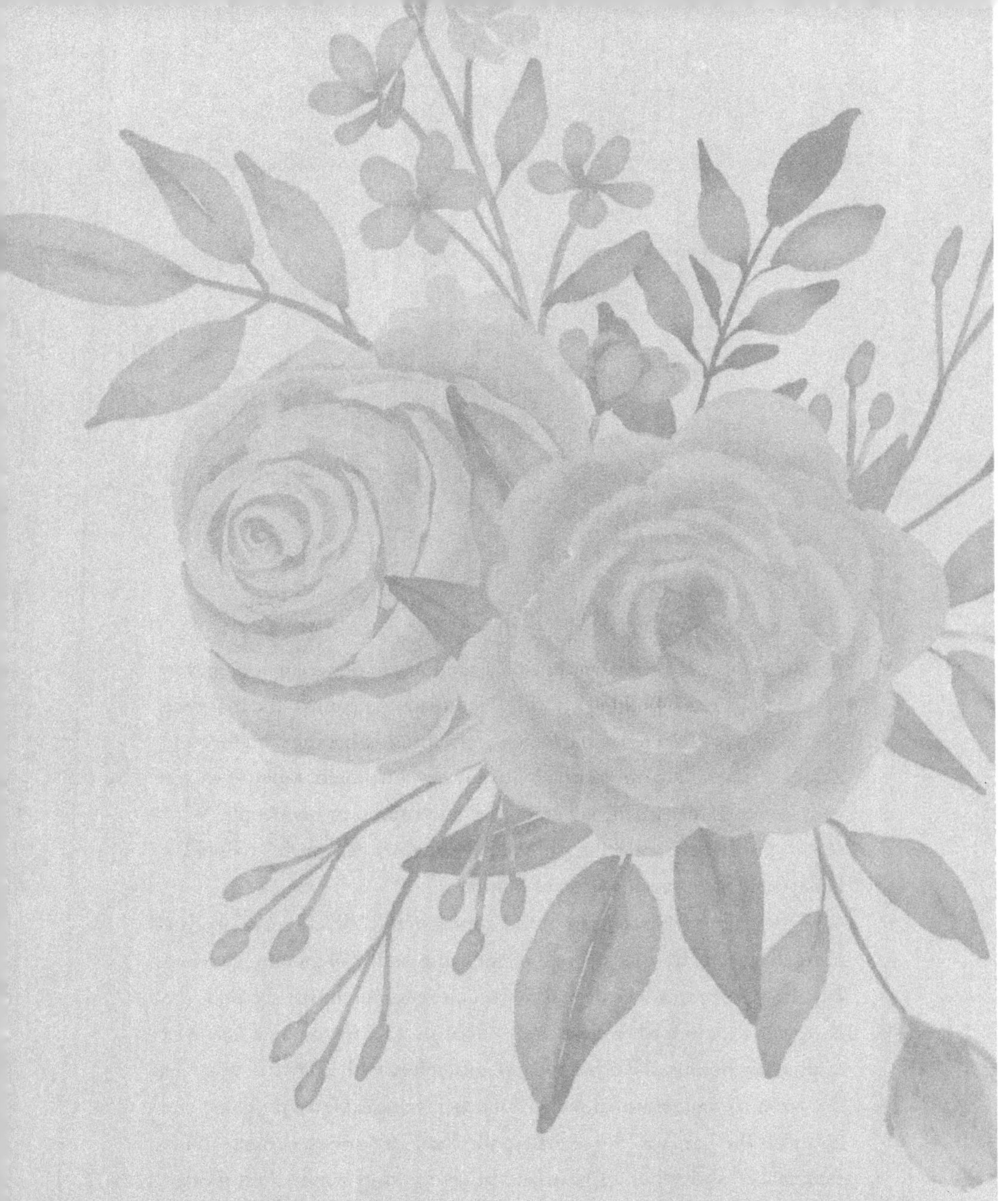

ABOUT THE CONTRIBUTOR

Jazimin is a globetrotting wordsmith, a connoisseur of experiences, and an unwavering French Bulldog LOVER. Her trusty companion, the charming Sebastian, has taken residence in her heart, infusing her life with love and a dash of playful charm. Jazimin's life journey is a vibrant tapestry woven with love, whether it's for her crafts, her adventures, or her people. With each stumble, loss, and triumph, she navigates her path with a twinkle in her eye and a contagious sense of humor.

Originally having roots from the vibrant streets of New York City, Jazimin's adventures have led her to the captivating shores of the San Francisco Bay Area. It's in this eclectic and dynamic environment that she finds the perfect backdrop for her creativity to flourish. Her words are a fusion of inspiration, humor, and profound wisdom, spiced with a pinch of mischief. But Jazimin's wanderlust knows no bounds. Having explored the globe, she now calls the Bay Area home, where she crafts her stories, dreams up her experiences, shares her insights, and of course loves boldly. And though her roots may be in San Francisco, her spirit is as boundless as the world itself. She's ever-ready to pack her bags and transport her charismatic presence to speaking engagements across the United States and beyond. With her, you're not just getting a speaker; you're inviting a whirlwind of inspiration, vivacity, and a whole lot of cheekiness to your event.

Bits of Her Heart...

Jazimin Garrett

Keep it movin'.
If you ain't helpin'
you ain't helpin'.

FUN FACT...

The two books that changed everything for Jazimin are Eat, Pray, Love by Elizabeth Gilbert & The Overstory by Richard Powers.

SECTION 6

WE ARE BOLD AND COURAGEOUS

I'M IN
by Jessica Baguchinsky

A VERY LITTLE KEY CAN OPEN
a Very Heavy Door
by Krista Lynn

#IHAVEAVOICE
by Nichole Palmer

COURAGE IS THE BOTTLE ROCKET AND GATEWAY TO LOVE.

I'M IN

BY JESSICA BAGUCHINSKY

This chapter is dedicated to the person who needs that final push. That last little bit of "go for it!" The person who needs to hear that they can do it. Jump in! If you really want it, you will make it happen. As Jimmy Dugan from A League of Their Own said, "Of course it's hard. It's supposed to be hard. If it was easy, everyone would do it. Hard is what makes it great."

I'm in!"

It's amazing how powerful two little words can be. Growing up, my parents always told me, "Ya know, you don't *have* to say *yes* to everything." I usually heard this after complaining about something I had optimistically committed to and was now angrily regretting. I'm sure whatever it was seemed fun or easy enough at the time, but we all know how that goes. The older I get, the more I understand and appreciate their message. Time is the most valuable commodity, and we need to spend it where it matters most! That's different for everyone, of course, and probably changes a lot along the way. I know what it meant for me ten years ago looks far different than what it does today.

I always like to end on a positive, so, in a world of good news/bad news, let's go "bad" news first. Sometimes, with as simple a statement as, "I'm in!"

you can completely lose yourself. I know I have. It can take you far too deep into situations you have no desire to be in: joining a committee you know you don't have time for, staying in a role that has long lost its joy and fulfillment, procrastinating the end of a toxic relationship (personal *or* professional), or buying a house you pretty much can't afford... okay, maybe that last one is just me?! Don't get me wrong... I am beyond grateful for the opportunities I've been a part of and look forward to many more, but sometimes there's just not enough bandwidth left!

> *"Most of the stress people experience comes from inappropriately managed commitments they make or accept."*
> David Allen

I read this quote many years ago, and it has stuck ever since. This was me! An invitation of some sort would come my way, and without a second thought or consideration, I'd commit. "I'm in!"

What did I have to lose?

My sanity, that's what.

Before I knew it, I was in too deep: stressed, overwhelmed, and furious with myself. Without fail, I'd hear mom and dad *ever so faintly* in the background, "Ya know..." *Yes, I know!* Although it seems harder at the time, how much easier would it have been to just say "no" from the start? Instead, I would over-commit (ignoring that little voice called common-sense telling me to pass), then quickly come to resent the task at hand. There's a special kind of guilt that comes from disappointing others because I decided to stretch myself too thin.

David Allen's words have become a personal mantra. I find myself repeating them when approached with something I fear may just become a dreaded task on the to-do list. I've come to learn it doesn't have to be a cold-hard "no." How about, "I'm flattered, but I unfortunately don't have the time right now." Or, "Wish I could! Thanks for thinking of me and please keep me posted on future opportunities." I like this. It's not a, "no," it's just a, "not now." All the sales reps in the house should appreciate that one! I've also realized that it's okay to allow yourself a day or two to decide. Think it over; how much of a commitment will it be and are you willing to spare that time? Much easier said than done, but I'm working on it.

I love words. I have always relied on them, in one form or another, to help me navigate the challenges I've inevitably gotten myself into. Song lyrics, movie lines, quotes or self-generated mantras, pep talks from friends, family, teachers and mentors along the way, inspirational memes seen while mindlessly scrolling social media... whatever it takes! I believe when something stands out, grab ahold and run with it as long as you need to. Jot it down, read it, live it! The right words can get you through anything. Even during my school years, I would choose an open-ended essay over a multiple-choice test any day of the week. Let me talk my way through it! I get that from my dad, and I'll be forever grateful to him for it.

I still get chills when hearing the Jimmy Cliff classic, "Sitting in Limbo." I *was* sitting in limbo. I had bitten off way more than I could chew this time.

A house.

I bought an entire house that I had absolutely no business buying. But I did it anyway. I saw it, loved it, sold myself on it (not hard to do), and then had to figure out how to keep it. I was alone (feeling somewhat paralyzed) in my living room I couldn't afford when the song came on. He sings about sitting in limbo and even though he feels like a bird without a song, he has a revelation.

"Sitting here in limbo, But I know it won't be long..."

A switch flipped. I played those words on repeat and knew that eventually, this moment would be a far-distant memory and a priceless life lesson painstakingly learned along the way.

Things were *tough* for a little while there. As I type this twelve years later, I carefully take myself back to the worst of it so I can both appreciate and share how far I've come. While I have blocked out a lot of the dirty details, I do remember a few. I remember coming up with excuses to work from home (before it was an actual thing in my world) because I couldn't afford the drive. There were days I was down to literal pennies in the checking account with *no* room left on the cards, for even just a *tank of gas!*

I remember having to repeatedly decline or cancel plans because there was just no fun-money left. *"What do you mean you can't make it?! You're always in!"* It almost cost me a few friendships. People took my cancelling personally, when in reality, there was just no way for me to make it happen. It's a tough pill to swallow and an even tougher pill to share with others, especially those closest to you. I remember having to call my sister and embarrassingly ask for help so I could make the mortgage payment that month.

That was fun.

"Hi, I'm supposed to be older and wiser, but can I borrow a couple bucks so I don't lose my house?"

There are a handful of amazing humans out there (you know who you are) that helped me more than they realize, and I'll be forever grateful.

It became a downward spiral I was trying so hard to get out of. Money was tight, and keeping my morale going was tough. Like, *depressingly* tough. And we all know how easy it is to work hard when we're depressed, right? So, instead of crushing it like I was used to, the sales were just not happening, which, in turn, means neither was the commission. One day, when my stress level must have been too hard to hide, a colleague offered to take me to lunch. He let me vent and listened with an empathetic ear. To this day, I will NEVER forget his response, "You're in sales. *Sell* your way out of it!"

I believe in some way, shape, or form we are all in sales. *Life* is sales. Every time you set, work toward, and achieve a goal, you are becoming and selling your best self to make that happen.

I don't have a magic pill that all of a sudden turned things around and saved me from financial ruin before the age of thirty. I put my head down, worked harder than I ever had, stayed positive even when faking it (which was quite often), and allowed myself an occasional meltdown along the way. Long story short, jbBungalows LLC was born.

The thought behind purchasing a house was to have a New Jersey "homebase", a place I would enjoy spending my time in between all of the world traveling I planned on doing. It could be a spot others would want to rent while I was off galivanting and living the dream. It's that simple, right? I was twenty-seven, making decent money for the first time in my life, and I *clearly* had big plans. So, of course, the next logical step was to rush into buying a house. Why rent comfortably for a few years when you can completely stress yourself out with a mortgage?!

It became quickly evident I had to "use it or lose it," so that's what I did. After applying a fresh coat of paint and hanging some cute beach deco, I wrote

"

DESPITE THE FEW MOMENTS OF PURE, SELF-CREATED PANIC ALONG THE WAY, HAVING THE CONFIDENCE (AND SOMETIMES BLIND FAITH) TO SAY, "I'M IN!" HAS BROUGHT ME SO MUCH MORE GOOD THAN BAD.

JESSICA BAGUCHINSKY

an ad for a summer rental, threw it on the world-wide-interwebs, and waited for the people to come knocking down my door. Believe it or not, they did! (Shout-out to Debbie H if she's reading this… my first official tenant and now life-long friend!). Just like that, my best four-legged friend, Duke, and I were couch-surfing from May through September, and the vacation-rental business of my dreams had officially started.

Thinking back, I easily could have given up and almost did a few times: thrown in the towel, admitted defeat, and sold the house for whatever I could get (in an absolute terrible market). But I didn't. Instead, I hit the reset button, came up with a plan, and refused to fail.

Saying "I'm in" is not for the faint of heart, but it can be rewarding. Despite the few moments of pure, self-created panic along the way, having the confidence (and sometimes blind faith) to say, "I'm in!" has brought me so much more good than bad.

During various periods throughout my life, "I'm in!" has served me well!

It sent me traveling through Italy for two weeks and to Mardi Gras, twice!

It led me to the University of Delaware Women's Rugby Club, a sport I knew nothing about and, to be honest, seemed slightly barbaric. (It is. And it's awesome!). Four crazy years of play and twenty years of life later, I still consider those teammates the best friends a girl could have.

It found me racing outrigger canoes and completing an Olympic-distance triathlon. It brought me on a five-day, life-changing walkabout at a surf hostel on the island of Eleuthera, bodyboarding some of the scariest ocean I've ever been in. It had me running the Honolulu Marathon!

It also led me on a two-month cross-country road trip covering 12,000 miles, 32 states, 21 friends and family visited, 12 national parks, 8 campsites, 3 hotels, 7 universities, 6 nights in "Hotel Jeep Cherokee," 5 state capitals, 4 cases of CDs, and 2 boxes of AAA guidebooks (thanks for the stats, Kelby!). Literally, one of the most amazing experiences of my life. We were a few weeks from graduating college and feeling *all* the feels. Reminiscing on the past four years and uncertain of what awaited us after cap and gown, my friend and soul sister brought up a trip her older brothers had taken after their college graduation. Without a second thought, myself and our third amiga yelled out, "We're in!" and that's how "CC03," the world's most epic road trip, came to be.

I'm In

In July of 2004, "I'm in!" brought me all the way to Hawaii. After taking an unexpected opportunity to housesit for a few weeks on Oahu, I quickly found myself falling in love with the island, its culture, its people, and pretty much everything about it. I wasn't ready to leave. I had a brand-new teaching degree in my back pocket and figured I might as well put it to good use! I started out as a substitute teacher. This seemed the best way to learn my way around, understand the school system, and make a little money while doing it.

My first call was to cover a 5th and 6th grade Hawaiian Immersion class at an elementary school in Hau'ula, a small community on the edge of the island heading toward North Shore. *Hawaiian Immersion.* That means Hawaiian was the student's first language and English was their second. I was terrified, but of course, "I'm in!" I arrived, fresh off the plane from New Jersey and sporting my best Gap cardigan, hoping nobody would see how truly terrified I was. As the class eyed-up their new sub, there were some anticipated smirks and snickering throughout the room. I took a quiet breath, brushed it off and started the day. Eight hours later, this amazing group of students was writing a note on their blackboard, asking if *Kumu Jessica* could come and teach them again. I was hooked.

After a few months of covering different classes all over the island and loving every minute of it, I was presented with a week-long opportunity at a local high school. This particular assignment was to cover a fully self-contained (FSC) classroom. These students were with you for their four main subjects, unable to handle transitioning between classes with the rest of the school's population. It was a small class—4-8 kids at any given time, and they each had a skills trainer assigned to help navigate their daily challenges. I found it to be a slightly terrifying yet ridiculously exciting opportunity. Plus, it was five guaranteed days of work.

"I'm in!"

At the end of a week filled with ups and downs, I was asked to consider staying through the remainder of the school year. Unbeknownst to the administration, I was a certified special education teacher on my way to obtaining Hawaii state licensing. It was a match made in heaven and where I called home for the next two years.

As 2006 was coming to an end, it was clear that my time on the island was as well. Things in my world were changing, and signs were saying it was time to head back to "da mainland." As much as I loved teaching, I was born and raised in the world of sales. My dad was a salesman turned small-business owner. I saw what he and my mom were able to create, and I wanted to do the same. I could not have asked for better role models than my parents. They are the real-deal version of "work hard, be good to others, do the right thing, and the rest will follow."

Upon my return to New Jersey, I started applying to any and all sales positions I could find. A few weeks into my search, I received a call. This individual said we *had* to meet. She had seen my resume and couldn't believe it. Her career also started in education, and even more coincidentally, on Oahu. After her time there, she returned to New Jersey, began a job in sales, and was now a professional recruiter.

Obviously, "I'm in!"

That conversation eventually led to the right job interview and six rounds later, I was offered my first official position in sales. Actually, it was more like, "Well, you can certainly talk the talk, let's see if you can walk the walk!" No pressure. In the end, I like to think it worked out nicely for the both of us.

Ok, I got the job! Now what?

I did *not* go to school for business. I did *not* know the world of spreadsheets, databases, prospecting, pipelines, or quotas. But I *did* know how to talk to people. So, that's where I started. My manager suggested I look into local networking groups. I visited a few and was instantly drawn to one, in particular. They invited me to join and as the story goes, "I'm in!" I was quickly asked to take the position of Events Coordinator, which led to serving a term on the Membership Committee and eventually, group president (ahem, "I'm in!"). I got more out of that group than I ever imagined. Beyond finding business contacts and clients, I met and have remained friends with some amazing people—people who seven years later and completely unbeknownst to any of us would wind up introducing me to my future wife.

Fast forward to 2014 when my dear friend's daughter is graduating high school. I was honored to attend the ceremony and, of course, the after party. There was a euphoric air to the night. Everyone was just so proud to be a part of the village we had created and thrilled to be there celebrating together. We floated through the night and on to bacon, egg, and cheese bagels the next morning. I went home to recover when my phone dinged with a text message from an unknown number.

I'm In

"Hi! It's Melissa from the graduation party. I'm sorry we didn't have a chance to talk much last night, but would you be interested in grabbing a drink sometime this week?"

Ummmmm, "I'm in!"

Nine years together, six years married, two houses and one adorable daughter later, I'm happy to say it was the best "I'm in!" of my life.

There will always be ups and downs, but I have so often found that the risk is truly worth the reward. On that note, I'll leave you with a few of my go-tos when the "I'm in!" doesn't turn out *exactly* as planned:

1. Relentless persistence can't be beat; put your head down, blinders on, and keep your focus on the big picture!

2. Bet on yourself; it's as close to a sure thing as you're going to get.

3. Failure is not an option; learn from the mistakes, but don't let them define you.

4. Just do the right thing, even when it seems like nobody else is.

5. It's okay to hit a wall, but when you find yourself running into that *same* wall over and over again, it's probably time to rethink your game plan.

6. Rely on your network and share your goals! Remember, they don't know how they can help unless you tell them.

7. Everyone needs more cheerleaders.

8. The only consistency I have found is inconsistency.

9. Set small goals to help achieve big ones and celebrate the little wins along the way!

10. Just because it's right doesn't mean it will be easy. Good things take hard work, too!

11. Just because you can doesn't mean you should.

12. You really do become what you think about.

13. Fake it till you make it; act like you know what you're doing and eventually you will.

14. Don't go through life wearing rose-colored glasses; you'll miss the red flags.

15. When you feel like giving up, remember why you held on for so long in the first place.

Now, it's your turn. How will you get off the sidelines and dive into life? What do you need to say, "I'm in!" today? What lessons have you learned from the "I'm ins!" that didn't turn out as planned? What mantras have helped you through? I'm sure you've said, "I'm in!" to many things that turned out to be amazing, too. Recognize how simply awesome this life can be when we all go all-in together!

> **A NOTE FROM THE CONTRIBUTOR:**
> I want to thank the people who have helped pave the path I'm so grateful to be traveling. My parents: the two most influential people in my world. My sister and brother—who, even though younger, have taught and inspired me more over the past 30 years than they'll ever know. The friends that I'm so lucky to call family and the mentors who have dropped their priceless nuggets along the way. And finally, my wife Melissa and daughter Eleanor. They are the reason I take on each day the way I do... relentless and insistent on forward motion. Although slower some days than others, I've come to realize that every step I take is progress, no matter how big or small. Thank you for choosing me, girls! You are my forever home-team.

ABOUT THE CONTRIBUTOR

Jessica Baguchinsky has been a sales consultant for over 15 years. She currently works in employee benefits at *Sequoia Consulting Group*. She owns a small vacation-rental business, *jbBungalows LLC*, based out of Beach Haven West, New Jersey. In addition, Jessica recently started her own consulting company, *Is That Gluten Free LLC*, with wife and business partner, Melissa Javorek. They are helping businesses and individuals integrate simple and cost-effective solutions to gluten-specific dietary needs. Jessica and Melissa welcomed their daughter, Eleanor Anne, in October 2021.

Jessica thrives on creating a community within her network and is truly excited by helping others create, implement, and achieve their goals.

Bits of Her Heart...

Jessica Baguchinsky

Luck is where hard work and opportunity meet.

FUN FACT...

Jessica is a born and raised parrothead and has seen Jimmy Buffett in concert over 50 times. If she was going away and could only bring three things, it would be her sunglasses, a hat, and a cold beer!

17

A VERY LITTLE KEY CAN OPEN A VERY HEAVY DOOR

BY KRISTA LYNN

This chapter is dedicated to all the latchkey kids. Honor the latchkey kid within so you never forget this one simple thing, I DESERVE TO HAVE MY NEEDS MET.

I'm sitting at my desk. It is a dreary Tuesday afternoon. Stacks of orders surround me. The embroidery machine runs in the background. Crystals, beads, paints, and clay embody the shelves in my studio. My studio is my sanctuary. It is my place to heal and create. I come to notice that I am feeling slightly overwhelmed. Will this all get done? Then I am illuminated by a thought; I sit back and realize I am an extraordinarily lucky woman! I am a single mom with two amazing boys living in my own home doing what I love and getting paid to do it! And then, feeling blessed I reflect and I ask myself, "What brought me here?"

Taking several moments and pondering this question, I remember a question asked by my Communications 101 professor, freshman year of college at Pace University back in 1990: Who are you and what makes you who you are today? Our assignment was to write an essay answering this question. At that time and at the age of eighteen, I was like WOW this is a hard question... who am I? I looked at all of the experiences and parts of my life that had happened thus far. My parents divorced when I was very young. My father was non-existent in my life. My mother worked, was hardly home, and did what she needed to do to support me and my younger brother. Through this internal search for answers to define myself the words *independence* and *self-reliance* surfaced.

Digging deeper, I thought about these words. *How did I get to be so independent? What made me so self-reliant?* And then a symbol came to my mind. The key. That key I wore every day around my neck for ten years. That's it. A latchkey kid is what I was... this is a child who returns to an empty home after school or a child who is often left at home with no supervision because their parents are away at work. Who knew that the symbol of a key would spark and open up the foundation that I built at such an early age? And then the essay came to light.

A Day In The Life Of A Latchkey Child

My independence began when my mother handed me the keys to the house and said, "Now I hope I can trust you with this set of keys and to stay out of trouble when no one is home." Having this set of keys, I was able to open the house on my own. I would come from school, walk up to the door, and try and open it, forgetting that no one was home. I had to use my new set of keys to get inside. Now that I think of it, opening the door and facing an empty house turned me into a "latchkey child." Being a "latchkey child" has made me very independent.

Since my mother worked a twelve-hour day, many responsibilities had to be put on my shoulders. For instance, the laundry was a big task. Why? Just imagine a thirteen-year-old girl lugging armfuls of laundry down the stairs, cramming colors and whites into the washer, and putting capfuls of detergent into the machine. In the beginning, doing the laundry was one of the chores I hated the most, but after a while I got used to it. Although I never loved doing the laundry, it did teach me to pick up after myself because I knew that no one would be there to pick up after me when I was on my own.

A Very Little Key Can Open a Very Heavy Door

In addition, I had to start dinner. I would take frozen spinach out of the freezer, put it into the microwave, set it for three minutes, and then work on the spaghetti. I always seemed to fill the pot with too much water, which caused the water to bubble over and make a sizzle sound on the hot burner. Since the oven was a more complicated task, burning meat was my specialty for I always set the temperature too high. After several tries and pretty much teaching myself, creating special dishes became my forte. Dinner was always ready, and the table set as soon as my mother walked in the door. My mother and brother also seemed to enjoy my culinary creations as much as I did. (Looking back, I don't know if they really enjoyed it or if they were just being nice.) Learning how to cook taught me to depend on myself whenever I was hungry, for I knew later on in life I would not have a "cook" who would provide me with the essentials of a nutritious cuisine.

Another responsibility that was given to me at an early age was to watch over my younger brother, Kurt, and make sure he did not get into any trouble. He was one of the boys who could find trouble wherever he went. For example, I made sure he did not go out with the wrong people. What I mean by wrong people is other boys who had gotten in too much trouble already and would bring my brother down with them. Even though I was a year older, I had to play "mother" to him by telling him to clean his dishes, clean his room, take out the garbage, do his homework, and so on. Doing this taught me how to be in charge, like an authoritarian. When I had children, this trait would help me a great deal.

For these chores, my mother gave me an allowance of twenty dollars a week. With this money, I had to make decisions regarding whether to save or spend it all. Most thirteen-year-old girls would probably spend it on makeup, clothes, costume jewelry, and all the other luxuries with which teenage girls were fascinated. On my own, however, I went to the bank and picked up some brochures on how to open up a bank account. I brought them home and showed them to my mother who was very impressed and started me off with fifty dollars. Every week I would put part of my allowance into my account. In this way, I learned how to budget money well because I knew it would help me later on in life. Starting a bank account and watching my money grow with interest and deposits showed me that money would always be there if I needed it in case of an emergency.

While I was doing all of this work inside the house, I never had a chance to be with my friends who were always outside playing and meeting boys. In a way I was jealous, but since I stayed in the house and was on my own, I learned a lot. I tended to do a lot more grown-up things, which my friends were not used to. Therefore, at the age of thirteen I was able to make decisions for myself. Since I was on my own without someone watching constantly over me, I was able to learn from my own experiences.

God forbid if I was ever on my own without anyone to care and look after me, I could always fall back on what I started learning at the age of thirteen. Today I am capable of doing my own laundry, cooking, budgeting my money, and in general being completely self-sufficient. All because my mother had the confidence in me as a "latchkey child." Thanks Mom!

I ended up getting an A+ on this essay and encouraging words from my professor saying, "You better wrap this and put it under the Christmas tree for her. I'd love to see her face when she reads it. Bravo Mom—you've got a great daughter!" I was so happy about my grade, and of course I took her suggestion and shared it with my mother. The lights glistened on the Christmas tree and a smile lit up my mother's face.

After graduating college, I followed in my mother's footsteps and started working in the corporate world. This lasted for about eight years, and then, in 2002, I took a giant leap of faith. I left a stable corporate profession where financially I was raking in abundance. Spiritually, however, I was starving. I was often physically sick and generally unfulfilled. I knew that this was no way to live, but I had no idea what to do next. Asking the universe for guidance, I was moved to take a sabbatical to Europe. For two weeks, I traveled alone, blissfully remembering who I really was and gaining valuable insight into the person I wanted to become.

Upon returning home, I was inspired to enroll in a course taught by Barbara Sher at The Learning Annex in NYC. The message being communicated

"THAT KEY THAT COULD HAVE BEEN THE ALBATROSS AROUND MY NECK IS NOW WHAT IS GOING TO OPEN UP THE BIG HEAVY DOOR IN FRONT OF ME."

KRISTA LYNN

was crystal clear—a person could do anything if they only knew what it was. So moved by this experience, I advanced my education, joining a Success Team led by Andrea Reese. Since as Barbara Sher says, "Isolation is the dream killer," this weekly gathering of supportive individuals empowered my vision for ArtSpa, a facility offering creative spiritual workshops to those in search of inspiration and healing. However, along with my dream came a degree of fear.

This fear then guided me to Julia Cameron's course, The Artist's Way. So inspired, I was then able to tap into my inner voice. Looking within, I wondered how I would make my dream of ArtSpa come to fruition. Encouraging words from Julia Cameron, "Jump and the net will follow," gave me the faith and confidence I needed to boldly move forward.

This led me to participate in an intensive yoga teacher training. This training enhanced my strengths and creative abilities in a way that would prove invaluable to my future role as Creative Spiritual Workshop Facilitator.

From these wonderful experiences, I was then divinely guided to design jewelry. My primary focus was to envision and design one-of-a-kind ceramic pendants uniting beauty, grace, and spirituality. Designing jewelry brings me to a peaceful place where the hummingbirds flutter, waterfalls cascade, and flowers burst into bloom against a warm azure sky. This is my HEALING! I have found my bliss! Krista Lynn Designs (as well as I) had awakened. Each one of my jewelry pieces tells a story. The process of designing and creating jewelry came naturally to me, and through this artistry I found something about which I am passionate. My passion to share and inspire has led me to truly become a "passionate entrepreneur." I know my early days as a latchkey child helped me to unlock this part of me. The self-reliance and independence I learned allowed me to take the leap from an unfulfilling career and explore deeper parts of myself.

So here I am in my adult life, raising two amazing boys, moving through life adapting to situations individually as they present themselves. I ask myself the same question my professor asked me back in 1990, thirty-two years ago, "Who are you and what makes you who you are today?" I can easily say the following: I, Krista Lynn, Artist, Jewelry Designer, Creative Spiritual Workshop Facilitator, Light Worker, Numerologist and Passionate Entrepreneur, was divinely guided to find my story. I have made it my intentional commitment that, through my jewelry creations, spirituality, and workshops, people manifest their own stories.

A Very Little Key Can Open a Very Heavy Door

Does what I do for a living define me? I think it makes up the being of me and comprises some of the keys to my existence. My job in serving others and sharing my light comes naturally to me... it is all I know. It has been my foundation that I instilled upon myself at such an early age.

Honestly, being an independent, strong, and self-reliant woman has also had its downside. Today, I look at the foundation of feelings that defined me of being a latchkey child as well as being a passionate entrepreneur.

In being a "*latchkey child*," I was often lonely and felt a sense of yearning. One image that comes to mind frequently is sitting on the sofa at night and looking out the bay window waiting for my mother to come home. Every headlight that shined upon the dark street excited me in hopes it would be her. I look at the "mother" role I had upon my brother. I was always looking out for him and his well-being. Neglecting myself and my well-being, I was sick a lot during my school years.

These thoughts and images are recollections of my perception of my life as a child. We all know that our perception is what becomes real to us at that time. Now, as an adult, I have grown and reflected on these memories and now know that what we perceive as a child is not always 100% accurate.

I was doing so much for everyone else and making sure that they were okay and happy. But was I happy? My mother and brother knew that they could count on me. *Krista could take care of it.* Being in control was exciting and new at such an early age. I felt important and wanted.

I see now that this foundation of being a latchkey child has become the norm for me in my adult life. I have a *Control, Nurture, Take Care of It, Put Everyone Else First* type of mentality. A childlike manner of imagination and freedom of being just a kid was not on the forefront. Though it was lacking then, I can see that my inner child has manifested itself immensely in my businesses today, and for that I am extremely grateful.

I grew up so fast... I was "adulting" at the age of thirteen. I have no regrets, and I am grateful for my mother and know that she provided what was needed being a single parent. She believed in me and had confidence in me and knew that I would be okay. I remember meeting my mother in New York City for lunch after I had left the corporate world, and she said to me, "You inspire me, Krista, for taking the leap. You are finding your own way, and I love that!" This brought tears to my eyes. I love my mother with all of my heart and know that this blessing of being a latchkey child has made me the woman I am today.

Looking back at my journey of becoming a passionate entrepreneur, the feelings of fear and unknowing consumed me. I constantly remember my upbringing of being a latchkey child and the facets of teaching myself how to do things. I am a seeker. I find things that I am curious about, and I take it upon myself to teach myself and learn along the way. I don't really ask for help. I know from such an early age that I was capable of doing it all by myself. And then through my spiritual growth during this journey, I turned to God and the Universe. I asked through many prayers to guide me toward what is next. I believe that there is one truth and there are many paths to get there. Whoever you believe in, know that you are not alone. I started trusting my intuition and kept saying to myself, "Pease divinely guide me to what is next that will bring joy and peace and open up the parts of me that I have not seen." This constant prayer became the key that opened up the light and inspiration within. I truly believe that the Universe provides, as long as you are open to receiving. I had finally started to realize that it is okay to let go and not be in control of everything. This still is a hard concept and journey, but every day it gets a little easier.

In 2022, I turned fifty. In Numerology, the number 5 is all about change. We add the 5 plus the 0, which gives us the number 5. The energy of the number 5 relates to making positive life choices and decisions and learning life lessons through experience. These days, the rawness and the vulnerability of being is a key that I hold close to my heart.

People have always told me, "You are a strong, independent, successful woman, and I admire you." My heart lights up with so much joy, and I know these words have become the foundation of my being. I understand this about me. This is part of me, but not all of me. There is so much more to discover. But I must say, just because someone carries it well doesn't mean it isn't heavy. I continue to be a work in progress, discovering, peeling away, and unwrapping all of the emotions and layers of loneliness, confusion, and yearning of who I was all along.

What is really going on on the inside? Am I running from something? Is there something I am afraid to see? Am I keeping myself busy so I don't hear the noise inside?

That noise inside is my inner critic, "No Krista, don't ask for help! That is weak. Don't let anyone see you weak, then you are vulnerable."

A Very Little Key Can Open a Very Heavy Door

I can't be vulnerable, I am strong! Right?
I don't need anyone.
I will get hurt.
I will crumble.
I will fall.
Well, I don't need anyone, or do I?
Is my inquisitive nature in asking so many questions a sense of striving for perfection? Keep asking questions and you will eventually get the answer you are looking for. If you have all of the answers you will never fail, and you will never be weak. Hurry up, shut the door! Don't let them in. You will give them control. They will fail you. You will get disappointed and hurt.

Perfection was the thirteen-year-old girl making dinner, doing the laundry and house chores while watching my friends outside laugh, play, and hang out with boys. I could not disappoint Mom; she worked so hard. I could not disappoint Mom because I wanted her to know she could count on me. I love her, but as I child, I interpreted loving someone means it is all about their happiness while keeping your sadness and fears inside. Relationships come and go. This has been the pattern and the way I have dealt with things. There is sadness, there is loneliness, there is addiction, there is yearning, there is the feeling of unworthiness, and so much more.

It is time for a change... that key that could have been the albatross around my neck is now what is going to open up the big heavy door in front of me. It is time for a new beginning. I am more. I want more. I now realize, "Yes I deserve more." Perception is all subjective. I want to change my perception and how I see me. I want to keep it REAL.

No more hiding. It is time to let go, and I am determined to accept and embrace what is within me, while accepting and embracing what I see in others for what they truly are. Life is super hard. There is no manual. We are all unique in our being, and that is what we need to hold on to. We must continue to search and grow along this journey of life, using keys when we are ready to unlock the parts of ourselves that are ready to be seen. Thank you, Mom, for all you are. All you have given me. Thank you for the strength, independence, and self-reliance you nurtured within me. It has taken me fifty years to get to this point, and I believe it is because of all those things you have instilled in me that I was able to get here.

I want to grow, I want to let go, and I want to release control. I want to laugh more. I want to discover what makes me happy, and I want to let people be who they are and accept them for who they are and all the gifts that they have to share.

I believe in the timing of life... everything happens when it is meant to happen. I am ready to give a new meaning to the key that once defined me. Our lives are layered, and our journeys are complex. The beauty is, it is our story... it is our journey... it is how we are magnificently made. It is our choice to unlock the parts that will grow us deeper into joy when the time is right.

This morning, I was feeling blessed and grateful wondering how I got so lucky, but the seeker in me knew I was ready to go deeper myself. Life to me is all about learning and growth, whether it is a person, place, or thing that brings the lesson. We have to be ready and tell ourselves, "I know there is something that can make my light brighter within and around me." So, I bring these questions to you as the reader, "What keys do you have access to? What doors can you open that will allow you to journey beyond what you already know?" I know that walking to the door and opening it up with the key that you have brings a lot of fear and unknowing but know this... you can always shut the door and move on to another. You have the keys within to go wherever your heart desires.

ABOUT THE CONTRIBUTOR

Krista Lynn independently owns and operates two businesses. She believes there is power and solace in creativity. Residing at the Jersey Shore with her two boys, three cats, and one dog, she continues to find the space of enchantment and embraces the findings. She invites you to join her on this passionate, creative journey at kristalynndesigns.com.

This chapter is dedicated to Lynn Engeholm, for being the mother you were and are through your hard work and dedication. You gave me the ability and opportunities I may have not had. You held the key, and you trusted me with it. Little did I know that this small, tangible object of a key would be so symbolic. I made the choice to embrace the "key" as an empowering "gift" in unlocking my growth and development throughout the years. The impact of this "gift" has afforded me the ability to be the mother I am now and am going to continue to be for my two boys, Alessandro and Luce.

Bits of Her Heart...

Krista Lynn

"Yes, I am imperfect and vulnerable and sometimes afraid, but that doesn't change the truth that I am also brave and worthy of love and belonging."
–Brene Brown

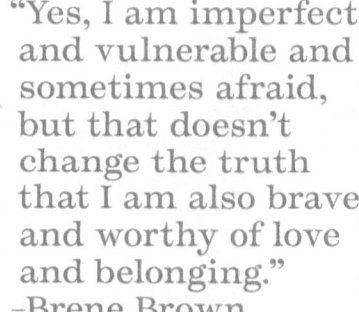

FUN FACT...

While living in Miami, Florida, Krista Lynn was on the HGTV show, That's Clever sharing her process of making ceramic jewelry.

18

#IHAVEAVOICE

BY NICHOLE M. PALMER

To the women and girls who need to remember they have a voice.
Use it. Loudly. Boldly. Without hesitation. #IHaveAVoice

...Stillness gripped me for six days...

DAY 1

My cell phone jolted me out of my regular writing routine. It was early morning on Thursday, May 28, 2020. Globally, life had been shut down due to the COVID-19 pandemic since March 13, and my middle school classes had thankfully ended for the year. Working as a teacher's assistant was my "in-between" gig as I searched for full-time writing/editing assignments; however, this classroom experience proved debilitating.

Being in the classroom wasn't new. In my hometown of Gary, Indiana, I had my own make-shift black-box theatre classroom from 2014 to 2017 of precocious and deeply soulful middle school theatre students at Wirt-Emerson Visual and Performing Arts High Ability Academy.

Together, we created new stories in a curse-word-free zone. We blended history with theatre, devised wickedly funny commercials, and tackled sensitive dramatic topics courageously. When tragedy struck our school through the suicide of one of our own, we created original short plays to work through the daunting emotions. Through the work, I had taught my students to own their voices on stage and in life; they taught me that our stories are worth the fight. Those were my kids; I think of them often with pride.

However, in my new classroom in Charlotte, North Carolina, the students were behaviorally challenged. This meant a daily barrage of inappropriate outbursts, name calling, cursing, and fighting from them. Many were a grade level or three behind their peers. Deep down, the students wanted to be with their peers in regular classes, but they weren't ready. Frustrated, they took their disappointment with life out on each other and us, the teachers.

Sometimes, laughter and enlightenment found us. Students would understand a concept, or simply finish an assignment well. Our smiles punctuating their success short-circuited any on-coming tirades. We all lived for those moments.

Having had only a few months of that experience, I opted for self-care that weekend: no internet or phone, just rest, nature, and Netflix. I needed to detox from crazy because the Wednesday night virtual prayer service was coming up. My church Bible study group had asked me to help lead prayer that night. I couldn't be influenced by whatever bombarded the internet that weekend.

So when my friend called that Thursday, I truly had been out of the world loop. She simply asked, "Have you seen the news? Been on FB?"

"No."

"I know you don't usually do that, but I need you to today."

"What's up?"

"Just read…"

Her voice so serious and solemn. She hung up. I sighed as I turned to my laptop…

• • •

I barely read the news anymore. Three years as a news copy editor spoiled it for me. From 1992 to 1995 during most night shifts, I helped edit all of the news at one of the local mainstream newspapers. Every beat had drama: political corruption, educational snafus, and financial fraud. But, it was the coverage on Gary—the lone predominately African American city in Northwest Indiana, which was predominately white—that knotted my stomach. There were more stories about crime, murder, and mayhem than I cared to count. Black joy rarely made headlines.

With only one African American reporter and two African American copy editors at the paper, our voices fought to influence how we reported the news. We were all under 30 with me being the youngest at 22. Sometimes, allies would question angles, engage in healthy debates, and challenge their own perceptions. Other times, the white American lens colored the news without a second thought.

After work on especially taxing news days, I stared at my apartment walls numb. Maybe if I toughed it out, I could become an editor of one of the news sections. Perhaps, I should just go straight into reporting. But, would I last with my soul intact? The assistant managing editor offered a third choice: a column. It was a natural fit. I shared my perspective on community happenings. Black joy finally had headlines! I also doled out hard lessons learned, which became the columns that drew the most attention. Even got some hate mail. Nothing like the putrid smell of self-righteousness and white fragility in the afternoon.

Later, as an assistant city desk editor, I led an award-winning project on the Civil Rights struggle across community racial lines. Both opportunities gave me great satisfaction, but my soul cried for more. I eventually left to earn my Master of Fine Arts degree from Tisch School of the Arts at New York University in film/TV/theatre. Family and friends joked that I leapt from the frying pan into the fire. I saw it as a way to control the stories I wrote.

...

Looking at my laptop now, I quickly typed GOOGLE.COM. Headlines screamed: Police! Murder! Knee on neck! *Stomach knots... dear God... stomach knots!* Cradling my phone, I found sanctuary on the bed in my boudoir. There, I swiped to the Facebook app but stopped short of pressing the symbol. Do I even want to know what happened this time?

There was always a "this time" when it came to racial injustice in America, yet white America labeled Black people's cries of unfairness as "whining," "overly sensitive," and "exaggerations." Weeks earlier, the murders of Ahmaud Arbery and Breonna Taylor occupied headlines. Their legitimacy for even being discussed flamed virtual and in-person arguments. I couldn't stand the back-and-forth bickering. Words dipped in poison darted like arrows always tagging their targets but never killing the arguments. This was why I used Facebook and social media in general sparingly.

Magnificently MADE

...

Former President Barak Obama helped me warm up to news again. Mama and I heard him speak before a packed gymnasium in Gary at Roosevelt High School in April 2008. We connected with Mr. Obama's voice—confident, modulated, preacher tone reminiscent of the Rev. Dr. Martin Luther King, Jr. At one point during Mr. Obama's speech, Mama and I looked at each other; we glowed with pride.

All the way home, we debated Mr. Obama's political points. We marveled at the hope his presidential candidacy brought and allowed our chests to poke out just a bit. Finally, we would be the leaders in the White House that our ancestors built and on land our ancestors helped survey. Thank you, Benjamin Banneker.

Our girlfriend connection gave air to my soul, because usually, Mama and I battled. She would say black; I would say red. She would want earth; I would want sky. She would see possibilities; I would see compromise. Our voices clanged like tin bells unable to find honest harmony; anger and frustration singed many of our conversations.

Underneath, we were just alike: headstrong passionate women of faith who had been verbally squelched and physically dismissed by a society never meant to accept us. We loved our people and being Black. We hated social injustices. We loved children and enjoyed teaching. We engaged in Christian ministry in our own ways—her community missions, my dramatic storytelling—yet at times, we couldn't find the space to give each other room to just be.

Looking back, we fought to love each other because we wanted a smoother relationship. We just kept stepping on each other's last nerves trying to get it. But that day, hearing Mr. Obama, our voices stopped warring and became wind chimes on a gentle Lake Michigan breeze.

Driving home, we couldn't wait to share this with Pops, who was a traveling pharmacist at the time. Yep, he was 69 years old and still working. He considered retirement a dirty word, but quietly, Pops worked because he didn't know the meaning of the word "rest." For him, retirement meant "slow death," and Pops believed he had the energy of the young people he managed and mentored. So, every morning, he got up and worked.

That sounds so easy, but Pops had a bum knee. When he was about sixteen

#IHaveAVoice

or so, he had a football injury, which left him with a permanently changed gait. His left knee rotated closer toward the right leg, so it always looked as if his legs created the letter K as he walked. As a "Big & Tall" man, Pops' weight exaggerated his walk even further. Over time, that knee shot excruciating pain into his body; the later onset of diabetes didn't help. Pops never complained. Publicly, Pops bore his thorn with grace and elegance. Privately, he cursed his body and his inability to do more.

My siblings and I grew up keenly aware of our father's limitations, but we never allowed that to diminish his place as king of our family. When Pops laughed, his voice filled the room with sunshine. When tired, his quiet voice brought us closer for an intimate moment. When angry, his voice thundered, kicking up emotional storms. When he dispensed advice, Pops' wisdom grounded us knowing that he would never steer us wrong. For 40 years, my father's voice moved us to action and feeling.

When we shared Mr. Obama's words with Pops, he glowed, too. His eyes danced to the rhythm of djembes. In his baritone rumble, my father exclaimed proudly, "Fantastic!" Then, silence. Mama and Pops stared into one another's eyes speaking a language only 43 years of marriage could have understood. Respecting their intimacy, I departed to my "basement apartment" giving them room to marvel at the possibility they never believed they would see, yet hoped to do so anyway.

Descending the stairs reminded me of how far I had fallen in life. For a year, Pops asked me to come home. Each time he asked, I said no; however, the last time there was something different in his voice. Then, the home phone number I had memorized since 1974 suddenly changed. My mother's conversations with me felt tighter than usual, and my sister alluded to some "challenges" at home. All of this, plus my inability to find sustaining work as a writer in LALA, as I called Los Angeles, made me throw in the towel. I had two degrees and still wound up living in my parents' basement! *Why, Lord, why?!* There in the basement apartment, I sulked, raged, regretted, and punished myself by replaying my mental Naysayers' Tape about my work:

"*Does the main character have to be Black or even a plus-sized woman?*"

"*This is really sophomoric work at best.*"

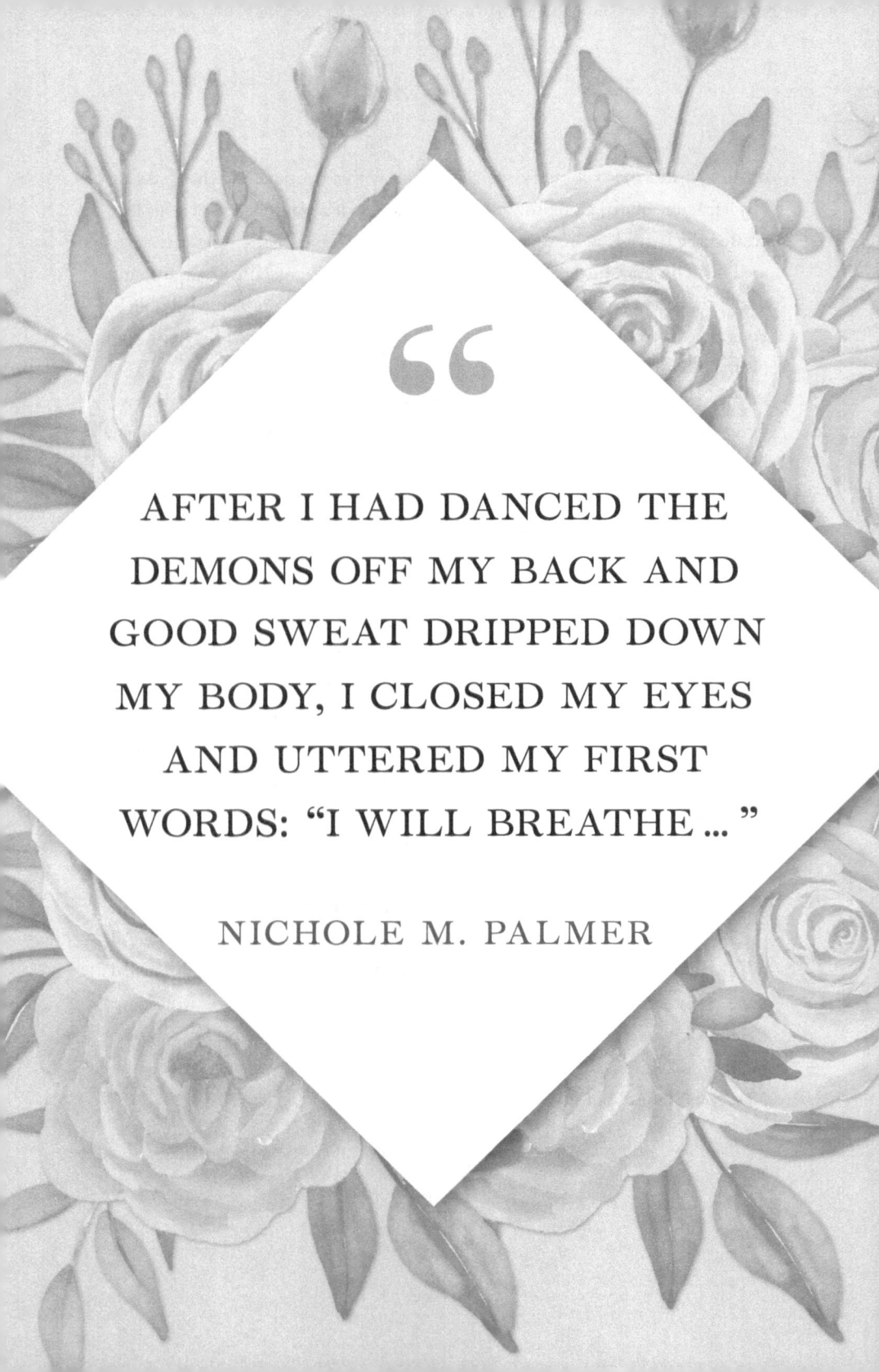

> AFTER I HAD DANCED THE DEMONS OFF MY BACK AND GOOD SWEAT DRIPPED DOWN MY BODY, I CLOSED MY EYES AND UTTERED MY FIRST WORDS: "I WILL BREATHE…"

NICHOLE M. PALMER

"Let's not even discuss the dialogue."

"This script doesn't make me SEE anything."

"It's really not funny, is it?"

At that time, I would go to the beach, sit in my car, and scream at God. Years before, Mama told me to get everything that I wanted in life, because when marriage and children came, my life would be all about them. I followed her advice, and yet, I felt cheated by the sacrifice. Certainly, there had to be more to life than basement living?

Other days, when the answers I sought eluded me, I praise danced. Sometimes, I'd dance to my favorite gospel music in the basement and praise my way out of dark, dank, debilitating emotional holes. On those days, I felt like Jacob wrestling with the Angel of the Lord to get his blessing. I had a routine: during the day I loved on my nieces, taught community theatre at local spaces, worked a myriad of part-time jobs, and helped my parents. At night, I prayed and danced the demons off my back.

Watching from a distance, my parents couldn't understand why their well-educated daughter struggled with work. She was smart, talented, well-mannered, and opinionated. Perhaps she was too opinionated? Had too many ideals? Their hushed whispers echoed my own unspoken thoughts, although they eventually leaked from my eyes drenching my pillow at night.

My parents and I spent the next few years laughing, crying, arguing, sharing, fighting, and loving on each other. With them, I learned not to be afraid of intensely passionate conversations. Loving people can be pushed to limits; real love allows room for the conversations and the work to find your way back to each other. Our love was real ...

By the end of 2014, my parents had made their heavenly transitions. Closing my eyes, I still see them doing a slow Chicago two-step in our old kitchen as '70s R&B sensation Lou Rawls crooned his song "You'll Never Find Another Love Like Mine" on the radio. I may have resented having to go home, but I'm so glad I did. They needed their warrior daughter who knew how to tackle a 21st century world; I needed adult refining that only loving parents could provide.

Now at fifty, remembering all I had been through, I looked down at my phone and pressed the Facebook icon. A barrage of angry, emotionally riotous posts flooded my sparsely populated FB page. At the center was George Floyd, who police allegedly murdered in broad daylight in Minneapolis, Minnesota. This time ... there was a video.

I found the video marked "sensitive content." *Ummmm.* Rodney King, Malcom Ferguson, Oscar Grant, and hundreds of others flickered in my mind. However, it was the death of my sorority sister Sandra Bland in 2015 that took me over the edge. Now, it's 2020. Taking a deep breath, I clicked on the video.

Eight minutes and forty-six seconds later...

Heart stopped. Words choked. Tears soaked. I trembled. I heard Mr. Floyd cry for his mother, and then say, "I can't breathe." Bystanders pleaded with the Minneapolis cop to get up. Smugly, he waved them off. Mr. Floyd died with a cop's knee on his neck.

THUMPTHUMPTHUMPTHUMPTHUMPthumpthumpthumpthump...

My world shattered underneath me; I fell really slowly inside myself. My apartment spun in slow motion. Viewing the horror had stripped me of words. Mama! Pops! I wanted to call them, but my familial safety net had long ago been torn asunder.

Instead, I read FB posts on my phone. Northwestern alums turned their FB platforms into spaces where stories of 400-plus years of second-class treatment and experienced overt racism poured from their fingers. Bravo! Friends of mine added their tales of being the "exception" and "you're not like them." Words like "white fragility" and Black, Indigenous, People of Color (BIPOC) littered their forums. Intriguing.

...ten hours later...

The moon's light had traded places with the morning sun. Suddenly, I remembered the day I stood before my fourth-grade teacher pronouncing my worth.

"Nichole, we lowercase the B in black," my teacher said about my essay.

"Why," 9-year-old me asked.

"It's the way it's done in English," she patiently tried to explain.

"Being Black is a proper noun. When you lowercase it, it looks like the color black. I am more than a color," I stated.

Mouth agape; cheeks flushed. At nine years old in the winter of 1979, I had dropped the mic before it was even such a thing to do.

At home, Mama made sure I read the classics: Phillis Wheatley, Paul Lawrence Dunbar, Gwendolyn Brooks, and Nikki Giovanni. We also had the big four magazines: *Ebony, Essence, Jet,* and *Right On!* History centered around Black excellence: Benjamin Banneker, Matthew Henson, Charles Drew, and Marva Collins. Reading them laid the foundation for my budding Black consciousness.

I had a voice then, I reminded myself. I opened my mouth to speak, but the words ghosted me. Instantly, my stomach growled. I hadn't eaten since breakfast. As if on autopilot, I cooked then ate. My eyes burned. My mind screamed. I turned off my phone. I turned off the computer. I turned off the lights. I slipped on my nightclothes, then I crawled into bed. I whispered in my mind: *God, what is Your response?* Hurt feelings and sleep wrestled; sleep eventually won.

DAY 2

God, I'm tired. I need You. What is Your response?

Two voices fought in my head: the wise woman within, and the cynical woman hardened by the world's ignorance and insensitivity.

"None of this is new," cynical me said. "Hell, we've been dying since we arrived on these shores. The only difference is that now we see it in real-time."

"The world sees it in real-time," wise woman said. "It's no longer an internal matter."

"Do you really think that's gonna make a difference," cynical me asked.

"Yes," wise woman answered. "America hates looking bad."

"She's got great PR people," cynical me quipped.

"And today, so do we..." wise woman confidently stated. The conversation faded.

I couldn't write; so, I read. The Black Lives Matter movement raged. CNN.com showed the country burning, protesting, marching, and looting. These images populated videos 24/7. People wrote signs that said:

Make America Not Racist for the First Time

When the Color of Your Skin Is Seen as a Weapon, You Will Never Be Unarmed

#Asians4BlackLives End the War on Black People

My Arms Are Tired from Holding this Sign Since the 1960s

Will You Still Stand for Us when #BLM Isn't Trending?

Mr. Floyd's word "breathe" pounded in my ears. I mourned. *What could our lives have been like without the shackles of racism? Yes, we've had victories. Yes, we've gained strength and mental fortitude from overcoming adversities. However, what if the playing fields had been level? Would we be the Wakanda of our time?*

"I will breathe..." Those three little words whispered to my soul and reverberated underneath Mr. Floyd's voice begging for air. Emotions boxed inwardly; pain clouded my mind. Then, I heard God call me like He called Samuel of old...

Write, Nichole...
Write what, Lord?
Write what your heart screams...

DAY 3

"I will breathe..."

The words echoed quietly in my soul. I kept my phone on silent. I turned to my computer and followed the happenings of life via the internet; I scanned, read, digested, and reflected. Memories that I had pushed aside as the cost of being Black flooded my mind:

Weeks before the George Floyd murder, a police car follows my every move for five miles. Foot shakes on the gas pedal. Knuckles turn white. Eyes peer at speedometer... under the limit. Eyes look in rearview mirror. Cop car tails me hard. Cars pass us up—speeding. I was in Charlotte, North Carolina, and 49 years old.

It's summertime, and I wear a colorful headwrap to work. My white co-worker insinuates that I look like Aunt Jemimah. I rip him a new one... professionally. Later, in the bathroom screaming, my Black co-worker asks what happened. I share. Before the day is over, my white supervisor approaches me. "Nichole, if anything like that ever happens again, tell me. It's not your job to handle that type of abuse. It's mine." Blink. Up until this point, I usually had to have my own back in the workplace. Here, in this office, I met one of my first allies before it had become vogue. I was in LALA and 31 years old.

Join a museum tour. Come to the Kwanzaa exhibit. Tour guide asks me if I had ever celebrated Kwanzaa. I am the only Black person in the tour of maybe 15 people. My stomach knots up. Naively, I say yes. She next asks if I might be able to explain it to the group. All eyes on me. Angry, but not wanting to make a scene, I explain the exhibit. As I leave the museum, the unpleasantness of my experience gnaws at me. I return, find the woman's manager, and express my displeasure at the woman's unprofessionalism and cultural ineptness. I was in St. Petersburg, Florida, and 24 years old.

Overwhelmed, I grabbed my iPad and played gospel singer Travis Greene's single "Won't Let Go." My head bobbed. My feet moved. My back jerked. I moaned. Like a healing salve, the music washed over me and my body let go. I let the song loop. Soon, I was in a trance. I was back home in my family basement fighting for my mind! My spirit screamed: *I am worthy! Valuable! Love-able! Strong! My life matters!!!* After I had danced the demons off my back and good sweat dripped down my body, I closed my eyes and uttered my first words: *"I will breathe..."*

DAY 4

Sunday. May 31, 2020. My pastor, too, voiced his outrage, despair, and hope for a new day in the lives of his people all across the country. As we prayed, I heard myself say "Amen" and "Halleluiah." Then, I heard the Holy Spirit whisper my favorite Scripture:

> *"Write the vision And make it plain on tablets, That he may run who reads it."*
> *—Hab. 2:2,* NKJV

Write the vision … Write the vision … "I will breathe … " Those words now exploded in my chest. "Yes, I will breathe," I spoke. "I will breathe. I will inhale and exhale. We will breathe.

"Breathe. … Black man murdered by Minneapolis cops … " A new poem! I heard a new poem! OMG! I hadn't written new poetry in a minute.

I snapped Zoom off. Church was pretty much over. I pulled up a new Word doc file and typed the words: Black man murdered by Minneapolis cops … The poem pushed her way up from my toes, rattled around in my gut, burst in my chest, and rushed up the esophagus …

"Make it STOP! Dear God … Make it STOP!"

Yeah. That's good. Blocked words tumbled from my soul. I feverishly typed every line. *I wrote. I imagined. I remembered. I cried. I screamed. I researched. I wrote …*

DAY 5

A friend called. She too had been gripped in silence. I shared that I was just coming out of a fog myself, but a poem was being birthed. *Chat later?* Sure. We hung up. I turned to the piece and wrote all day.

DAY 6

Chewing stale gum, I stared at the new poem. Raw. Real. Naked. My students would love that. I always tell them to "get naked on the page," if they want to truly connect with their audience. So, here I was using my own advice, but who was going to read it? Words, images, and memories lain bare for whom to experience?

This poem had to be added to the artistic conversation of the day, which meant only one thing: Facebook. Securing my resolve, I called a friend and sorority sister.

"I've written a new poem, and I will film myself reciting it and then post it on Facebook," I announced.

She waited, and in a measured tone, she said, "Okay." Later, she shared she didn't want to say more because I was a toddler taking my first steps into social media territory. Mothers know you don't spook the toddler. You just hold out your hands and say, "You can do it."

I read her the piece. "Powerful," she whispered.

"Yeah," I said. "I've been silent for five days. This is what finally emerged."

"When are you gonna post?"

"Tomorrow. I need to let this sit. Then, I will post. I'll let you know when I do it."

"Okay," she said. We switched gears, chatting about everything else.

DAY 7

Wednesday. June 3, 2020. Morning. I reread the poem. Got dressed. Put on some makeup. This was a huge leap for me. Years ago, I made a conscious decision not to major in broadcast journalism, because on-air female reporters were judged harshly about their looks. Being a curvy woman, who warred with her weight since middle school, I never wanted my dress size to determine my paycheck. I wasn't interested in that fight. No thanks. I am a fierce writer. No one needs to see my face.

"But I need people to see you say the words," God whispered. "Now is the time for your voice."

He was right. Turning to my bathroom mirror, I studied my gray hair, cheek mole, sun spots, and smile lines. *Beautiful.* Shutting off the light, I sat at my desk chair and tapped into my Zoom account. Staring at the camera, I spoke:

Magnificently MADE

"I Will Breathe"
by Nichole M. Palmer. 2020…

…BREATHE
Black man
murdered
by Minneapolis cops
17-year-old witness' video
goes viral
a nation erupts

damn… it's Emmett Till all over again
and FB is the open casket

MAKE IT STOP!!
MAKE IT STOP!!

…BREATHE
centuries-old rage
screams
in city streets
remembering
our Middle Passage Holocaust
2 million strong Africans died
11 million strong Africans survived
half-a million enslaved as labor
solely to make america great… ???

that was between the 16th and 19th centuries
…it's 2020…
shackles exchanged for handcuffs

MAKE IT STOP!!
…dear God…
MAKE IT STOP!!

#IHaveAVoice

… BREATHE
see,
Black blood soaked
in america's soil
SPILLED
in cotton fields & concrete jungles
Black bodies
STRUNG UP & SWUNG
wore nothing, rags, work clothes,
three-piece suits or military dress
Black minds
systematically CAGED
through educational brainwashing
of keeping Black history
a gray box, on a page, in a chapter, of a book
told to read once
in school … if at all

Black people are NOT immigrants!
… that is NOT our experience …
… BREATHE
these memories
knowingly or unknowingly
pump in the veins
of today's generations
of those Africans who survived

we march
we protest
we cry
we scream
we rage

… BREATHE

all of this
points to systemic & legislative
racism that america would
like the world to never know

TOO LATE

her shame like soiled panties waves in the air
she's not really the home of the free
at least for those of us
who look like me…
whose skin
ranges from vanilla to blue/black hues
all beautiful
all targeted
behind car wheels
& shopping carts
in america

…BREATHE
for months
years
decades
centuries
our cries for justice
fell on deaf ears
our tears for compassion
ignored as being
too emotional
too angry
too disturbing

but you hear us now, right?

american skies

choke on the smoke
of destroyed dreams
hopes
& lives...

looting & destroying neighborhoods
are never the answer
but... change must come
and when it does
George Floyd
Ahmaud Arbery
Breonna Taylor
Sandra Bland & many others
will rest
their deaths not in vain
their memories
the spark
that pushed Black people over the edge
and onto the streets
the news
& FB pages
with others who care
writing
speaking
marching
demanding

...to BREATHE..."

    I turned the camera off, then replayed the taping. Satisfied, I uploaded the video to Facebook and called my sorority sister from the day before.

    "I uploaded the video. It's done..." She screamed with joy; I screamed with joy.   "CONGRATULATIONS! You did it!"

    "Gurrrllll!"

"I know! Huge leap for you. But, it's out there. Your voice is out there!"

She spent time teaching me how to share the video. More than 3,000 people have seen my poem. Hopefully, my words have given them some air to breathe.

After years of ghostwriting, editing, teaching, and helping to launch others, I launched myself. No longer in the shadows or backstage. Now, I was front and center. Scared, trembling, yet standing strong. I had joined the world. My nine-year-old self applauded.

"Wonder what Mama and Pops would think of this," I questioned. And just as that thought crossed my mind, I heard my father's voice proudly exclaim, in his baritone rumble, *"Fantastic!"*

ABOUT THE CONTRIBUTOR

Trained journalist, dramatic writer, playwright, and published author, Nichole M. Palmer holds a BSJ degree from Northwestern University and an MFA degree in dramatic writing from New York University. This Gary, Indiana, native has helped birth inspiring storytelling voices for the multicultural, mainstream, and faith/inspirational marketplaces across America for more than twenty-five years.

She gravitates toward beautifully flawed characters who dare live out loud in spite of what the world tells them. She does not shy away from societal issues. In fact, Nichole prefers them because she says, "This is where everyday people discover how to live fully in spite of the devil. As a little girl growing up in Gary, Indiana, I decided that I wanted to tell the stories of forgotten people because there weren't enough characters who looked like me on TV." Her passion has always been to tell stories of forgotten people.

To learn more about Nichole and view her extensive body of work, visit her website at NicholeMPalmer.com.

Bits of Her Heart...

Nichole M. Palmer

Joy is... breathing life into my authentic creative voice and helping others do the same.

FUN FACT...

Nichole's latest commissioned full-length play PROPHESY to the BONES... and Other Stories Black Folx Whisper debuted in May 2022 to packed audiences at the Armour Street Theatre in Davidson, North Carolina.

SECTION 7

WE ARE WISE AND POWERFUL

PRIORITIZING & SELF WORTH:
A MILE MARKER MOMENT
by Alicia Marie Geczi

THE PRESENT IS A MOMENT
by Stacey Anne Wade

HAVING IT ALL
by Tracey Hall

INVITE A NEW INTENTION IN. IT'S THERE, JUST WAITING FOR YOU TO CALL IT INTO BEING.

PRIORITIZING & SELF-WORTH: A MILE MARKER MOMENT

BY ALICIA MARIE GECZI

To all those that have forgotten the way. All that you seek lies in your heart. Your soul remembers it all. God is always giving you the unconditional love and support you desire. It is time to awaken.

I get most of my ideas when I'm driving in the car. It's a time when I let my mind consciously wander and explore. I work through different themes going on in my life, and I try on new scenarios. Because I allow my heart and mind to be open, I often receive insights of wisdom during these drives. Nuggets of profound realization that open up my heart and soul to the infinite world beyond that is always waiting for me to listen, so it can drop in the message I need at the exact moment I need it. The other day, I had one of those moments.

I was driving back on my way home from a massage. It was great—until the end when I got off the table and realized that the massage therapist had kinked my neck. As frustrated as I was, and unfortunately in severe pain, it was the sign I needed as confirmation that I was meant to cancel my massage membership. I did have a doubt while I was on the table—the massage felt good, and I thought, *Why am I meeting such wonderful practitioners since I've made the decision I'm no longer going to be a member here?* I then thought, *Maybe I'm meant to stay.* Until I got off the table, in a lot of pain, I realized it was time to go.

As I drove, I reflected on how I am currently in a season of profound change in my life. I started a new business—a seed of an idea dropped in my heart that I planted at the end of last year. I never imagined how sharing my spiritual journey could equate into a business and yet here I was exploring that exact possibility. This new venture is requiring me to show up in ways that are stretching me. While the business is now my focus, the passion this new business has awoken inside me has asked me to step into a deeper story: *Will I create the life I envision? Will I fulfill my purpose?*

These questions have stoked the fire within me, and now I'm spreading that into all areas of my life. Because of that, I cannot do what I was doing before. In order for this new season of my life to blossom, I must change. The lesson of balance is now incredibly important for me to learn. I cannot move through this next season without it.

I had begun the new year with a planner, so I could write and create and see my tasks and my vision in my handwriting in front of me every day. This led me down a path of understanding how many areas of my life I'm juggling and the struggle to pour my energy into all of them. Without prioritizing I noticed I'm struggling to consistently keep the house clean or spend quality time with my husband in our newlywed year or run two businesses. I'd been grappling with this idea of balance and how to incorporate it into my life now that I have a new business and also a new marriage. I'd been told many times, from a spiritual healer I see, that one of my most important lessons I've chosen to learn in this lifetime is indeed balance.

It was in that moment in the car after the massage, stewing in my mind on the way home, that I made the commitment to focus deeply on my health for the next quarter. Despite my best intentions at the start of the year, I hadn't been very productive when it came to prioritizing my health. There had been many starts and stops. During the past three months, I signed back up at the yoga studio I belonged to and then I slowly fell off of attending classes. I wanted to go to the gym in the morning to start my routine but that didn't happen. I downloaded a

Prioritizing & Self-Worth: A Mile Marker Moment

yoga app that I could just do at home for fifteen minutes a day. While that seemed easy enough to commit to, it only lasted for a couple days. So here I was, in my car, making a promise to myself that this time I would take care of my physical body starting in April. I would make that the main focus because I knew I needed to in order to make an actual change.

And then I paused. *If my health—specifically physical movement—was my top priority for the next month, how was I going to continue doing everything else in my life?*

Eh, it won't be that hard—I'll just make sure I schedule it into the day. At least, that's what I told myself.

And I realized that physical movement is not scheduled into the day now, and I don't stop from the moment I wake up until the moment I sit down.

I'll be more focused with my time.

I told myself I'm already very focused on my two businesses, my husband, my home, and taking care of myself.

And so, prioritizing came into my mind.

It's a word I've heard a million times, and I've mostly heard it in relation to business. It's my understanding that it is the most efficient way successful people work, and because of that, they prosper. It is something that I have never been even remotely close to being able to do.

Prioritizing was the opposite of the way I lived my life. I couldn't imagine focusing my energy on just one task or area of my life and allowing the rest of my responsibilities to fall to the wayside. Everything was a priority in my eyes because everything was important.

Why was it that I felt like everything was important? Wasn't I supposed to make progress in all areas of my life and not just one? Then that would mean that other areas of my life suffered, right? Well, I guess it would just mean that some areas would just stay the same, and some would get worse. *I couldn't just let go of other areas of my life. That would be crazy.* Or would it?

This was where my heart and mind began to open. In one instant I understood exactly why prioritizing existed, why it was so important, and how it was done.

Prioritizing is about making the conscious choice to pour your love and energy into a specific focus. It means that the other things that aren't your focus will naturally maintain themselves at their current state or they will slowly decline. It

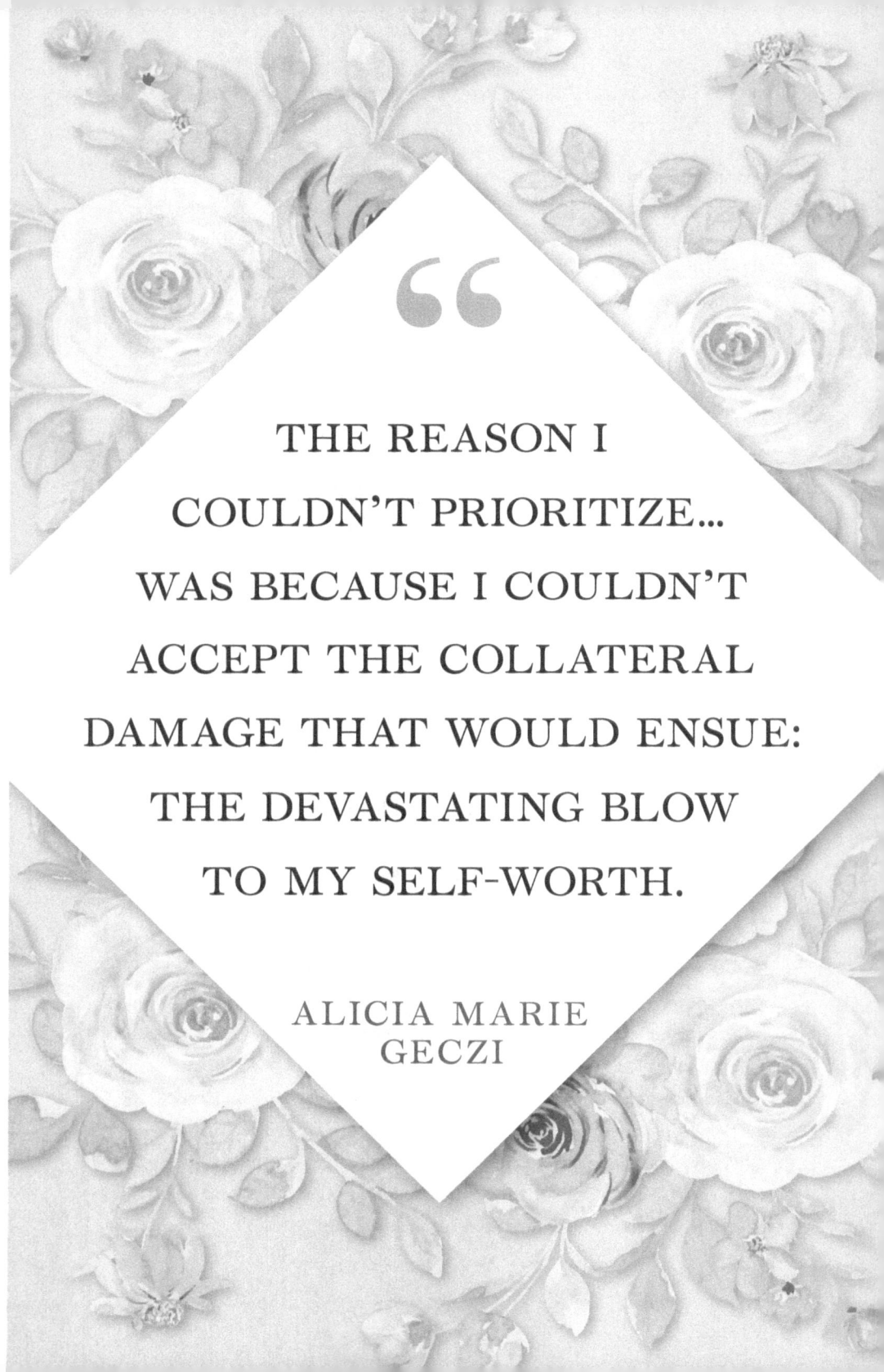

> "THE REASON I COULDN'T PRIORITIZE... WAS BECAUSE I COULDN'T ACCEPT THE COLLATERAL DAMAGE THAT WOULD ENSUE: THE DEVASTATING BLOW TO MY SELF-WORTH.
>
> ALICIA MARIE GECZI

Prioritizing & Self-Worth: A Mile Marker Moment

is the only way to move the needle on a specific focus because it requires more of your energy than you could give if you were focused on everything. It means letting go and surrendering and accepting everything else the way it is today, or worse, so you can focus on ONE goal.

And then the light bulbs just kept coming.

The ripple effects of this message proceeded to reverberate throughout my life. It felt like time stopped, and in my mind's eye I could see this message zooming down pathways to arrive at a moment of time that would then play like a movie. So many puzzle pieces clicked together all at once. It was a solution to a puzzle I didn't know existed, so I didn't even know there was a solution or even that I was trying to solve it. Once that puzzle came together in that moment that felt like five minutes but was really five seconds, another realization happened.

The reason I couldn't prioritize wasn't because I didn't understand the concept. It was because I couldn't accept the collateral damage that would ensue and the devastating blow to my self-worth. Incredibly surprised by this answer, I paused and listened. The answer was astounding.

Somehow, the acknowledgement of surrendering and accepting the status of the non-priority areas of my life was tied deeply into my self-worth because it was a threat. It felt like failure. It felt like I was giving up, and it felt like I would lose the battle I was waging to prove my worthiness. It meant that I would have to be okay with the areas of my life that I was working on improving. It was like I was accepting a permanent freeze on those parts of my life so I could grow in another.

So. Many. Emotions.

I followed this thread of prioritizing and self-worth down one of those message passageways my mind's eye had created to a moment when I was in college.

In college, I had a job working for two brothers who owned a bunch of commercial properties. I was hired part-time as an administrative assistant. In my free time, and out of boredom, I organized the copier room, created spreadsheets with tenants' lease increases and expirations, cleaned up their files, and learned bookkeeping. The CPA who was renting space from them saw what I was doing, and she hired me part-time too. I was working forty-hour weeks, splitting my time between both the CPA and the property management company, while also attending school full time. It was a lot of work and a ton of hours, but I loved it and I learned so much. I became such an invaluable asset that the brothers offered me a full-time job after graduation with the idea for me to run the business while they slowly phased themselves out of the business into retirement. It was such an honor to make such an impact on a small business like that. In all the years I worked there and all of the time I spent improving the business, the only negative feedback I received from one of the brothers was this: "You aren't very good at prioritizing."

That phrase has stayed in my mind all of these years. Sometimes it floats in when I struggle to find the time to do something or when I realize I should've done something sooner than when I was actually doing it. Other times it just pops into my mind out of nowhere.

Roger (one of the brothers) and I had such an honest relationship because we truly learned so much from one another that the one piece of negative feedback I received in our very casual annual review didn't feel like judgment at the time. As we sat at his desk, absolutely covered in stacks and stacks of paper that had accumulated over the decades in the one room in the office I couldn't organize, his sincere honesty and also confusion of why I couldn't prioritize was so innocent. It was amazing to him that I could do all that I would do and take the initiative on other tasks he couldn't have thought about asking me to do, and yet I still couldn't prioritize. I couldn't understand what was important and what wasn't. I couldn't understand how long something would take and by default, understand when I would have to start that task. I still remember the puzzled and flabbergasted look on his face, expressing that he just didn't get it. It didn't make sense to him.

I was self-aware to some degree at that time, so when he said it, I acknowledged that he was right. I knew this was one of my biggest obstacles. If I set my mind to something I would go to the ends of the earth to make that thing come to life. If someone said I couldn't do something I would ask them when they wanted it done by and I would do it sooner. I was unstoppable. I was driven and ambitious with an unlimited energy source to create and organize and continue to pursue and achieve. It was a deep fire within me that I couldn't turn off, and I brought that into the areas of my life that I enjoyed. That's the key word here folks. If something brought me joy, I was all in, no questions asked, and I never looked back. If it didn't, it was like pulling teeth to get me to do something. Which is why Roger couldn't understand why one of the single most important tasks of my job—to go to the bank every day to deposit the rent checks from the

Prioritizing & Self-Worth: A Mile Marker Moment

tenants—was the task I absolutely hated. I could create spreadsheets and organize files and review the finances for ten hours straight without even blinking. But the thought of going to the bank to deposit the checks every single day? Oh my goodness I didn't want to do it. So much so, that Roger actually spoke to the bank and discovered that they could install an electronic check scanner in our office for FREE. (Roger's favorite word).

I couldn't prioritize. I didn't want to. I didn't know how to. I didn't know why I couldn't do it. I didn't honestly even know what it meant. *How was I supposed to decide that this one thing was more important than this other thing? Isn't everything important? Doesn't everything need to be accomplished? Why does it matter if I do this one thing now and that thing later? Does it really make that big of a difference?*

Those words rang through my mind as I returned to the present moment, driving in my car. It was something I've known wasn't my strong suit all of these years and I couldn't figure out why. Now that I knew the root of my inability to prioritize, preservation of self-worth, I needed to understand where this root came from and how it got there. *Why couldn't I differentiate between something important and something not as important? Why did I believe everything was equally important? How would I feel if I deemed something important and something less important? Why would I feel that way?*

I believe we all have a soul, and we all have an ego. Our spirit or our soul is always speaking to us, and it is often difficult to hear because it has lost its prime spot. The ego has taken over and has stifled the voice of our spirit. Our ego is the voice in our minds that has lots and lots of thoughts throughout the day—mostly negative, even if they are disguised as positive. The inner knowing and the guidance from our connection to spirit has been pushed away to nothing more than a whisper in most of us. Over the past five years I've been working with a spiritual healer so I can hear my spirit more clearly and understand how and why the ego does what it does. This realization of my self-worth being tied to my inability to choose a focus was a perfect example of the ego work I had been doing. I followed the thread once again to see where it led me.

I became aware that my lack of ability to prioritize is a trait of my ego. I learned that the root of this character trait was not just tied to my self-worth, it was about the even deeper still preservation of my self-worth.

I could finally see how my ego had woven itself so deeply into this character trait that it took something that was a gift—my perseverance, passion, and dedication—and sabotaged it. By not allowing me to channel this energy pointedly into a single focus, I was setting myself up to fail.

Every. Single. Time.

By not allowing myself to accept where a certain aspect of my life was today, I was never able to shift my focus away from that to pour my energy into something else. It led me to believe that if I wasn't trying to improve everything, I was failing. If I was failing, I wasn't worthy. If I wasn't worthy, I would never be loved. *If I was never loved, what was the point of being here?*

I peeled the curtain away from of all of these defensive thoughts to see what was hiding behind there. Much to my surprise, I found my aching heart defined by the level of improvement in all areas of my life all the time. My self-worth was intertwined so deeply that it would rather do everything a little bit than to do one thing a lot. It believed that my worthiness was tied into every aspect of my life and to consciously put one aside would be accepting failure. It believed I had to focus on everything—work, home, family, and self-care—all the time. If I made the decision to put my energy into one or two of those four things, it would mean that I was okay with allowing another area of my life to maintain or decline, and my ego clearly wasn't okay with that.

I told myself I couldn't allow that to happen. I must do a little bit to everything all the time. I must focus on everything. I couldn't drop the ball in any areas of my life. I couldn't make the decision that one thing is better than another. I must get better at everything. I must spread my energy to everything. I must make improvements everywhere. I must keep going. Everywhere. No matter what.

These were the beliefs my ego tried to justify.

I was convinced of the fallacy that I should be improving in all areas of my life. If I'm not constantly focused on improving, then what am I doing in my life? I would scold myself, thinking about everything that is going to suffer because I'm too busy focused on one thing. I chided and judged myself constantly. *You should be going to yoga; summer isn't that far away. You should be spending time with your husband since you are a newlywed. Your house is going to be a mess if you stop cleaning it, and that's disgusting.*

Fear was the emotion I felt when I thought about letting go and accepting

Prioritizing & Self-Worth: A Mile Marker Moment

mediocrity, which was how my ego was framing the idea of the other areas of my life staying the same or declining. So, I followed the thread of fear.

In all of these statements I saw the fear that was being defended by guilt. Guilt is often the emotion my ego uses to manipulate me into action. I've come to learn that under the hard shell of the attack, sometimes anger or guilt, there lies another emotion, the root emotion, that is being defended. For me, it is usually sadness, and that sadness is usually tied to the belief that I am just not good enough. This is a lie the ego has told me for a very long time and something I've spent the past five years unraveling. This scenario with trying to learn how to prioritize and focus was no different.

Underneath the fear of surrendering the other parts of my life so I could focus on one was the real reason I felt fear. The fear was because I believed that I am defined as the person I show up as in the world. If I stop taking care of certain areas of my life to focus on another, how I am defined will look different—messier, less put together, disheveled, and embarrassing. My ego decided this would be the unacceptable result if I surrendered. *If this was how I would show up to the world, how could anyone love me?*

This is the thing with shadow work; you never know how the ego has woven its lies into your life and how you've been a slave to them without knowing. You also don't know that when you get to the core of the lies, how deep that one statement really hits. As I'm typing this, weeks after I had this epiphany in the car, I can still feel the gravity of that sentence, because I'm not done with my ego work, and that belief that I'm not enough is still alive inside me. It has less pull and less control over my life now, but it's still not gone just yet.

I felt the sadness of that little girl inside me who still believes that she is unworthy of love. I poured lots of love into her heart and spoke to her, telling her that she is worthy, and she is so incredibly loved. This is one of many moments I've spent with my inner child, assuring her that she will make it through and live the life she's always wanted and that God didn't abandon her. It all had a purpose, and, because of that, she is going to do great things because she already has.

I slowly and mindfully followed the thread back out to my original light bulb moment about prioritizing. As I embark on this new season of my life that requires me to be authentic and open, I know all of the healing I've done and will continue to do is even more important. One moment in the car daydreaming about how to focus my life on what this season is asking of me led me down a path of profound realization.

In order to prioritize my health for the next few months, I have to make room in my schedule for it. In order to do that, I must accept that there are certain areas of my life, like my businesses, family, or home, that will stay the same or decline from that decision. This means that when I make the decision to truly focus on my health and allow the other areas to not be a priority, I am accepting them for what they are today. I'm accepting that these other areas are, like me, enough.

The only chance anything actually gets better is if you DO prioritize it. In order to move the needle, that aspect of our lives needs time and love and energy. It requires us to show up and be present. It requires us to be mindful and be with it consistently, wholly, and without distraction. It demands for us to be there with it so we can work with it to become the vision we know it can be. That is impossible to accomplish if we are only giving it just enough attention to get by. The needle will never move. The changes you want to see will never happen. The vision you see for that part of your life will always stay just that, a vision. It will never be a reality. It will never be created on this physical plane. It will remain a seed in your heart, a tiny hope, without the love and care and nutrients it needs to become the flourishing life you desire.

There are a few moments in my life that I can say *from that moment forward, I was never the same person.* This is a moment when I realized I just put myself on a new path because of what just happened. For me, this moment in the car was one of them.

I began writing this story to share with you how in a single moment, God can drop a message right in your path that changes the trajectory of your life. We have these moments every single day. Some of them go unnoticed, and others become mile markers for your journey. I have had several notable mile markers in the past five years that have changed my life and that led me to be writing this chapter that you are currently reading. Before that, I was just trying to get through the day, doing a little bit of everything, and failing at it all. I didn't have trust that the Universe would catch me if I fell. I didn't have faith that God would show me what this season requires of me and that He would give me the tools to thrive. I didn't know that I was hurting, and I was living my life in a way that was tailored to protect myself and shut everyone else out.

Prioritizing & Self-Worth: A Mile Marker Moment

If we listen and let go just enough, we can hear the whispers of our spirit within us and the spirit world around us. They are always guiding us and supporting us. They are always delivering messages: in music, in our dreams, in a conversation with a friend, in a thought out of nowhere, or in a kink in the neck. You are not alone. We are not alone. Don't be afraid to prioritize yourself. Don't be afraid to share. Spirit is always listening.

ABOUT THE CONTRIBUTOR

I'm Alicia. I write. I practice yoga. I rearrange my home often. I am a wife; a fur mama, and I am an extremely spiritual person.

I wasn't always this way as I am sure you weren't the person you once were. I used to live my life in a constant state of anxiety. I was constantly seeking approval and always waiting for the other shoe to drop, believing that nothing was actually as good as it seemed.

I had a session with Intuitive Jack, and I walked out of that session awakened and ready to show up and do the spiritual work that I knew I was here to do. I now reflect back on my life as "before" and "after" that session.

I have spent the past five years healing. I am learning to have a deeper connection with the world around me, heal the trauma that has woven its way into every area of my life, and commit to an unbreakable faith in God. Each day I am learning, and I will continue to learn. I am so grateful for where I was and where I am now.

Bits of Her Heart...

Alicia Marie Geczi

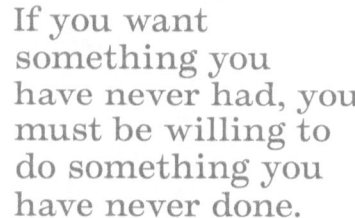

If you want something you have never had, you must be willing to do something you have never done.

FUN FACT...

Alicia loves love so much that she actually created a brand called Twelve Moon Studios that supports couples to craft their dream weddings.

THE PRESENT IS A MOMENT

BY STACEY ANNE WADE

This chapter is dedicated to those who wish to embody and embrace the ecstasy of being on your own.

As soon as you heard the gentle tinkling sound of the wind chimes, you knew it was time for yoga. The soft tintinnabulation of the chimes continued to linger as you announced your name followed by "Here for class." Little did you know your decision to practice yoga was going to change your life. Often it was an effortless subtle change; you learned how to soften your shoulders when you exhale, releasing a world of tension. Other times you may have left class in a daze with a feeling of *What just happened in there?* and thinking *I need more of that in my life*. Then there were days that the practice effectively changed your life from the first breath to the final pose, and it all happened in one of life's simple moments.

This is when profound things begin to happen; this is a story of how that happened for me.

The wind chimes at my studio, Yoga Bliss, became a well-known sound that no one really talked about but everyone knew of. It's like the air in your lungs is there, but you don't realize that in the moment the air is what's keeping you alive. I often refer to my yoga practice as what keeps me alive! Yoga has saved my life countless times and continues to dramatically walk with me, comfort me, love me back, and be there for me, no matter what. I have been practicing yoga since the '80s, and I can boldly state that, not including my children, yoga is truly the love of my life. It's the only thing that's ever remained consistent with the utmost discipline. It's never been the motivation that got me on my mat, but rather the joy of the outcome from the practice.

After becoming a certified yoga instructor in 2004, I immediately began teaching yoga in a spare room over the garage in my home, offering it to ten of my brave friends and acquaintances who were willing to try something new. Yoga had been gaining popularity but was still very foreign to most people. They agreed to eight classes, came in fresh with little to absolutely no experience or ideas of what yoga was. Before they were done exploring, I was quickly signing the lease to rent a space for yoga because I knew this was in fact the purpose that had been assigned to me from the universe.

The funny thing is I had no idea that my offerings of teaching yoga in a space outside of my home would be footsteps away from my doorstep. At the time I lived next to a Women's Club in a home that was built on an old horse farm. As a kid I always loved riding my bike for miles and miles and often wandered off to explore new places. One day along my journey I discovered a plot of land with which I fell in love. It was an open area not very developed that I repeatedly went back to for a while so I could simply ride around and imagine building a home on this secret spot one day. There were just a few homes there at the time, and I still remember staring at the land with all my childlike imagination streaming over like magical stardust and rainbows. I later learned that storms come before the rainbows and explosions before the dust.

Ten years later my husband and I built a home on the land, and three years after we moved in, I opened *Yoga Bliss* at The Women's Club next door. The Law of Attraction was doing its work on me during those bike rides. I knew I'd live there, but what I didn't know was I would begin my life's work there. My belief is show up, the story is waiting for you, and sometimes you just become brave enough to tell it.

I bought a large sign with moveable letters and arranged the words, "Sign up for yoga here, Saturday 9 a.m." I set up the space with candles, yoga deities, my yoga mat, and a clipboard for students to sign in on. On the very first Saturday for

The Present is a Moment

my first official class, the door opened and the most enthusiastic woman came in. All these years later, I still remember that moment. It wasn't a saunter or a stroll of curiosity but more like a quick scurry to the sign-up table because the sprint of her joy was so intense that if her feet followed her heart, she would have run right past me. Her words were simply, "You're offering yoga here? I'm so excited I can hardly breathe!" Her smile stays with me now as I reflect. She introduced herself and from that day forward she fondly became known to me as my first official yoga student at Yoga Bliss.

I will keep her name to myself and simply refer to her and that moment as a reflection of Goddess Lakshmi. Lakshmi is the goddess I became interested in during one of my yoga journeys. I meditated on her power and found it to be the most relatable to my own spirit. Lakshmi is the divine power that transforms dreams into reality. She is a perfect creation of a self-sustaining, self-contained nature: A delightful delusion in a dreamlike expression of divinity that makes life comprehensible and worth living. Lakshmi's energy is unlimited and abundant. In all her auspiciousness, the spirit of Lakshmi was with me in every session I taught thereafter and still is today.

Every time I taught a class at The Women's Club I had to set up and take down 50 chairs; 25 to the left, 25 to the right, 5 neat rows of 10 across with an aisle in the center. The space was shared with a church for worship on Sundays and used for events, meetings, and parties.

Although this was a pain in the neck, it was a methodical moving meditation that claimed me a huge space in which to offer my students a yoga class several times a week, and if you've ever gotten into yoga, you can understand and appreciate the vibe of a room. This took me extra time to set up and tear down, so I began a practice for myself of always being mentally prepared for a class.

At the time it was a means of mental toughness; if you want this space, you literally must work for it every single class. The task also involved the setting-up of the props, the altar, the music, the lighting including candles, setting the temperature, clean sweeping the floors, and making sure the bathrooms felt tidy. I set up my yoga studio one class at a time. Eighteen years later, now writing this story, I reflect on the profound experience it was to be setting my studio up every single session I taught. You see, practicing yoga is new every single time if you allow it to be. The mat is your canvas, and your body is the brush. What pours from your soul is the art you create, the masterpiece you take with you, and the story you leave behind, either to tell or wash away in the river.

Practicing yoga often comes with tears, joy, sorrow, grief, agony, and laughter, but always in the end, relief, gratitude, love, and light. The physical aspect and benefits are another topic entirely. I can't tell you how many times I heard thank you for the class I've received over the years, but I can tell how many I didn't hear. Hundreds of thousands because yoga does that—it offers you something you can't buy or be given. You must create it yourself, and it's yours to keep and use whenever you like. When you cultivate a practice of yoga you create a toolshed within yourself. You notice how you can stand on your own two feet and feel strong. You can close your eyes and see your heart's desire; you can take a conscious breath and at the end of your exhale you have the answers.

What I'm describing to you and ultimately prescribing to you to start yoga is to begin with a pose called Tadasana–Mountain Pose. In my yoga professional opinion Tadasana is the antidote to everything that ails you. Here is when you witness the present moment. I mean really notice everything—all your surroundings: the sounds, the smells, the feelings, the emotions. All your senses light up and are electrified. If you believe you're born with everything you need to survive a situation, and you don't quite know what that means, I'm telling you five breaths in Tadasana is the key to self-discovery and unlocking it all.

BREATH ONE

Inhale - Stand up tall on your bare feet, spread your toes and feel your legs fire, your chest expand, and your ribs awaken.

Exhale - Notice your body start to empty out and surrender.

BREATH TWO

Inhale - Firm up your quadriceps, elongate your tailbone and lift your kneecaps slightly, roll your shoulders back.

Exhale - Lengthen your arms turning your palms to face out and reach your fingertips to the floor.

> "
>
> I ROARED OUT LOUD, DANCED AROUND THE ROOM, BREATHED THE FRESHEST AIR I EVER TASTED, WRAPPED MY ARMS AROUND MY HEART, AND FELL IN LOVE WITH BEING ALONE.
>
> STACEY ANNE WADE

BREATH THREE

Inhale - Widen your collar bones and allow the crown of your head and sternum to lift to the sky.

Exhale - Melt your shoulder blades down your spine and lower your chin parallel to the earth.

BREATH FOUR

Inhale - Feel the roots beneath your feet and your breath cascading all over your body.

Exhale - The weight of your body slowly dissipates, and you feel like a sunrise.

BREATH FIVE

Inhale - Release the last bit of tension around your face, close your eyes, unclench your jaw releasing it from bearing anymore emotion.

Exhale - Notice the ears numb to the outside world, your eternal listening is dialed up, and it's time to begin.

I want to share a story of when I noticed this for the very first time, honestly and whole heartedly. With the core of my existence, I felt the truth of what I had been practicing for all those years. It wasn't just mild and subtle like the usual beginning of the romance, it was an, "Oh my God, is that you?" type of notice.

It was a Saturday morning in late spring when I witnessed and fully embraced the ecstasy of being alone. A true introvert, I feel much more comfortable focusing on my inner thoughts and ideas rather than what's happening externally. I don't mind alone time or not being at the best party, and I rather enjoy small groups and deep conversations with less external stimulation.

However, I had many bouts of terror fearing the alone time, which was beginning to come more often.

I had taught yoga that morning at my yoga studio, as I always did, then I came home to make myself breakfast. This morning was different, however. It wasn't just one thing; it was many. The new normal, which didn't feel normal for many years beyond this story, was that my kids were not home. I dreaded coming home to the sick feeling I had in my stomach knowing the house was a different type

The Present is a Moment

of quiet. My children were not just out and back soon from an errand or a playdate; they were gone for the weekend and would be every other weekend to follow. Just months before this particular day I'd come home to a house full of kids in pjs waiting with hugs and kisses, playing with toys, or running around out in the yard. Going off to teach yoga at my studio was the one place I felt alive in, a woman that only existed there. Coming home to my three children connected me to a whole other part of my life that also beautifully existed. A life I created with my heart, my children, and my home was everything. Studio life was very separate. It was work, yes, my passion, indeed, but I left it behind to come home and be their mom.

This wasn't the first time they had gone to their father's for the weekend, and it wasn't new that I was all alone with my thoughts and fears and issues. I was separated with divorce in the wings and my life as I knew it on the chopping block. Everyone said it would get easier, but, to be honest, it didn't for a very long time, and even then, it just became different. I love spending time with my children, and, in most cases, I'd rather be with them more than anyone else. A student of mine once told me after class that unconditional love is only found in the love you have for your children. I've learned he is correct, and even the greatest romance cannot compare to the love of your children. As my heart continued to break open, I continued to learn more of how my yoga practice supported me in the longing for the losses I was beginning to generate.

As this process unfolded, I discovered there is a gift at the end of fear.

This particular morning, I felt a new happy coming on. The spring air smelled sweeter, the sun was shining bright, and I felt genuinely at peace. I was excited to go home and seek a new adventure. This home was a third move for us as a family, and it still felt fairly new in its discoveries. It had the most magnificent kitchen with lake views, counter tops of mahogany and marble, custom-painted black cabinets with glass doors, and appliances any chef would dream about. The aesthetics of the home were glorious; however, they have nothing to do with the joy I'm about to express of this day. I was preparing my standard favorite—fried egg whites, avocado, multigrain toast, and fresh fruit with coffee made by yours truly.

I'm not one for going out to eat much or picking up coffee. I rather enjoy making my own meals for myself and for my family and serving them with spectacular love. When I prepare a meal for myself, I always use a special plate that I have just one of, a glass or mug that makes me happy, and occasionally I even treat myself with a cloth napkin. When I sit at the table with this completed meal before me, I feel in that moment all is just right in my world. I have lived my life with this one core value, "Love is in the details."

I distinctly remember the sounds that day—the pan hitting the stove, the cage free eggs cracking open on the side of my Le Creuset, and the aroma of EVOO heating up like a warm hug you can't let go of. That day the sizzle was particularly exotic, the oil temperature was just right to seize the pop and crackle ensuring me a proper flaky edge. I prefer my eggs a little well done, brown on the edges and firm in the middle, always salted and peppered while the egg is still cooking, giving it a coat of gentle spices for my morning palate to enjoy. Next, after I slide my eggs onto my special plate, I slice the avocado into a thinly layered fan across my eggs, topped with more salt and pepper, although now in present day I'm loving Trader Joe's Everything but the Bagel spice. Grass-fed butter on my toast, and a bowl of assorted organic berries and melons. I really appreciate a colorful plate of fresh food; it just feels like a symphony.

I lived on a dead-end street in a unique, quiet little neighborhood. Our home was a beautiful custom-built farmhouse that sat lakeside on the east coast facing the sunrise. The roads were more like paths: one-way, very windy, and constructed of uneven cement. Each home was a piece of art detailed and decorated by the heart of its owner. It looked like something a child would draw out of crayons on crumbled-up, colored construction paper. None of the homes were new, but several were reconstructed like ours from their original building materials, as living on the water can be a brute on maintenance. The charm and whimsy were never lost, and I always felt like I was part of a fairytale. We had just moved there about eighteen months prior, and it was from the get-go a mysterious, seductive source. Our lake home is fondly referred to in our family as "The Blue House." It was a brief journey filled with mountainous emotional peaks and valleys. It was the perfect hardcover for my story to unfold … little did I know the stories that occurred in my life where there waiting for me.

After my breakfast was prepared, I sat alone at the head of the table facing the water with my back to the kitchen. Any Italian mom would tell you the closest seat to the kitchen is forever her seat. I got lucky here today with a beautiful view in lieu of the empty seats surrounding me missing my family members. The dining room wall I was facing was filled with French doors overlooking the water; the doors opened inward, which was kind of unique. In a symbolic sense, open doors mean opportunity, and in a Biblical sense, an open door from God is one that allows our faith to be stretched and strengthened. This day was not about me walking out the door; in that case the door would have opened out. I had to stay there a little while longer to be stretched and strengthened, and there is where I needed to be still and know.

I began to enjoy my meal, my alone time, the view, and the vibe—it was all amazing. Then I realized I wasn't alone. I arose, mystified, my bare feet clinging to the cool aged pinewood floor as I slowly walked around the house. There was not a peep from the tiny neighborhood or a sound from my children to be investigated. As I approached the sitting room, the sound got louder and louder causing me to pause mindfully, listen, and be still. Just my eyes were now moving and wondering if this was the moment I'd lost my mind.

I closed my eyes like I do when I'm teaching yoga to feel the energy in the room. I stood still and took a deep breath in Tadasana. I opened my eyes, then I saw it: the glass home of our pet fish, Cutie. It's a tiny clear bowl of water with blue gravel set on the bookshelf and inside was a blue Betta fish with brilliant orange fins staring at me. Betta fish are naturally territorial and must be housed alone. If you place another Betta fish in the same home, they will fight to injury often resulting to death—interesting plot twist at the pause of discovering being alone in this home is probably best for the moment. Well, the sound I heard was our fish chewing its food and chewing quite loudly; he was also eating his breakfast. I came face to face with one of God's creatures, and despite the fact that amongst all things happening today including this fish chew in the silent pause of my changing life, I was witnessing one absolute thing ... The Present is a Moment.

I was so incredibly present and available to the stillness that I could hear a fish eat underwater in the other room. I roared out loud with laughter, danced around the room, breathed in the freshest air I ever tasted, wrapped my arms around my heart, and fell in love with being alone. It wasn't just the fish, but the intimacy of listening to everything that day. Hearing the fish represented hearing everything. You're never all alone. My ears became my eyes, and my broken heart suddenly had an antidote. I had many times taught with my eyes closed, capturing the energy of the room, and guiding my students through an experience, but this came to me that day and gave me something I will never forget: to fall in love with myself, graciously and consciously.

I fell in love with my heart that day. My efforts of nurturing myself that morning, being still, using my tools, grounding my feet, taking my breath, noticing everything within me and around me didn't compare to this moment. I woke up and became alive in a way I had not yet lived. It was bigger and more profound than the practice on my mat. My yoga practice saved me once again and allowed me not to die that day, but to live eternally.

ABOUT THE CONTRIBUTOR

Stacey is living a life of presence and availability…Showing up for the Storms and the Rainbows…Making room to bear witness to the unfolding life that she's meant to live.

One day at a time she steps into the unknown with complete vulnerability…Sometimes feeling alone, friendless and without love, she catches a faint reflection of her truth revealing that she can love her way, without rules, expectations or a need to show up in any other way other than as herself. Without judgement her love prevails…

Bits of Her Heart...

Stacey Anne Wade

When you're ready, you'll find that the connection you seek is well within your reach.

FUN FACT...

Stacey hysterically riffs about life, putting words to pain and having it come across as funny and lighthearted.

21

HAVING IT ALL

BY TRACEY HALL

This chapter is dedicated with love to my younger self and to all working women who are juggling a full-time career, raising children, and maintaining a healthy marriage and a happy home life.

The year was 2017. I wish I could say I was in the hospital because of a broken leg from skiing the Alps or a broken arm from falling off a camel in Egypt, but the sad truth is I was hospitalized because of a perforation in my appendix that was threatening to tear and unleash untold numbers of bad bacteria into my body.

So unglamorous, but there I was, in a hospital bed waiting for my infections to subside before surgery could be done to remove my appendix. Hooked up to an IV and consuming only a bland liquid diet, I was pretty miserable. Sleep was nearly impossible in the hospital, although one afternoon I woke up from a nap to find a prayer card laying on my stomach. I guess someone stood over me and prayed, but I never saw or heard them.

At the time, I was employed by a small media company in southern New Jersey as a sales rep tending to the needs of very small advertisers. The area I covered was literally full of senior and 55+ communities and the doctors' offices that catered to them. Most of these doctors didn't need to advertise because their waiting rooms were always full.

But being a road warrior meant this sales position had to be done mainly in person, on my cell, and by communicating through emails. Prospecting and cold calls were necessary evils, and I was very good at being able to start up a conversation with a complete stranger, eventually working up to getting them to advertise with us.

In my delusional state awaiting surgery, I figured I could continue servicing my clients while in my hospital bed and during my recovery. I had nothing else to do, and it just made sense to be productive. "Made sense" seems so silly now as I was battling quite a nasty internal barrage, but I thought I could still work. I was hooked up to wires, monitors, and tubes and couldn't leave my bed without bringing all of that equipment with me, but despite those obstacles, I thought I could do it.

Looking back, it made no sense really, and my employer wanted no part of it. They kept asking when I would be returning to work, and, of course, I had no idea. I had all the tools I needed for work in bed with me. I could make and receive calls to clients. I could prospect, cold call, and manage my schedule on my laptop. But one day when I tried logging in to my business accounts held by my employer, I realized they had blocked me from accessing my emails and client information! I called for an explanation and was basically told to go get on disability.

I was furious! I had business pending and knew it was all going away, which it did. My employer kept the revenue from my accounts and closed the pending contracts in my pipeline. They wound up giving me a small percentage afterward, but we both knew I wasn't going back.

The most interesting part of this story is that I didn't even like that job! I hated my territory! Our office was in an old decrepit Victorian house that was chopped up into office space. It was dark, depressing, and smelled funny. We joked that the mold would eventually do us all in if we didn't fall through the floors first! My coworkers were all nice people, though, and I guess that, and a weekly paycheck, is why I stayed. It seemed my work ethic certainly outweighed common sense back then. I had carefully cultivated that mindset through years of struggling to "climb the ladder."

Prior to that job, my career was the epitome of "here today, gone tomorrow." The tremendous effort I put forth to achieve success in my field brought me to a sales position at one of the world's largest media companies. We had all the bells and whistles, from company cars and expense accounts to exclusive access into the elite world of C-Suite clientele and all the perks they brought to the table. My sales team was made up of high-achieving women like me, and we worked great together. It truly was "the dream job." I planned on retiring there until massive layoffs became the norm in all things media. Our group, along with countless others, were suddenly unemployed. So many of my colleagues and I had to start all over from scratch.

We took lesser positions for a lot less money and prestige; some left the field altogether, and some simply retired.

The one thing we weren't prepared for was how disposable we all were. And still are. Corporations answer to shareholders, and the bottom line often comes at the expense of the workers. I've been caught up in several layoffs and business closings throughout my 40-year career and never really thought of the emotional toll it took on me.

Today, we hear so much about self-care and self-love. That wasn't a prescription in our work health years ago. I really believed I could work through a major illness! It was ingrained in us that women who wanted to make it to the top of their companies knew they had to work harder and stronger to be taken seriously. It was suggested that "you can have it all," meaning a successful career and a wonderful home life, but the only way to do that was to work yourself sick.

That lousy, misguided information caused a lot of burnout, and women took the brunt of it. I saw women working through so many difficult circumstances. Full-time employment meant that in addition to the 40-plus hours women gave to their company each week, they would also be juggling their own health or difficult marriages or caring for aging parents while managing sick and healthy children. "Having it all" was extremely stressful. I had one friend and colleague leave the workplace altogether through a "psych leave." Her mental health had deteriorated to a dangerous point from the pressures she was under both professionally and in her home simultaneously.

After returning home to recover from my surgery, I was so burnt. The truth was I couldn't have it all PERFECTLY. Something was bound to give. In this case, it was my health. And I was so angry! Angry at being locked out of my accounts, angry that I had to grovel for a job I didn't like, angry I got so sick, angry that once again I had to start over, angry at the whole long, hard, and backward road that my career path took me on.

> RELEASING MY OWN HUGE SELF-EXPECTATIONS LED TO A SLOW DISCOVERY AND ACCEPTANCE OF THE SELF-LOVE PRESCRIPTION.
>
> TRACEY HALL

Having It All

I don't know what I was trying to prove. I didn't understand that I was putting way too much value into my work-self and not nearly enough into myself. Validation was important to me, especially when working in a goal-centered career. I wanted to make my sales goals; I was driven to make it!

It wasn't until all of this was taken away for the umpteenth time that I finally realized perfection is an illusion and that being just okay was okay. Releasing my own huge self-expectations led to a slow discovery and acceptance of the self-love prescription. I knew I was replaceable at work, and that was a tough lesson to absorb. Truth is, we're all replaceable at work, but we are irreplaceable at home to our loved ones, and that's what truly matters.

My time sitting home in recovery made me question what really was important and what did I want to do with my life. I knew I wouldn't be going back to that job, but I had nothing else lined up, and I was tired of turning myself inside out to make money for a company that only wanted more and more from me. Salespeople are the revenue generators. In what used to be a lucrative career, sales jobs became a joke. Many companies decided to only pay commissions, not a salary or expenses. Basically, the time a salesperson needed to close a deal wasn't of any value anymore. Only the close mattered.

I can't think of any other profession that does that. Can you imagine saying to your doctor, "I'll only pay you if I'm cured" or to your college professors "I'll pay you after I know for certain a good company is going to hire me"? As I scoured the job listings, I knew I was overqualified to be a commission-only rep, and I also needed to earn an income.

In a sink-or-swim moment, I decided to launch out on my own and created my website, *Jersey Shore Scene*. It wasn't an easy decision, but I knew I had the foundation and skills to do it. I knew so many good people who could help me with everything from designing a logo to who I needed to call to actually build my site. I can sell ads, but I don't know code!

I knew writers, photographers, and designers. I knew what the competition was and still is, and I knew what was missing from our local media landscape. The "local" part. We have plenty of touristy websites and magazines, we have glossies and newspapers, but we didn't have a website dedicated to this beautiful part of New Jersey that talked to the locals through content written by the locals.

I finally understood that my crazy career happened for a reason. I learned so much from the successes and failures; I remembered what worked and what people liked to consume through the media. I knew what they didn't want too. I was determined to not put out any negative posts or images on *Jersey Shore Scene* because I didn't want people leaving my website feeling worse than when they clicked on it. We were and still are surrounded by bad news. My site was purposely designed to shed light on and share all the good things we have happening right here at the shore.

But starting your own business isn't for the faint of heart, and sometimes I questioned myself, "What were you thinking?" It took so much preparation and work to get all the pieces together for this digital puzzle I was creating.

People wanted to help me though. It was amazing what they said "yes" to, and I realized that all you have to do is ask. What's the worst thing that can happen? They say "no?" So, then you find someone else!

Jersey Shore Scene officially launched in October of 2017, and I haven't looked back since. I've met the most incredible people on this journey. I've interviewed locals of every possible profession you can think of. I've featured authors, artists, musicians, dancers, yogis, chefs, teachers, environmentalists, wildlife experts, historians, farmers, and so many more. Every day I am excited to present all these amazing people to my readers. There are so many talented and dedicated professionals who live on and around the shore.

You may wonder, "What's the upside to all of this?" The answer is that I control every aspect of my life now. I work for me, and I'm a damned good boss! The downside? Well, those dips tend to be of my own making, and I've been learning how to avoid unnecessary pitfalls. There is a brutal honesty that envelops you as an entrepreneur because everything that happens is a direct result of what you do or don't do.

If you choose not to be a business owner, you can have fulfillment in your workplace too. Women have evolved so much since my early days in corporate America forty years ago. I love seeing the heights that women are attaining WITH the support of other women. There is still more that can be done, but I hope my struggles and the struggles of all the women who came before, after, and with me opened many doors for our younger sisters.

I believe the clearest lesson in all of this is that the "you can have it all" myth has been replaced with finding the right balance that works for your life. Understand that you need to make the time for rest, relaxation, healthy eating, and exercise the same way you would schedule sales calls or any other work activity. Ultimately, I learned the hard way that loving myself is just as important as loving my family, friends, and my career. I can still see myself lying in that hospital bed, trying to ignore the pain and all the devices I was hooked up to, trying so hard to be a good worker bee but so unable to focus on my own healing instead.

Protecting my health and energy is a top priority now. It never used to be; I burned the candle at both ends and paid a dear price for it. Know that you don't have to do it all. Ask for help and be open to receiving it. I'm here to tell you that "having it all" comes at a steep price without backup and support from your inner and your professional circles. Know that you can define what you need to feel balanced in all aspects of your life, and there is no one size fits all.

Consider the notion that yes, you might be able to have it all, just don't expect it to be perfect and not all at the same time. There's freedom in flexibility and acceptance of what is.

Most importantly, remember you will get through the tough times. A long career is one of many peaks and valleys. Celebrate the peaks; learn in the valleys. Surround yourself with loving and supportive people to help you journey across this life. Don't take things so seriously because they can change in a heartbeat.

Remember to never undervalue yourself as I did by only seeing through a career lens and not seeing the whole picture of my life. We all need to make time for those we love and to give back when we can. I now will say "yes" more often and not feel guilty when I say "no."

Take time outside of work to nurture and nourish your head, your heart, and your soul. Along the way, try to nurture other women in and out of your circle. They too, carry large loads and may need someone just like you to lean on. Share your warmth, your wisdom, and your encouragement. When one of us succeeds, we all succeed.

At the end of every day, I am truly grateful for all the lessons learned, even the hard one in that hospital bed, and I hope that by sharing my story, my beautiful sisters will rise even higher.

ABOUT THE CONTRIBUTOR

Born and raised in New Jersey, Tracey Hall is a kid of the '60s, complete with memories of listening to music on 45s with a portable record player! Raised by a working single mom after her parents' divorce, Tracey learned so much by watching her parents, and she saw what to do and what not to do in personal relationships and at work. Later married and after having three sons, divorce happened again, and Tracey became a single working mom herself. But, as luck would have it, Tracey remarried gaining a "Brady Bunch" kind of story with two blended families.

Working in media was always a part of her life, but after having been part of downsizing and closures, it became apparent that starting her own media outlet was the way to go. Tracey is a writer, publisher, content creator, mom, wife, and Jersey Shore resident, so she combined all of these talents and traits to launch a digital, local lifestyle magazine called *Jersey Shore Scene*.

Tracey considers the magazine a place to hold and share wisdom from local writers, business information from the local community, and beautiful images to inspire readers to stop for a moment and read the content. And it all began with a leap of faith—*Jersey Shore Scene* was born from years of learning and watching what her employers did, then taking the best of those experiences and going for it!

Bits of Her Heart...
Tracey Hall

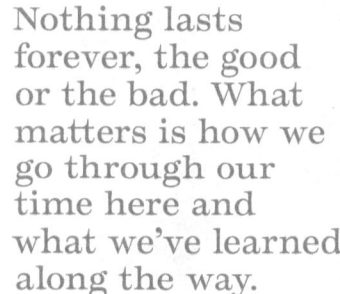

Nothing lasts forever, the good or the bad. What matters is how we go through our time here and what we've learned along the way.

FUN FACT...

Tracey loves to write poetry and draw with colored pencils. Her guilty pleasure, aside from an occasional butterscotch sundae, is napping.

SECTION 8

WE ARE READY TO SOAR

MY YEAR OF YES!
by Emily Yablonski

FEAR NOT: THE COURAGE TO RISE UP
by Frankie Winrow

LEARNING TO FLY
by Dr. Veera Gupta

> PURPOSE IS WOVEN INTO EVERY BREATH YOU TAKE.

MY YEAR OF YES!

BY EMILY YABLONSKI

This story is for the woman pushing through life and making it all happen, in every area of life. The woman that when asked, "What did you do for yourself today?" stares blankly back. It's for the woman who stands in the shower or parks in the driveway, staying there a little longer to catch her breath before moving on. She's the one you need to say YES to and listen to, and she is yearning for your attention.

Ever feel like you're on a merry-go-round and it's time to get off? Like you're living the same life and thinking the same thoughts week after week, month after month, year after year? I do.

I need to change the way I eat. I want to feel better. I should really be more organized.

The list goes on and on of why I am not good enough and why I must improve, while forgetting who I really am and losing myself even more in this hustle and bustle of life.

For years, I would do things to keep very busy. Sometimes, I would even run away from myself, so I didn't have to hear myself think. I would clean, do laundry, start a project, and reorganize. I'd sit, read, walk, drive, or talk with a friend. I'd cook, go food shopping, and do more laundry. This was all in an attempt to block the mental noise and make the inner critic stop.

I remember when I was a child, I liked getting lost in thought. The thoughts weren't so critical then, though. Thinking and wondering were what I'd do as I looked out the window during car rides to here or there as a child, or often on our way to dance class when I was younger. It was just music and the road. No phones. I remember sometimes talking, but not always. I loved a rainy day and watching the drops collect on the window. When one drop got too heavy it came down the window picking up other drops in its path. I would try to guess the path of the heavy drop, kind of like the Plinko game from The Price is Right. I would just sit there while we were on our way to wherever and watch.

There was always a question and answer inside my head, until one day, the curiosity switched to criticism.

When did it turn from wonder?

I can remember the first day I wore my brand-new Strawberry Shortcake glasses into Mrs. Magnuson's first grade class. Just days before I had gone to get my eyes checked, and I was super excited to try on new frames.

There were a few different ones to choose from, but my favorite was the Strawberry Shortcake glasses. They were brown frames with two teensy-weensy strawberries at the temple, and when I tried them on, they had a little Strawberry Shortcake decal on the front frame. I was happy with that pair, and we were told to come back in a week when mine would be ready.

We went back downtown to pick up the glasses, and everyone was excited for me to see better with them. But when we got to the big reveal, I was just really disappointed.

These aren't the glasses I chose. Where is my Strawberry Shortcake? She is no longer on the front, no decal?

The man doing the fitting said something about obstructing my view, but all I wanted was the decal back. He pointed out the strawberries on the side, but I was bummed. This was not the pair of glasses I thought I was getting. I recall walking out of the shop and to our car parked out front, and the road seemed to slant.

I told my mom. "You just need to get used to wearing the glasses," she said. We drove home, and I looked out the window.

Wow! This is what there is to see!

I could see the leaves on the trees. Not just a blob of leaves, but every single leaf and all of its detail. Wow. I was amazed and in awe of the world I could only now fully see. It was beautiful. But that all changed, the next day, when I had to go to school in my new glasses. For some reason I didn't want anyone to see *me*. I didn't want to be different.

It was a rainy day. I recall it being dark, and the rest of the students were lining up in the all-purpose room. I didn't want to go. My dad walked me to my classroom that morning. I sat at my desk alone. My stomach hurt, my dad talked to my teacher, and I waited for the children to come into the classroom. I don't really know why. I liked the glasses, but I didn't want to be seen as being different. I think deep down I always felt I was different somehow, but now I was taking that feeling and putting it front and center on my face with a tiny pair of frames. Was this when the little voice started? The little voice that makes you feel less than? The one that says, "You're different! And that's not good." The little voice tells us we're different, and the things that made us twirl and smile all of the sudden make us curl down in shame. It's similar to the story of Adam and Eve being completely fine with being naked in the garden until they bite the apple and want to cover up. There is that worry of being seen. Is that shame?

Ooooohhh. Shame. That's a loaded word.

Deep breath.

Shame. Being seen. Don't talk about that. Look neat. Get good grades. Be polite. Smile. Children should be seen and not heard. What if I had something to tell you? Wrap it up in a perfect little package and tie it with a shiny bow. They'll never have to see you then.

So, I did. I kept it all under a perfectly wrapped package pleasing others and making everyone happy. I lived my whole life that way, but I just didn't realize it.

The little girl that loved twirling and leaping around during dance classes turned into the woman that took a different type of leap—I left a corporate job to open my own dance studio. My long day at the dance studio was always Saturdays, and on competition weekends I would leave on Friday while my two boys were at school and try my hardest to be back Sunday before bedtime. On weekdays, they would come to the studio after school, and there would good night hugs at 5:30 p.m. when John would pick them up from the studio to go home with him. When we moved further south, and they could no longer come to the studio with me after school, I tried for a quick hello when they got in from school, left dinner for them, and hoped it all worked until the next morning. In this hustle and bustle of working and kids growing up, I tried making it to all of their sports games I could.

One winter day, when my son Mason was in seventh grade, I made it to his Saturday morning game by rearranging my schedule. John always coached him. They had a really good father/son and coach/player relationship. We played hard but took the loss. The boys were smiling though, feeling like they did all they could. I checked in with Mason and John after the game, said my goodbyes, and headed off to the studio. I left right after the game, because I had to be at the studio by noon for rehearsals. My mom was there and was staying for the second game, and John mentioned his sister and nephew may come also.

Great. Exhale. It's all going to work out.

I made it to the studio and did my rehearsals as costumes were coming in, and dancers in and out; there was lots of hustle and bustle. My last rehearsal was just about to begin when Joan, our studio manager, came to tell me I had a call. Jen, John's sister, was on the line.

"Hang on, there are costumes I'm pinning," I said kind of casually. But then I realized, *Jen is on the line?* My heart sank. My first thought was that something happened to Mason.

I rushed to the phone.

"John? Wait, I'm confused. John, you said?" I was nearly repeating every word she spoke in shock.

Ambulance. Dehydrated. Hospital. Mom has the kids. Meet you there.

Words and thoughts rushing in. In a fog, I walked back into the studio and told whoever was listening that I had to go, and shaking, I grabbed my keys. I jumped in the car to head to the highway, back on the road for the forty-minute drive. Forty minutes of wondering what the hell was going on and feeling scared, sad, angry, and confused. I got to the hospital, and he wasn't in the room. They had taken him in for a CAT scan. He came back into the ER and was lying in pain. The ER doctor came in and told me he had blood on the brain, and then called in the team to help. It would be thirty minutes or so, and the surgeon was rushing to get there.

How did we get here? Blood on the brain? I am not okay.

My dad had had a large blood clot on his brain years ago right before my senior year of college. I remembered that panicked ride from my internship to

"

DON'T FORGET WHO YOU ARE AND DON'T LET THIS WORLD CHANGE YOU.

EMILY YABLONSKI

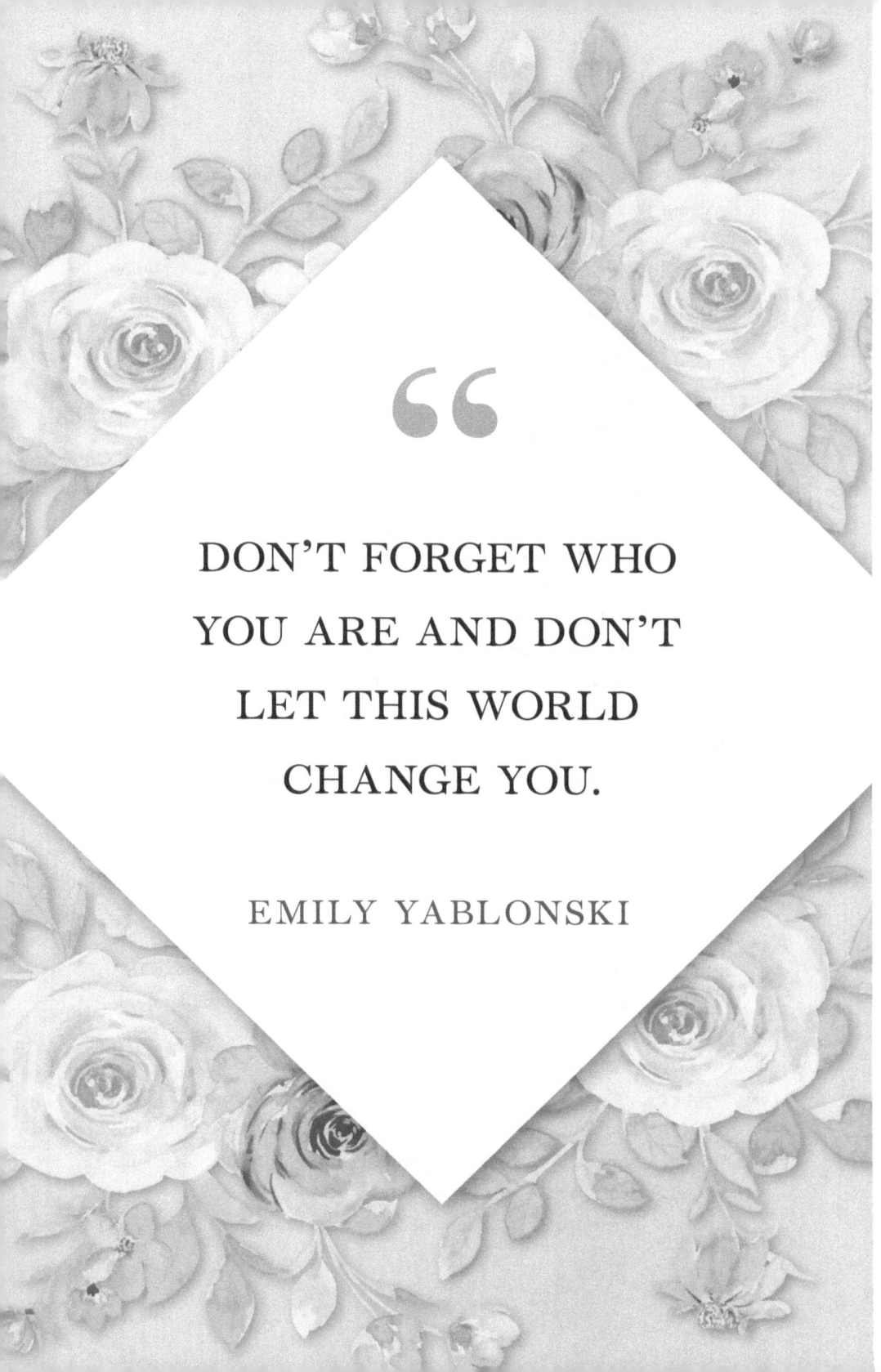

the hospital: we said goodbyes ... just in case. I hadn't met John yet. My father survived, but I felt like I was living the nightmare all over again.

Why? How are the boys? Where are they? Do they know?

John pulled me close to tell me about the papers. "No, John, we aren't doing this," I said. "It's going to be okay. You're going to be fine." John's sister was with us, deciphering everything the doctor said. Moments passed that felt like eternity as we waited for the neurosurgeon and team to arrive. Jen and I were on opposite sides of the bed hardly speaking. John was in pain. A lot of pain. Finally, the surgeon came in. We were signing papers, moving swiftly through the back halls of the hospital.

Where are we going? He needs surgery now, oh my God. Will he be okay, like fully functioning, okay? How long is it?

The surgeon didn't have clear-cut answers because there were a lot of variables, and they would be looking for an aneurysm, the source of the blood, so they could clamp it. We waited in total disbelief. I believe I may have had a sandwich but tasted nothing. I had to meet the boys to give them the keys to the house. They needed some things since they were staying with my brother-in-law.

Hi guys, just smile. Dad's with the doctor. How was the game? McDonald's? Cool, have fun.

I was calm with them like just another day. Inside I felt like I could buckle and go down myself any minute, but I needed to be strong and put together for them.

John had a subarachnoid hemorrhagic stroke that afternoon, right in the middle of coaching a basketball game. My son's game, with my mother and sister-in-law watching. He lost the ability to drink or speak. In a flash he had the thunderclap headache, and the ambulance was called.

In the weeks to follow he remained at the hospital and came home with a walker. He couldn't walk, and his muscles were so tight. We later found out this was caused by the cholesterol medication they put him on. He did not have high cholesterol, but the medical team thought anything to keep the blood flowing easier while he healed would help. The full recovery was made in three months' time. My boys didn't miss a beat. They were in school, playing basketball, and I never missed a game. Our new town surrounded us with such care; the people we loved pitched in as well.

This was a huge wake-up call. How quickly life can change on a dime, and how in some instances people don't have the three months' recovery time but a lifetime without their loved one. His surviving this was a gift. Yet, if I am completely honest, inside I felt heavy and burdened. We have so much that just happens to us, and I like to think that our life is happening for us. This experience was the beginning of my reawakening so to speak. I had my first strong awakening before I turned forty a few years ago. I was really into mindset, focusing, getting healthy, working out, and eating right. I wanted to start my new decade feeling good, and I freakin' did!! Once I got into my rhythm, I remember thinking it was easy too.

Big sigh, where did that go? Flood of emotions. Where?

It's not that I hadn't had some really happy amazing days. It's just I am not sure I have the words for it. I felt a heaviness that was like a robe of heavy. It was like a weight, and I was not fully sure when it began or where it came from. I mean, it had to have come from me. We are the ones responsible for how we think, act, and feel, but I really really wanted it off. It reminds me of the saying, "You know that mountain you've been carrying? You were only supposed to climb it."

But I could not figure out why I was carrying it.

Put it down! Now!

It was some time after John's stroke I had a breakdown. I finally was able to cry. I couldn't cry throughout the ordeal, because, I don't know, sometimes you don't during a crisis. You just do the things. And I was doing ALL of the things. I had lots of help but felt so very alone. So alone. I sat on the stool in my kitchen, and I cried and cried. I cried over everything. There was so much inside. John hugged me, and I felt guilty dumping this on him or having any feelings with all he had just been through.

And I never hated myself more.

Pause.

I wanted to run away but knew I couldn't because I would still be there. I had gained weight and felt terrible, and I wanted to somehow unzip myself and jump out of my skin and run away, so very far away from myself. I felt trapped and scared, and I didn't know how to get out. I wanted to crawl in a ball and scream for a million years as loud and as hard as I could.

But instead, I just sat there and cried.

So here he was, with a renewed sense of life. The stroke was a turn, for him, for the better. He began enjoying life and taking nothing for granted, and once he was better, he began to work again. He was in awe of the outpouring of support from our new community, from old dear friends, and from people whose lives he touched in the past who reached out. He was renewed. I was so there for it. I always wanted him to see the good in everything. It just depleted me to get there.

We continued on, and I just kept going. I never took a breath or came up for air. I just kept going. Life happened, and the boys were growing. Mason was moving on to high school. My sister and her family moved to our town from across the country, and I put one foot in front of the other. There was a small song singing in my heart and a knowing deep within that there was more; there was more to come, and I began to poke around and look for it. The days passed, and I grew heavier still. My body was acting off, but I wasn't sure why.

Luckily life happens, and life saves us. You get distracted in the busy and that can be really good when all you want to do is hide and cry.

When the pandemic hit in early 2020, things began coming to a boiling point. There was so much disconnection and disease within. My body was acting off, but I still wasn't sure why. It's truly remarkable that the body can force you to pay attention, and it will. With all of the pressures, we couldn't sustain dance virtually, so the dance studio was closed for good that fall. I lost a part of myself when the studio closed. It was my identity for all of my adult life. It was what I did, what I loved, who I loved, and who I was. My outer world felt unknown, and my inner world was disconnected. It was a rough place to be. I didn't know who I was, and I didn't dare ask myself what I wanted.

How do I even begin to ask when I have become a stranger to myself?

It was the following springtime, about a year into the pandemic. Mason was home on virtual school since he had to have knee surgery to correct an injury. I couldn't stay in one place with younger eyes on me. I started to force myself to go out once a day. I would go out and order food and talk to people, even for just a quick pick up of a meal. I sat outside a bunch and joined another online course on self-development, thinking I would find my new path. I lost a part of myself when the studio closed, but it was a blessing. Owning the studio came with a ton of people-pleasing tendencies that ate away at my trust of who I was authentically. I was looking for confidence and to be seen again. Mason required three days a week of physical therapy, and that was a ride away, so I would drive and join in my classes, and each day I would get better and stronger as he was too.

Summer came, and the world was starting to feel a bit more normal. Mason was walking without crutches and healing, and so was I. While I still was on my journey, I was doing new things and trying to get out and lay new groundwork for my next steps. I met with a holistic doctor to find ways to heal my insides and figure out why I was growing in size, especially in my middle. I went to a daylong retreat and the healer began talking about our inner child. I cried a lot that day. What a release! We let our inner child reveal to us what she had been holding on to, and I spoke that day. It was such a beautiful day on the beach. I spoke about always feeling like I had to take care of everything and everyone, and that I had felt the pressure to pull everyone together and make it work for all, even if it didn't work for me. More accurately, I didn't even check if it worked for me. The greater good for everyone else was more important than I was.

And thus was the story of a lot of my life.

But it wasn't just affecting me. I'll never forget a dear friend saying to me when I told her of the studio closing, "Good for you; you really must have needed that. You always put the studio first before everything else."

That hit me. All along I thought I was the only one sacrificing, but my kids were too. Some of it they are better for, since there were things they needed to step up for, but as for the rest, I don't know what they will take away from it all. In all of the taking care of everyone else, I lost myself, so much of myself, and practically all of myself.

So, that growth that I told you about in the tummy area? I had a very large uterus from uterine fibroids. It was very large, like a four-month pregnant sized uterus. I called it my resentment baby. I could guess it began growing five years prior, right before John's stroke when I just was so damn busy people pleasing and hiding my true self and my true feelings, just like I did when I was little with those Strawberry Shortcake glasses. That fibroid represented to me every single bottled-up worry, hateful thought, wronged feeling, fear of lack, not enoughness, and the questioning of decisions that I have had over the last few years all wrapped into this giant heavy ball of flesh. It was as if my body was screaming for connection. It was poison, and it's so gross to say, but for the longest time I wasn't ready to let it go. Or was I just not yet ready to reconnect? It kept me safe somehow, and it weighed me down physically and emotionally. It was so very heavy to carry. I thought about it every waking moment, from what I wore to how heavy it felt. I could feel it through my stomach while lying down. It was a hard disgusting mass of negativity. I finally got the strength to let it go. I had had enough. And this past fall, I had a partial hysterectomy.

It seems only some years back, "I was woman, hear me roar" heading into this new uncharted decade ready to take the bull by the horns with no more littles and sleepless nights, nor finding our way as new parents. I felt like we had arrived, we had it together, and we were a strong family with some cash in our savings. But then to have that all chipped away little by little or chunk by chunk, I didn't want to let it happen. I really thought I could hold it all together, alone, without ever checking in on me.

I have spent the last year and a half putting myself back together, piece by piece, and I am clinging to what Rumi said, "The wound is the place where the light enters you." I am hopeful this wound fills me with the light that I have needed. I have also read that the Japanese fill cracks in broken pottery with gold dusted lacquer in the centuries-old art of Kintsugi. By adding beauty and uniqueness to what is broken, they emphasize the fractures instead of hiding them. I have loads of cracks in this full-on repair. And, thanks to my body breaking down and forcing me to acknowledge things I have not wanted to look at, I now have had time to discover who I am again and what I like, with my very own opinion that has nothing to do with what works for anyone else. I have a voice, my own voice, that doesn't need to match yours, and I am not here to make your life more comfortable at the expense of myself.

I'm giving up that feeling of needing to take care of everyone, and I'm releasing what everyone's opinion means to me. I can no longer be that person I once was, and, even better, I no longer want to be her. I want to take all that was good and start building it back again. It has taken some time, but little by little it's all coming together.

I have time for the new vision, and I am so very grateful that I am afforded this time. I would be remiss not to thank John for being so supportive and not overbearing on days when I know that he knows I literally got changed right before he came home so it looked like I was doing something that day. I'm thankful for the days John understood when I didn't really have much to say, and the days the same story was on repeat. He listened and gave me space, and for that I am so very thankful. He told me I could do anything, when he really wanted me to do something, and he knew how sad I was and just wanted me to be happy again.

So thus begun my YEAR OF YES. But not yes to everyone else. YES to me.

I started joining new things, like a book club and a speaking group. I went on a weekend retreat alone to a new city; I went and ate at a restaurant by myself. I sat at the bar and talked with the people there. I started living. It felt really good. I was walking a lot. I grounded myself, listened to podcasts and meditations, began working out and eating right, going to mass, and sleeping when I needed it. I added all of these things into my life this year, and although I'm starting from a different place now, the healing is coming, and the days are much brighter. I got my real estate license, and I am working with clients and love helping new and first-time buyers find their homes. I am writing, something which I never gave any thought to being good at, and I even said YES to being in this book! I am in a super amazing women's group with like-minded women, and I'm in a yearlong women-centered coaching program that aims to help others like me find their footing again. I am really excited for the future, and I know there are brighter days ahead.

If I could talk to that young girl again, I would tell her to take chances, as many as you can, and I would also tell her to not lose herself. Don't forget who you are and don't let this world change you. Take the time to be your own best friend and really connect to who you are. Know who you are, keep that wonder, and use your voice.

My year of yes is a time of saying yes to me.

Yes, you are worth spending time on.

Yes, you have a voice.

Yes, you deserve to be seen.

All you need is to start. I started with small steps and then a new door opened.

Yes to possibilities.

Yes to enjoying this one wild and crazy life.

And who knows? With this fresh perspective, maybe it's time for a new pair of glasses. I'll waltz right into the optometrist and buy myself the frames I love. I might just add those strawberries.

ABOUT THE CONTRIBUTOR

Emily, a graduate of Rutgers University's School of Engineering, has more than twenty years of experience as a successful family-oriented business owner and entrepreneur and has educated, coached, and mentored many people to incredible personal and professional success. Emily has built strong values in commitment, collaboration, and community, while feeding her entrepreneurial spirit. She is an enthusiastic dreamer and an experienced doer, taking leaps and building wings on the way down.

Bits of Her Heart...

Emily Yablonski

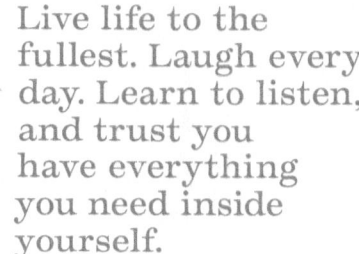

Live life to the fullest. Laugh every day. Learn to listen, and trust you have everything you need inside yourself.

FUN FACT...

Emily is a night owl. She loves listening to music, sitting on the beach with a good book, and learning about physics!

FEAR NOT: THE COURAGE TO RISE UP

BY FRANKIE WINROW

This chapter is dedicated to anyone who is being put to the test.

I remember when I lost my first tooth. Oh, the pain I felt! My wobbly tooth was hanging on by a thread. My mother, knowing what was best, said to me, "It will hurt for a minute, but you will be just fine." Somehow, I found the courage to let her pull it out. Courage can sometimes surprise us like that. It comes in when we need it most and reminds us that everything will be ok.

Growing up in a faith-filled environment made courage just part of the way we lived. There were so many small things to overcome back then. I see all the hurdles as blessings now. We moved and had to start school in a new place. It took a lot for me and my sister to dig up the courage to be somewhere so unfamiliar. Not knowing anyone at all was scary for me and my sister. We were the youngest of seven, just four and five years old. But we were taught to "fear not, for God is with us." Our mother and aunts instilled in us that it takes courage to grow and learn new things in life. God was shaping me; and always is to this day still shaping me. The challenges we face are the chisel if we so allow His mighty hand to do the work in us.

> COURAGE CAN SOMETIMES SURPRISE US. IT COMES IN WHEN WE NEED IT MOST AND REMINDS US THAT EVERYTHING WILL BE OK.
>
> FRANKIE WINROW

Fear Not: The Courage to Rise Up

Throughout my young life, I heard, "Be strong, have faith in God." This was so that I could stay alert enough to stand and fight the things that are right and wrong because bad things happen when we are not aware of the devil. I am an imperfect human, and I did not always have the courage that I have today. I was not always alert. Sometimes things happen, and we take different path then what God has for us.

It has taken some time to grow deeper in my faith and strengthen my courage, but the desire to do so makes all the difference. Deep faith does not happen overnight. It happens over time through building our relationship with God. When we have a strong relationship with God, we fear not. We have the courage to rise up and do everything in Love, even when the devil is working hard to keep us from the path that God has chosen for us.

Never give up; fight for what you think is right.
Even when we walk in darkness don't be afraid, God is with us.

I know because He has been there for me in my darkest days, in my trials, in my tribulations, in life and in death. And all I know is that having just a bit of courage helps me summit those mountains and gets me to the next level. I know it will do the same for you.

God has plans for us all. We may go astray, and it is hard when we give up on ourselves and think that the devil has won. Trust me, that little mustard seed of faith is just enough for the mountain to move, for the tides to turn, for heaven to open up. It is funny when God comes out of left field and says, "Not a chance in hell will you take my child!" He is there as our protector, even when we don't always see it. God has courage in us.

Why can't we have courage in ourselves and fear not the darkness?

It's hard to understand why negative things happen but again, our courage and faith in God will conquer and we shall all overcome the things that we fear. Courage, I pray for in my life because I know that without it the devil is lurking amongst the living.

I often think about how different my life would be without the courage that I have today. If my mom and aunt didn't allow us to be uncomfortable and instill these great values in my siblings and me, where would I be? But rather than dwelling there, I keep coming back for God's endless love of courage. Over, and over again, he replenishes the well. And I am there to help myself with courage and faith and love.

It has been said that we give up, but God never gives up on us. God has so much to offer us starting with courage and faith, but most of all love and the light to see us all through the darkness.

ABOUT THE CONTRIBUTOR

Frankie Winrow is married to Dean Winrow for thirty-four years, and is blessed with a beautiful family. She has been President and Vice President of the Board of Trustees at Hope Academy Charter and Academy Charter High School, as well as a Catechists teacher for over twenty-eight years. She has been a member of St. Vincent de Paul for over eighteen years and President of St. Vincent de Paul for the past six years. A dedicated woman of the church, Frankie is also a weekly communion steward, who many community members immediately recognize as soon as they see her radiant presence and giant smile. Known for her big heart, selfless generosity, and helping those in need, Frankie works tirelessly to give back and spread love.

NOTE FROM THE CONTRIBUTOR

I would like to dedicate this chapter to all the women in my life, young and old. You have helped mold me into the woman that I am today. I pray that I have set a good example to my own family to have Courage always trust in God.

Bits of Her Heart...

Frankie Winrow

I am not asking you to live your life right. I'm asking you to give God a chance.

FUN FACT...

Frankie is a community servant. She volunteers her time at the church and in the food pantry making sure all are well fed and feeling the love of God. She is known in her town as "Asbury Park's Heart."

LEARNING TO FLY

BY DR. VEERA GUPTA

To anyone who has ever wanted to feel weightless, free, and centered in this very moment. Yes, I am talking about you.

The universe will teach you a lesson in every way it knows how until you finally hear, see, taste, understand, feel, and implement its great teachings. And since this is the universe we are talking about, it knows plenty of unique, creative, and crazy ways to get its point across.

This is especially true when you have made a clear and defined declaration to the powers that be. I may have proclaimed out loud and to anyone who would listen that "My life's mission is to serve humanity as best as I can by improving the health of as many people as divinely possible until I am 100. I want to see patients on my 100th birthday and then watch the sunset over the ocean with my family!"

This made the universe turn its rather large head in my direction and ponder for a moment. Here was a girl who originally wanted nothing more than to stay in her little bubble and die young while laughing hysterically. Now she doesn't want to leave this planet until all her human brothers and sisters are as healthy and happy as she can make them. And she wants at least a half a dozen more decades of life in which to do this. She's got to learn to fly.

Teaching me this was a tall order, but the universe was ready to serve it up.

It decided that I needed a quick boost or acceleration if I was going to hit that profound goal of mine.

The universe also knows that if it plans on teaching me anything, it may need to simultaneously bang a gong, have angels sing, and have a neon light up sign that says, "Here is your lesson!" for me to even realize it is trying to teach me something.

Well, for this particular lesson, the universe gave me a hat trick, three different perspectives of the same exact thing, and I finally got it. I needed to see my lesson from three totally different angles to really appreciate its nuisances. I had to serve athletes on a trampoline, take salsa lessons, and climb a snowy mountain in little more than my underwear. Hopefully, you will know how to fly by the end of this chapter too, and you won't have to go to Poland like I did to learn how.

PERSPECTIVE #1 OF FLYING— TRAMPOLINING WITH TEAM USA OLYMPIANS

The universe started my lesson in flying by lulling me in with the most lovable, adventurous, charming, hardworking, and hysterical athletes on the planet—trampoline gymnasts and tumblers. As a sports chiropractor and a person who loves people who do things I consider fun and insane, like flying in the air after sinking deep into a trampoline, the universe held me at attention.

I remember when I was a little girl, I had the most amazing, realistic dream. I was in my backyard, in my red corduroy suspenders, and I ran full speed through the lush green grass. I leapt up in the air and put my arms out in a perfect T as the wind swept me up, allowing me to fly. I was flying around trees and through the brilliant blue sky. The wind was carrying me effortlessly wherever I wanted. It was just a dream, but I remember the feeling of flying, even all these years later. I have always loved airplane rides; even rocky, turbulent rides in small airplanes and helicopters thrill me. And here was a sport that literally scores people on "flight time."

If I was going to help these guys be the best they could possibly be, I had to understand their sport. What better way than to get on a trampoline myself?

I step on up. The trampoline is an unstable surface about six feet off the ground, wobbling like an earthquake under my feet. I was taught to warm up by tightening my core and taking a few practice jumps. Each one sank me into the trampoline further, with the kinetic energy shooting me back into the air for a few seconds of flight. While the trampoline is about six feet off the ground, some athletes hit it so hard that they need it to be six feet off the ground because they may sink into its surface over five feet upon impact.

The first thing I had to learn was that there is potential energy in the trampoline itself, and I could use that energy to vault myself. Sure, I knew there was energy all around me, but harnessing it was something completely different. There is no physical "grounding" from your feet. I wasn't a very good student in physics, but here was my chance to really understand Newton's third law of motion: "For every action in nature, there is an equal and opposite reaction." The harder I bounced into the trampoline, the more energy it gave me back. They should have just let me bounce on a trampoline in physics class and I would have thought of Newton as a friend I really understood. Okay, cool. *Step one to flying: harness the energy under those feet.* Got it.

As I stepped off of the trampoline, I realized that every barefoot step I took on solid ground allowed me to harness the power underneath me. I had never thought of it before. I had never thought that while I am thumping my feet down on the ground, if I am mindful the ground will help propel me to my goal—standing up to gravity and moving forward in the simplest of motions, walking. The first step in my lesson was to learn what a step really is—it is the mindful gathering of the energy supporting you from below.

Athletes competing on trampoline are judged on three parameters: 1) skill difficulty, 2) distance traveled from the center mark on the trampoline, and 3) the time they spend in the air, known as flight time. Hit your mark, the cross in the middle of the trampoline. Stay centered and within your core at all times. Well, I *thought* I knew what that meant. The centering, however, comes from within. Focus and extreme body awareness allow you to stay on your mark, the coveted center of the trampoline. Stay in it, and you get the greatest marks.

I know all about focus, and I didn't do half bad at staying in the center, but going up higher? That requires three things simultaneously. First, you have to be extremely present; you cannot worry about the skills you did not do perfectly a second ago, or the perfect routine you had yesterday. You have to feel the immediate connection of your feet to the trampoline's surface with every jump you make. There are so many variables that demand your real time attention that what happens in the future or what has happened in the past cannot take any of

"

DO NOT DANCE WITH
THE GHOSTS OF YOUR PAST; DO NOT
CARRY THINGS YOU DO NOT NEED.
DANCE WITH THOSE AROUND YOU,
CALLING UPON THEIR STRENGTHS
WHEN YOUR OWN FALTER.

DR. VEERA GUPTA

your mental bandwidth. All of you must be present and alive to the energy of the moment. The second ingredient is to transduce any energy you have (of fear, of failure, of the pressure of being watched as you fly through the air by yourself) to the energy of intentional action. It is this energy that allows you to go up and down. You have to be okay knowing you are going to sink low and go deep, only to be thrust sky high. You will oscillate from low to high and high to low with each jump. The third ingredient is the one the universe wanted me to cook with in all aspects of my life—how to let go. You see, only when you let go of extreme rigidity and stop trying to control the trampoline do you really go as high up as possible. You have to let go and trust that the energy in and around, the energy of the universe, wants you to fly.

PERSPECTIVE ON FLYING #2– TAKING SALSA LESSONS WITH CHRISTIAN AND DEVON.

The word core is Latin for heart. It turns out that the body has two hearts—the one we call heart and our core, which is the atomic epicenter of our physical existence. The core is the group of muscles that stabilize the spine and the pelvis, consisting of everything from your obliques and gluteal musculature to the muscles that line the spine. The pelvis is the major weight bearing joint of the human body, and it has to have crazy strong muscles to be stable.

While our actual heart is the one that pumps blood, it is this Latin-named other heart, the core, that keeps us going against gravity. The core is consciously activated and utilized only when you tell it to be. One heart working automatically and one heart that needs your constant awareness to fire—these twin hearts in sync allow you to be centered.

If you suck your belly button up and in, that little point in between your belly and your back is your very center. All motions, all movements, all actions should pass through here when you are in perfect alignment and using stellar biomechanics. This little dot is like an atom. It is the dot where all energy flows should rotate around. *Step two to flying: find your center.*

As someone who previous tripped on her own feet from being pigeon toed, I was not rotating around this middle spot much, until I started dancing every day.

Finding my center was essential if I didn't want to fall flat on my face. I had two instructors, Christian and Devon. While Christian taught me how to stay upright, Devon taught me how to root into the ground. With every single movement of my toes, feet, knees, pelvis, torso, and head, I had to be in perfect alignment with my center. And that energy had to keep moving all the way from the ground and my toes through my arms. To be centered is to live life in the place where energy simply flows without stopping. To watch Christian and Devon dance together is to see the embodiment of perfect, harmonious flow.

And that is when it hit me—no matter what you do in life, it should be aligned with your entire body. If you want to say something, did your heart say it was okay to say? That alone will stop a lot of the mean things we later regret saying. When we sit in a chair, did we hold true to our core or did we let it all hang loose, forgetting to activate and initiate our second heart? That momentary lapse in awareness will give us pain later because the core is what generates our stability. Any movement you do should be one that comes from the very center and radiates out in perfect alignment.

When we move, are our motions choppy and linear or do they curve and flow like water in a stream? If you want to fly, you have to allow everything to move and change, but always be mindful of your center. The center is like that first drop of water that breaks the stillness; it causes a ripple effect that emanates out from us and shares our energy with the world. What's more, is that even when we've forgotten it, all we need to do is remember it, and it can prepare us for the next great thing we are meant to be. It can prepare us to fly.

PERSPECTIVE ON FLYING #3 – GOING TO POLAND TO MEET THE ICEMAN

Being a trampoline gymnast is intense and physical with 18 times your own body weight going through your feet with each jump. I wanted to give these guys everything I could think of for performance and recovery. This involves allowing them to get out of their heads and into their bodies, and to do that, I needed a master of breathing and extreme focus. Who was that master? The Iceman, Wim Hof. Using a breathing technique, cold exposure, and intense mind focus, Wim is able to withstand extreme cold and has set Guinness World Records for swimming under ice and previously held the record for a barefoot half marathon on ice and snow. He even ran a full marathon in the Sahara without drinking water.

Learning to Fly

The guy is the champion of human potential, and if I wanted to help these gymnasts, I needed to learn from him. He starts his online, interactive breathing app by saying, "Breathe in, breath out. Fully in, and then let go. Breathe into the belly, into the chest and then let go. Make it circular, like a wave."

Having learned the secrets of core from Christian and Devon, I thought he was talking about breath, but that was only the most superficial of his meanings. I learned this when I actually went to Poland to meet him. Upon arrival, I was put into a group with twenty-four humans, just as daring as I am! We spent four intense days getting to know each other through a series of adventures. During the days we jumped into icy rivers and spent hours breathing in sync together. At night, we would sing, play music, and I would do chiropractic work on my fellow adventurers. I also brought an entire extra suitcase filled with snacks in case anyone needed one. I had no idea what the food was going to be like before the trip, but I thought it best to bring enough snacks for everyone. In short, I was prepared and ready to serve. I felt powerful with a great sense of peace from helping my new friends.

That was until the day we had to climb Sněžka.

I thought it would be the cold that would get me, but it didn't really touch me. It was negative ten degrees outside, snowing, and I was in my hiking boots, hat, shorts, and a sports bra. It turned out that the lack of clothing was freeing. My backpack on the other hand was weighing me down, making it difficult to breathe.

Nora, my best friend and seasoned hiker, had warned me to train with the backpack I was going to use for climbing. But instead, I just took my husband's pack on the trip, shoving it in my suitcase without another thought. It would be light anyway, only carrying emergency clothing, a bottle of water, and a couple of snacks. It wouldn't weigh more than a few pounds.

I couldn't have been more wrong. With every breath I took, that pack was slicing into me. I felt like a carrot crisply snapping in half with each breath. It was clearly the wrong size, and I was not used to it all. Halfway up the hike, its weight became too much.

That is when my instructors and team rallied around me. Shamir and Speedy Sticks, two amazing Brits on my team, stayed behind me every step of the journey up telling me, "You've got this! You can do this!" One of my instructors, Ben, stood beside me on the left, taking each and every breath with me from that point on. To my right, my partner for the climb and friend Aga was formidable. I am fairly certain she would have carried me up that mountain by throwing me over her shoulder if she had to. She told me story after story on the trip up, taking my mind off of my discomfort.

Shamir and Sanjay spotted my mistake and helped me correct it immediately—they took the things I was carrying off my back, and in one quick second, the pack was off and the weight was gone. I was able to move back into the flow, traveling up the mountain with my group.

Step three to flying: you have to let go of the extra things you carry and be willing to let others help you. That goes for all of life: any extra baggage you carry, whether physical or mental, weighs you down. Holding onto the negatives of the past and not living in the current moment can actually shorten your telomeres, which live in your cells and allow them to divide. In shortening them, you literally shorten the health span, the years you spend healthy, of your life. Physically, the weight of old baggage is tremendous and can manifest into the body as aches and pains. I had to take off the backpack. I had to let it go.

The number one risk factor in a less than timely death is not smoking—it's not even drinking. It is social isolation. Life itself knows we are better, healthier, and stronger when we are together. Not only do we need to let go, but we need to let others help us carry the load when it is too great.

This moment is when I truly understood what Wim was saying. Breathe into life fully, with every single breath you take. Be there, be present. And then let go of everything, let that moment stand alone, giving life the full, undivided attention it deserves. Do not dance with the ghosts of your past, do not carry things you do not need. Dance with those around you, calling upon their strengths when your own falter.

The moment the backpack came off me and Sanjay took it while smiling at me warmly, the universe gave me my banging-of-the-gong moment, with angels singing and neon lights flashing. The pull-me-down energy of the backpack was replaced with the energy from my friends in the form of love and overwhelming support. I could not feel the cold; all I felt was the love. I could laugh and smile, breathe better, and enjoy the company of my comrades. They rallied around me, moving just a little slower to the summit so I could catch my breath.

To reward me for finally learning this step on how to fly, the universe gave me an extra gift. *Step four to flying: the art of drafting.* Drafting is an aerodynamic technique where two moving objects are caused to align in a close group, reducing the overall effect of drag. Drag is exactly what you think drag would be—moving slower, heavier, and less efficiently. Especially when high speeds are involved, drafting can significantly reduce the average energy expenditure required to maintain a certain speed and can also slightly reduce the energy expenditure of the lead vehicle or object, or in this case—me. When we are in alignment with each other and ourselves, we can go faster with less effort. This is why birds fly in a "V" formation: they are drafting off each other.

Flying isn't just about getting into the air; it's about aligning with others. It's about the give and take, helping others as often as you can and then allowing them to help you. When we got to the top of the mountain and were having warm soup and hot chocolate, I told my friend Shamir that I felt bad about being the weak link, the one who needed help.

His response was profound. He told me he was grateful because taking care of me helped him forget how cold he was and made the time go by quicker. He took my experience and guilt and turned it into a show of love and empowerment in one of the greatest shows of alchemy I have ever seen.

That is when I learned not just how to fly all by myself, but how to draft and to reach even greater heights with fellowship and love. Sometimes you will be flapping, and other times those around you will be the wind beneath your wings.

Through three crazy, off-the-wall experiences, the universe showed me the four steps of flying with finesse and poise:

1. Use the energy around you to ground yourself.
2. Find your center.
3. Let go of the extra weight.
4. Learn to draft off the flock.

And so as a Doctor of Chiropractic, the universe knew I could help my patients for many more years if I learned how to fly, and, if I could pass the lessons I learned along to my patients, they could live to one-hundred doing the things they wanted to do. Learning to fly will help us live our own best lives. For me, living my best life is about doing the work I love, for you it may be something totally different! But no matter what it is, I promise you that learning to fly will help you with whatever your heart desires. And the next time you ask the universe for something, be prepared for the lessons it brings to deliver exactly what you need, even if it means taking an ice bath, salsa dancing, or jumping high into the air!

ABOUT THE CONTRIBUTOR

Dr. Veera Gupta is an award-winning, multi-faceted licensed Doctor of Chiropractic who has helped thousands of patients serving the Manasquan, Brielle, Point Pleasant, and Wall communities.

Dr. Veera has in-depth knowledge of neuroscience and philosophy. With this unique combination, Dr. Veera works extremely well with athletes, including Olympians. She has spoken in front of groups of all sizes and has appeared on camera and podcasts dozens of times. She is a relatable, down-to-earth, and "tell it like it is" expert in her field. She believes every human being is a hero, and by using their innate strength and activating the brain, anything is possible.

Bits of Her Heart...

Dr. Veera Gupta

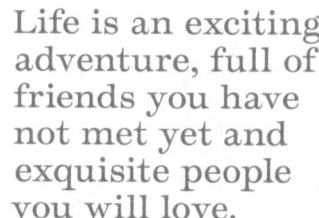

Life is an exciting adventure, full of friends you have not met yet and exquisite people you will love.

FUN FACT...

Relaxing to Dr. Veera is reading an anatomy book, singing her heart out to '80s and '90s tunes, or watching something mindlessly funny like the movie Dodgeball.

SECTION 9

WE ARE DEEPLY POETIC

THE EMBRACE
by Terisa Taylor

POETIC NOTES TO SELF
by Laura B. Ginsberg

THE STARS IN MY CHEST
by Kayla Harris

WE ARE EACH THE WHOLE UNIVERSE: A MIRACLE IN MOTION, EXPANSIVE BEYOND MEASURE.

THE EMBRACE

BY TERISA TAYLOR

*I hate clichés and antidotes. Conventional would not describe me.
I really had to figure life
out for myself. Keeping so many secrets including my faith.
This is truly written for me!*

*For the inner child in awe of nature and the freedom we
take for granted in our youth.
To acknowledge all the humiliation, fear, and
hurt we surrender to as teenage girls.
Then to appreciate the woman I have become and t
he wisdom I am capable of sharing.*

*I read something in a book given to me called,
Blue Denim and Lace by Dr. Jack Hyles.*

"Anybody can measure a fallen tree; character measures the tree while it is still standing. It isn't death that makes something sacred; it is life."

Thanks, mom, for leaving the book behind and turning down pages and underlining verses.
It gave me an idea of the woman you were and the woman I wanted to be.
This piece is dedicated to the memory of Diane Jean Zawadsky-Leppert and all the motherless daughters of every age.

The fairytale is possible. Have faith.

She stepped out into the morning dew, grass shimmering, the breath of the morning fog still hovering over the lake, the cool still air of the night meeting the dawn. Her eyes devoured the moment as she exhaled. She caught her breath joining the mist as if they were becoming one.

She had been coming here to these woods as a baby held in the safety of her mother's arms. Then she was kept in the safety of her view; it has been seven years that the spirit of this place had watched her grow.

She was seen by the woods and welcomed into its presence. Ready and invited to become part of the dance.

She stepped down off the safety of the cement platform to the steps of the cabin where her family slept.

The kiss of the dew, the coldness of the grass, the softness of the dirt meeting her bare feet, evoked a stirring to run free into the paths that lead to the woods. As she ran toward the lake, the fog wrapping her in its arms, every step was as if dancing in the clouds as she disappeared into the vastness of the woods, relying only on the sounds of her steps as her feet remembered each placement of earth beneath them. She took in the smell of the leaves as they crumbled beneath her feet. She knew the dance as the music met her energy engaging her heartbeat—each beat faster than the next, a methodical rhythm of energy and excitement … the music of life within her.

She heard the spinning of a nearby fisherman's reel being cast. It screamed out in the silence. The bobber invisibly hitting the water disappearing as it was eaten by the fog still engaged in the dancing across the lake. The smell of the embers left from the campers' fires lingered through the air, the smoke still billowing and joining the party with the fog just as my breath did.

Four years had lapsed … as I came to the end of the path and the woods opened and cast me out; the hand of my Prince Charming slipping away, "The Embrace" gone. I heard the cry of my name. My mother's voice echoing through the wood. She had just learned her father had passed away in those moments as I danced with my Prince Charming amongst the trees.

I felt the hardness as my feet hit the pavement of the road and the fog disappeared.

Unknowingly, that would be the last dance and the last time I would hear her echo my name unto the wood. She would die four years later.

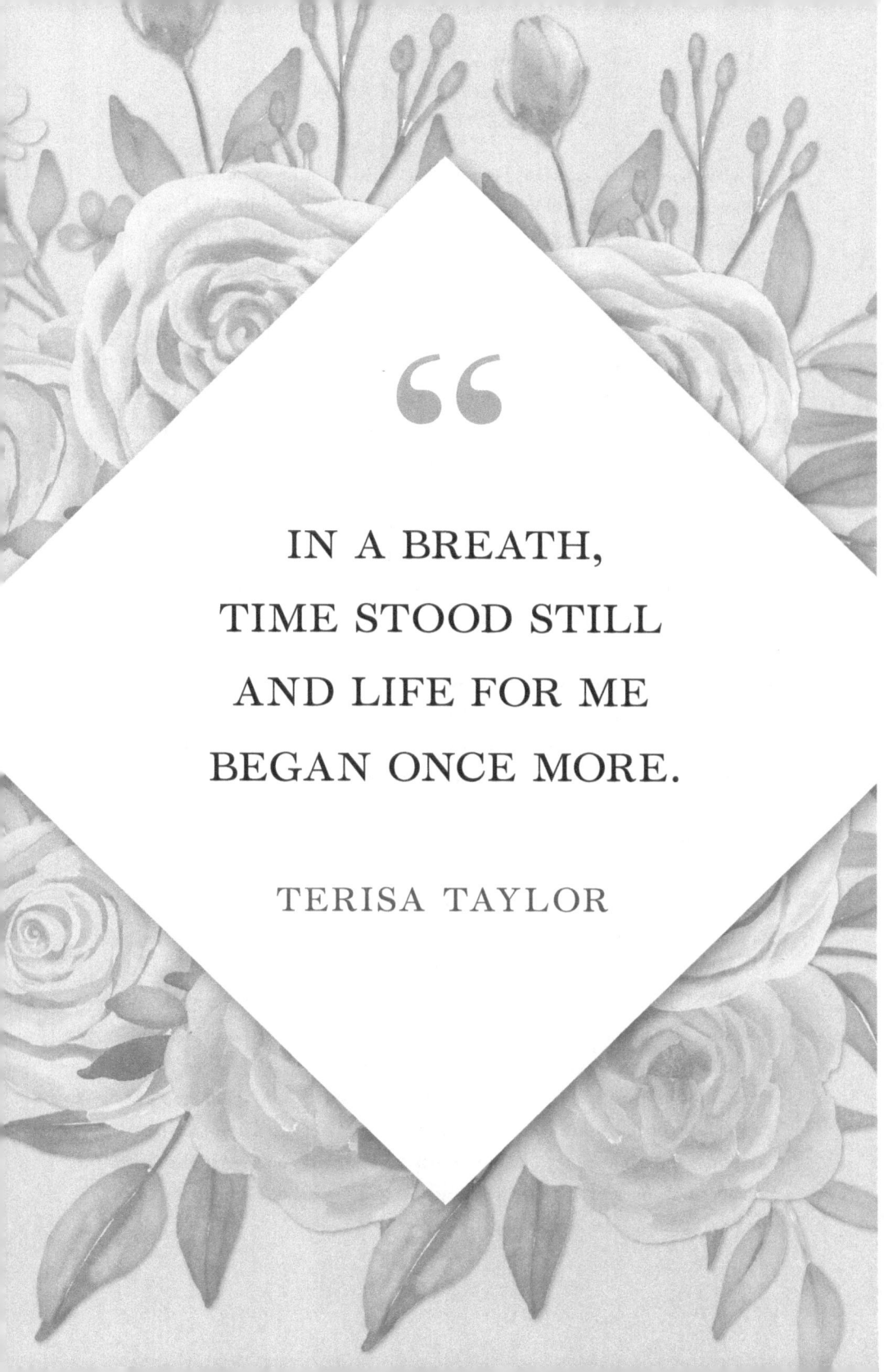

> IN A BREATH, TIME STOOD STILL AND LIFE FOR ME BEGAN ONCE MORE.
>
> TERISA TAYLOR

Days become weeks, weeks become years filled with the wonder of learning, embracing life only like a child can. There I stood scrawny, wildly alert blue eyes, stringy untamed blond hair streaming down my back. The girl from the woods had come to visit her Prince Charming. Alone once again. I noticed a painting. There HE was on the wall in my brother's room, my Prince Charming. HE had never left me. HE was here on the wall the whole time, and I never took notice distracted in the turbulence of becoming a teenager.

The morning was still as he stepped into my thoughts. I had been longing to dance with him once again. This time amongst a veil of white. It had snowed throughout the night. The snow always brings a hush to the world, my world. Time was to stand still. I grabbed my jeans and a sweatshirt, socks and boots, and a quick scarf and hat knitted by my mother's hands. The hands that embraced me as a child were still finding ways to keep me comforted. Opening the door of our two-bedroom apartment, remembering where my family of six had once happily lived. The rush of the cold air slapping my face, I could barely squeeze through the opening of the screen that had been sealed with an icy glaze; the snow forced against the frame of the door keeping me imprisoned in its memories, safely comforted by its grip. I scurried through wildly wanting to escape its control. I floated across the top of the snow as if walking on water. There in the wind and chill stood my Prince. We ran across the tops of the glistening water leaving just mental footprints that were quickly danced away by the wind.

Twirling, laughing, and jumping.

Letting go of all my shame and fear. Falling through hands of time, a million touches each hand grabbing, taking, abandoning, beating, stealing, betraying, and raping leaving its mark on my spirit. I let it all go and fell into the forgiveness of the white untouched virginal snowfall. Flickering flecks of glistening water continued the dance, stinging my cheeks as the warmth of my tears met the cold. I brushed them away with the softness of my scarf; I could feel a tender touch, my mother's hand wiping away my tears. I felt her embrace and then I heard the comfort of her voice in the winds, "Don't cry, you're okay." Time stopped! I peered into the bluest of eyes, a mirror unto my soul as I gazed upon the face of my Prince smiling as he reached out his hand awaiting me once again. I exhaled and all my shame and fear had disappeared. I took his hand. He lifted me from the cold isolation. It was time to go.

The Embrace

"The day came when the risk to remain tight in a bud was more painful than the risk it took to blossom."

Anais Nin

Before the bloom of the first flower, I left that place and all its teenage carelessness, never a regret. I had grown to become a virtuous woman.

In and out of the garden I'd go.

Everyone I met the song remained the same. I could love you just for today. Then their song would whisk them away. This new rhythm captured my heart. I took root to the beat of his drum. His words, his family, his ways. I bared to him my soul. Our passion for life combined in what seemed to be an unending embrace echoed in the verse, "If I had the world to give, I'd give it to you long as I live, laugh, dance, and cry," and we spun away building a place of our own.

I welcomed his past into our home to give it a future only true love could offer. I raised him and embraced him as my own. The son I would never have, given the love of a mother that wasn't his own.

Then with my soulmate, together we breathed life into the universe, not once but twice. We were gifted two daughters. Overjoyed that our song would continue through eternity.

Yet I always knew his past still held tight to carrying on his name. Always drawing him away to dance to a different rhythm. Sometimes my love longed for the freedoms of his childhood home. He flirted between two desires, never truly loving and accepting completely into his heart the home he had created, so he would dance away every so often but would always return. The music called him to a place he would not allow anyone else to join him in. His dance filled with secret embraces that fulfilled his heart's desires.

Then the unthinkable became real. The beat of the drum became heavy and threatening and the perfect music we had created became raw and a resounding cry for help.

What we believed would be for eternity, the song that would remain long after we were gone from this place, became a deafening silence. We were overcome with fear, time warped ... the life and joys as we knew them, the dreams for our daughters had been taken from me. Their song had ended before I even had time to teach them about the dance. I felt lost. His embrace was cold. Tears pierced my spirit like a million daggers destroying my inner child. Seconds, minutes, hours, days, weeks, months, years rushed by. I struggled to walk, let alone even imagine the dance. It became a sorrow, and my whole world seemed to endlessly weep. In the silence, I sat, a mother cradling her two daughters; one who had crossed over and returned. Questioning, "Why me?" The other pleading for understanding and comfort from seeing the unimaginable. Death through the eyes of a child. She was left alone questioning also, "Why me?"

In the turbulent confusion, once again my Prince appeared this time before my family. I wanted to ask, "Why me?"

I looked to my chosen love, clutching his hand ever so tightly, begging, come with me, dance with me again, as I reached out for my Prince.

The hand of my chosen love slipping from my grasp. I watched as he danced away to his drum once again, a stranger to me. An embrace I would never know again. Our song had ended.

I pleaded with the universe to keep the music playing, holding tightly to the hearts of my children and the comforts of the family we had built. Keeping them safe in my embrace. Memories burst across the skies.

First kisses.

Hot air balloon rides.

The perfect dress for the magical moment.

Paris.

Time kept moving forward. It seemed faster and faster. I struggled to keep pace. I became tired and had forgotten how to enjoy the dance. The music was vanquished, background noise, by the voices day after day demanding me to do their works, meet their needs... listen... hear only them, follow them, the steps paved before me.

The day was hot, and the sun shined bright in the sky. Even with my eyes closed I could see and feel the goldenness of the day. The sand warm passing effortlessly through my toes. I sat still listening, questioning still.

"Why me?"

Feeling so alone amongst such a vast world.

I heard him, my Prince, in the roll of the waves, "I'm here!" He questioned me, "In your whole life have you not known me? I have never left you. I am your Prince of all ages." I looked deeply into his eyes. A beautiful sky of blue! I was held in his

The Embrace

Embrace. I heard the tender sounds, giggling, of what I thought were some else's children off in the distance.

It was my daughters.

Running past me, embracing each other as they ran childlike to the water's edge. The vastness of the ocean mesmerizing and enticing.

Both falling freely into the waves, each one crashing joyfully, one after another inviting them into the dance. The mist of the water against their faces. I opened my eyes and, in that moment, I saw it in their smiles. Joy! That peace that only came when I danced with my Prince.

In a breath, time stood still and life for me began once more. I was again filled with hope and my regrets had been washed away. I realized in that moment that my daughters had invited Him to their dance. He was now their Prince. Their fairytales had begun.

He danced with them along the water's edge. Danced amongst the most opulent sunset of blue, yellow, and pink. I knew from that instant that long after I am gone, they will never be alone. Ineffable was that sunset! They had learned through the turbulence to embrace their faith. They had found the man of their dreams: "Jesus." Every girl's Prince Charming.

The fairytale is real for those who choose to believe in it!

ABOUT THE CONTRIBUTOR

After losing her mother at the age of 13, Terisa Elizabeth Taylor navigated her way through life, one faith-filled step at a time. This strong, self-made woman became a success in her own right in the financial industry. She worked her way up to being a respected Regional Banking Officer in the banking industry before she even turned 30!

When she became a mom, she decided to take those skill sets and apply them to volunteering in the community, balancing her time at home with helping others! And now she also continues her success in the private financial platform helping businesses oversee and organize their offices.

Terisa's greatest blessing has been being a mom of three extraordinary children Steven, Claire, and Sarah, and teaching them to be empowered to live life by her favorite words, "Be the change they want to see in the world."

Terisa believes that with love you can conquer anything, even the worst situations, and if you truly love GOD with all your heart, the journey your faith leads you on will always prosper.

Bits of Her Heart...

Terisa Taylor

If someone needs a friend, be one!

FUN FACT...

Terisa is a longtime member of Girl Scouts of The Jersey Shore where she continues to believe in the empowerment of young women!

POETIC NOTES TO SELF

BY LAURA B. GINSBERG

To any person who has been told that creative efforts aren't going to pay off in the long run. Believe in that poetic voice inside you and follow it beyond what other people believe poetry and art can add to your life and your future success. I try to write something in my journal of randomness every day, and these thoughts were taken from those daily writings. I hope they help you as much as writing them has helped me.

Always be fearlessly friendly to yourself and to others.

Sometimes, in the morning, before the noon billows, the deep mortality of the world outside yourself translates your mindset into something more perishable, dragging the joy away from your grasp.

Sincere and mortal, you cannot squander any opportunity to fully enjoy the delicious and brittle delight of confidence.

To estimate the collective laughter, you would have to find some numerical construct to house the manipulation of pleasure.

The intimate shape you've accomplished is remarkable.

Magnificently MADE

The support of your determination makes your boundless love indestructible against space and time.

You are unbroken.

The continuous value of your empathy spins beyond measure.

The sum of fear is hard to calculate on any given day, especially when you feel like an unknown entity, but all it takes is for one kind soul to shout out your name in the darkness to command the universe to stand at attention and circulate the acknowledgement of your talents.

You don't need their permission to take this infinite guidance on how to forget to be so secretive with your ability to hide your cosmic complexion from those who might dare to judge your worth.

Without fail, they will reduce you—if you let them.

When you are clumsy with intention, you must grow with your own will and walk steadily in that direction despite the weight of vulnerability.

You must look at what you have and understand that each piece is an answer to a previous wish, so leap into the animation of what you have already received from the gracious hands of the universe.

Stack those hopes like plates and get to washing those dishes.

The shapeless silence divides us into blunt but explicit forms, terminal and irregular, but you have to understand that a symmetrical life would be boring—a paradise of perfectly tapered dullness due to a lack of clarity.

Mortality and its stylish lethality keep you sharp and compassionate as you constantly and miraculously heal.

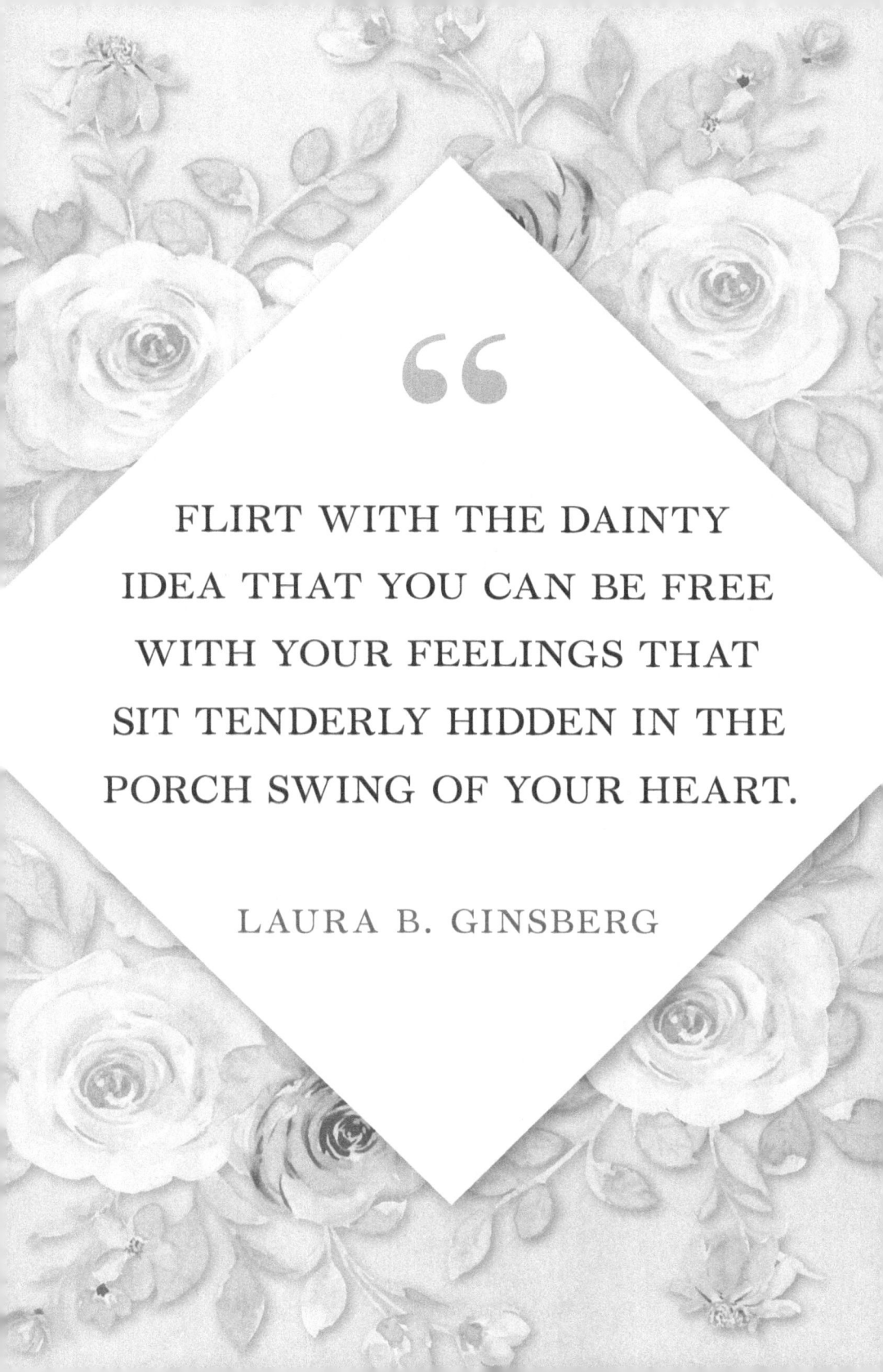

> FLIRT WITH THE DAINTY IDEA THAT YOU CAN BE FREE WITH YOUR FEELINGS THAT SIT TENDERLY HIDDEN IN THE PORCH SWING OF YOUR HEART.
>
> LAURA B. GINSBERG

Recognize proportional sleep as fragments of dreamy silhouettes that are unfathomable in their genuine confusion, bold in how shamelessly they focus on the frivolous and fluctuating shiver of superficial ignorance.

That sickness will vibrate and convulse you into a trembling and unstable contour when ashes replace those who once loved you in a physical state.

An eternity of unvarying stress surrounds any big decision because envy and the idols are empowered to skew the ideal, an epidemic of a cycle that keeps you from remembering how to be a rivalry of the similar and to nurture everything beyond what you think might be a parallel fascination with balancing desire and attraction.

Beware the invasion of the entourage.

Roles of youth run counterclockwise when it comes to the development of play—more aggressive when tauntingly dangerous and perplexingly undeveloped in what can end up being decadently terrible.

You will twist at the mouth and try to murmur your way out of every frightful conundrum, and you might temporarily be able to catch your footing, but the puzzling wonder of your inexperience will topple you into an incoherent foolishness if you prop on the falsehoods that obscure your true self.

You must work hard to brighten and understand the smudging realities of others.

Enduring kindness to yourself is always possible.

External pressure is a false motivator, so explore that place inside yourself and inspire your own intrinsic permission to stop holding back.

Find the tasks where love can solidify.

Protect and defend your blissful kitchen from the crystallized cruelty that might stare at you through the screen door of yesterday.

Poetic Notes to Self

Grapple to find a voice in all of the rooms where the first response is always no.

Dance with the demand of skill and effort that it takes to fully exist where all of the humbled exertion transforms into the artistic maneuvering it takes to appreciate your own knowledge and abilities.

Do not carry the disposition of someone who works too hard for no fanfare.

The biological urge to regret outlines a diet of depictions and designations toward an appetite of boxed coldness and division.

Exhale the clock.

Articulate the difficulty of what has happened.

Hours of sorrow will dissipate with a moment of sympathy.

Elaborate on the conic sections of how your perception of minutes and seconds often spirals into a rudimentary explanation of the fundamentals.

The gauntlet of your memory is unraveling, and the miscalculations of that remembrance leave much to be misinterpreted, so find a way to exist in what's left of now.

The distance of the miscellaneous will jumble your history of errors.

Always use patience to mitigate whatever illusion you might injure.

The assurance of gentleness helps encourage the promise of growth, so be receptive to the momentum of tomorrow.

Oddly oceanic, the idea that the perfume of hard work reveals itself as a sequence to be performed rather than an occupational invasion of our decisions.

The outrage of life is being concerned with the vanishing flatness of what tomorrow might not hold.

Make it your responsibility today to improve your creative self.

Feel compelled to make a kinetic impact, because only you can stomach the strength and coerce the requirements of your next big accomplishment.

Reveal whatever beauty you are holding back.

A ruthless truth will sometimes break your humor and crack open some insecure despair.

To hope for security within reality can warp the voyage toward authentic protection and certainty.

The filters of your bruised sense of self and societal repercussions will lock the mechanism that controls what you say out loud for those vulnerable souls.

The sparkle of cruel walls and flagrant greed are there to disguise the cold-blooded political calculation.

Think about what sort of impression you will leave in this world if everything you do is false.

You are gentle at your core.

Find some hollow piece of yourself and perform your exaggerations as you embrace someone else's love.

Blunt thunder stuns the breathless blunder of your flesh against some statistical shadow within the hour of fashionable daybreak.

Poetic Notes to Self

Stand up against the scorching future of numb fantasy and suspicious discouragement.

Smother confusion with daylight and recycle the glitter that celebrates the daily tumult inside.

The border of loneliness includes a description of violation.

We all just want someone to listen to our vivid monotony and the hazy aching of not knowing what to do.

Some days you just have to appreciate the glossy seclusion surrounding the translation of a damaged emptiness, longing in plain sight.

It's perfectly normal to be quietly confused about the unmistakable doubt that anyone will care about the things you have to sell.

You should sing about being heartbroken.

Answers will eventually mark the limits of the absolute void.

Sometimes, in an attempt to help, there will be the dread of a blinding mistake.

You can walk away and cry.

The loveliest distortion of drawings can be an exhibit of your feelings that are finding it hard to be forgotten.

The street corner can sometimes be an ocean.

The error of interpretation is something that can be fully squandered.

Magnificently MADE

Raw emotions are sometimes deep enough to wade in, so veer toward those delicate rhythms and sloping enjoyment.

Your observant eyes make dandelions possible.

Take your breathless and vertical extension of self and irritate the enemy to force the momentum of combat that will leave decayed fragments of consequence and illustrate the absurdity of their hostility.

Flirt with the dainty idea that you can be free with your feelings that sit tenderly hidden in the porch swing of your heart.

That delicate tarnish of fear will burn away in lacy sunlight.

The exquisite collapse of your bravery happens sometimes.

The blemish of your weakness seems to mangle every timid attempt to show the bruises of your past.

Misfortune might just scorch your battered earth, and your pride might fade into a horizon of the shrinking embankment, but let those things wash away the tide of destructive frustration and reveal your charm, fragile and petite.

The mythology of the night sky uncovers the simplicity of your designations and the secrets that the constellations failed to mention.

Stretch every midnight into a slender narrative.

Glimmer against the tolerance of shameful danger.

Scatter stars into the artless nothing with every handful of suggestions.

Belief can get you through this mystique, unreal and familiar all at once.

Poetic Notes to Self

Play and accomplish the teachings of every cloud within the dizzying slice of a crescent moon in the exposure of the shared sky and the silver wane.

You can endure the lunar tides of luck and division.

Chapters produce the kind of endurance that can happen only when you accept the faint elimination of your expectations.

Your wobbly self must continue to learn and split cells until healed with the medicine of the ancients—the passage of time.

Natural law requires your heart to continue beating in order to survive and inspire.

Imperfection is your most complex and fascinating companion.

The familiarity of such narcotic doubt should no longer attract you.

Prepare for the frailty of fortune.

Keep being awesome.

ABOUT THE CONTRIBUTOR

Laura Ginsberg is a content strategist, design fiend, conceptual creative, editorial magician, and poetic storyteller. Her childhood afforded her creative and unstructured days and language skills until some Journalism and Creating Writing professors at The University of Alabama really split open some hibernating creatures of the poetic sort. Dreams of New York City ransacked the mechanical stability of a career in magazines, so Laura followed a few friends up to New Jersey and stumbled into a marvelous book editing job in education publishing. Cancer happened. Marriage happened. As for Laura's own writing, she has made a hard slant toward poetry in the past few years and has a master's degree from Johns Hopkins. Her book, *Poetic Emergencies* was published by Inspired Girl in 2022.

Now, Laura lives in Asbury Park, New Jersey, and she teaches writing courses, works editing magic, and owns a college prep school! Beyond that, she randomly attempts to paint some dimensional acrylics and thoroughly enjoys unstructured days that start with a strong cup of coffee and an ever-changing view of the vulnerable ocean.

Bits of Her Heart...
Laura B. Ginsberg

 Be fearlessly friendly.

FUN FACT...
Laura loves soap. She buys Amish soap in bulk, and if she was going away and could only pack three items they would be two books and some soap!

27

THE STARS IN MY CHEST

BY KAYLA HARRIS

For all who have yet to find the majesty within. It's in there.
I dedicate this chapter to GG, my mother, and Emma.

"To feel, and to question feeling; to know,
and to agree to wander
utterly lost in the dark, where every
journey of the soul starts over."

Jane Hirshfield

TWENTY YEARS OLD

Once, a lost girl at the hands of the world. Now a princess in my tower. I searched for myself under the brush, beneath the copper bridges, and in the creeks, feet deep. The state park nuzzled next to my dorm building.

I was in a kingdom of books and sins. Days in the library were spent turning pages, and nights were spent on the town, causing trouble. I was fulfilling the princess fantasy with a slightly different happily ever after. I found myself.

I moved to the towers to study at my local university. It was my second year at school away from home. Tucked in the corners and under archways were hidden exhibitions displaying fossils and paintings from centuries ago. The professors taught us how to fulfill our dreams. The philosophers made us ponder our existence. The art on the walls called us to jump in and have the splash soak us with that corner of the world.

Crowded rooms with keg beer and loud music were the place to be when the classrooms emptied. Late nights were spent wandering the main street's rental homes and creating new stories to be told and written. We danced in small basements. We climbed trees, monuments, and fountains at 2 a.m. We walked the long path home to the books and class in the morning.

Before the walk, the parties raged on. All the faces in a room lit up as the lights flashed on and off. I craved for eyes to stop at mine and ask me anything. Hoping someone would look and choose me. Hoping someone would find me worthy. Hoping this night would be different, and I would find someone who loved me. The party played on. I'd crawl into my small twin bed in the cold early morning. I was all alone, not even with myself.

Another weekend was spent dancing in a crowded backyard with friends, beer, and sunshine. Just another Saturday. I found a gaze. A nice smile and loving demeanor were all I needed to leave the party hand in hand, skipping through campus, and grabbing flowers on the way to lunch. He left me searching the small texts in the few minutes between us. Was this love? My mind was isolated in the crowd of college, not even receiving the glow of my own warmth. I was without my own standard of loving myself. Each day I was lost on how to show up for myself. Let alone demand someone else show up and love me.

One night in bed with the lover reaching for the stars. The night took a turn to a path unseen. A short instance left a mark for years to come. I never suited up for the dark woods of battle but was pushed into the gender war by others. A precious stone ogled too long for a beauty she shouldn't have to provide. A gift my temple blessed with the power of soul genesis. May your hands be tainted for forcing god without permission.

By the morning, the man I found at the backyard party had abandoned me. He could not handle the dark woods of battle. I wandered the woods to crawl out bloody and disassociated and alone. Another long walk back to my dorm felt surreal. The bus pulled away from the curb, the elevator opened, and other students passed. My hands opened the door. My legs moved forward. Where was I?

For months and years, I walked in and out of post-traumatic stress. All I could

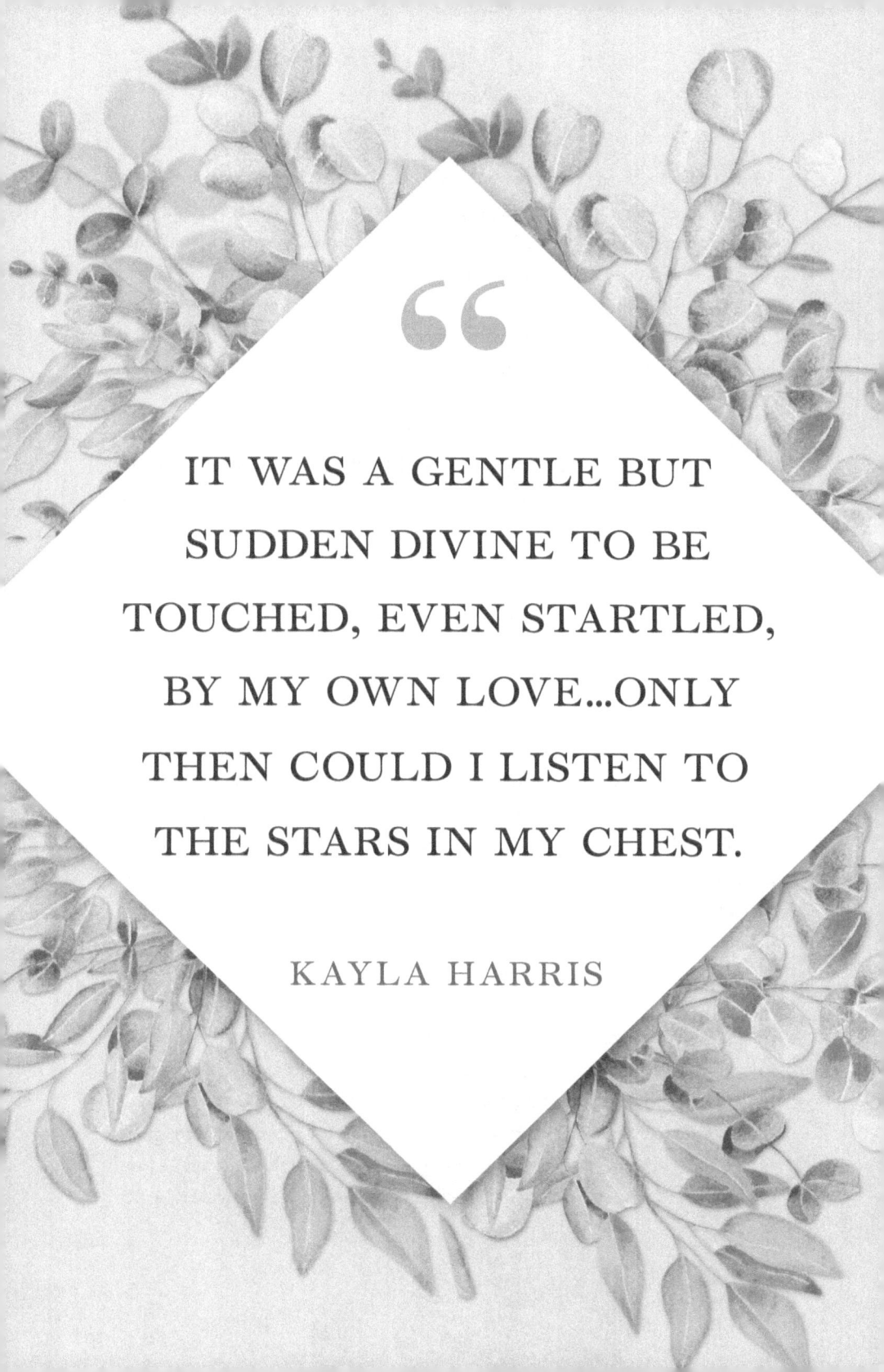

> IT WAS A GENTLE BUT SUDDEN DIVINE TO BE TOUCHED, EVEN STARTLED, BY MY OWN LOVE...ONLY THEN COULD I LISTEN TO THE STARS IN MY CHEST.

KAYLA HARRIS

feel was emptiness. My crown lowered. My body continued to be seen for how it was shown on the TV and on the magazine covers. The fatty curves held bones and were drenched in the tradition where we do not praise a woman but take her.

I knew I had to abandon what I had been taught about my own body. There was shame from when teachers told me I had to leave class for what I was wearing. There was fear when a strange man's hand grazed my back. There was a beauty to be hidden and preyed on. I found the strength to abandon these ideas of sexuality and redefine everyday standards for my own self-love.

My own mother and I, experiencing fear in our childhood homes. The pain from one trauma triggering another. What if I called the police like I used to? When I stood helpless at my parents' locked door. My mother screaming and the police banging. Did the post-traumatic stress cloud my state of being? Quickly, it all rushed back as I sat alone on the bedroom floor.

> "The wound is the place where light enters you."
> **Rumi**

TEN YEARS OLD

The bricks of our home slowly fell off. Two fucked up kids fucked, and then there was me. Teenagers turn parents, both from abusive homes, entangled in beach sand. My parents' monsters chased us throughout the pinelands and up and down the east coast. We ran from ghosts building in these beach bars for generations. Our grandparents sat on the same bar stools pushing away feelings and living in negativity. On the weekends, my parents sat there as I ran between the arcade and sucking oysters.

We skipped the shore like a stone across the bay. We flew like seagulls spreading their wings, looking for a new horizon. We never found the right nest. We only saw the same problems everywhere we went. We brought the storm with us to new places. My family was hanging by a thread in the changing wind. Sometimes we were flying; sometimes we dangled behind a boat at full speed.

The train rides to the racetrack, and hot days on the boardwalk were quick to end in a night of abuse. My father drank, and he took his demons out on my mother, leaving me, their child, a bystander to horror. I'd be awoken by her screams to call the police or her outstretched arms to pick me up and take me away, anywhere else.

In the middle of the night, we escaped to find solace at family and friends' houses. I'd wake up with new sisters, the daughters of family friends, willing to take my mother and me in. It was only so long before we'd have to run again. We'd curl up in another shore home. Another pocket of dune grass to nuzzle and hide from the wind and lightning. We followed haunted patterns that our grandparents paved, a path so hard to escape that it lingered and marked us as we slept.

Each house would only last so long before my parents were back together. This house or that house all had suburban sidewalks with sand in the cracks and bodies of water nearby. Even a couple times, our *own* rental bungalow along the shore, where nights got old, and my parents stayed young. I'd be awoken by loud music or screaming or screaming loud music. I'd find empty bottles scattered on the counter that led to my parents' bedroom. My dad's face was red. I could hear bodies thumping against the walls.

Until it was done. Then, my mother would crawl into my bed, and we would cry together.

I started to call 911. I was hoping the cops would take my father away. His violence exploded into the room to the point it bruised and battered my mother. Sometimes bystanders would run to get help.

My mother and I were numb after they ordered protection around us, still afraid of every sound. Creaky floors. Wind in trees. Loud knocks made us shiver in fear. But it would only be the police knocking for signatures on the restraining order or my great-grandmother coming home. I was always afraid he would come through the window at night.

The towns tucked along the mid-Atlantic coast had their own different personalities, and they soothed me throughout my trauma. The towns, like aunts and uncles, held me between the carousel and the inlet, my favorite rides and crane games. I was held by many midnight drives along Ocean Avenue, wondering where we would stop.

Lost along the Jersey Shore, the tourist summer hit us harder than some. The locals all felt flooded with ocean water and excitement to be steps away from the weekend vacationers and time for celebration. But the amusement ride's screams slowed after summer, and only the locals remained to keep the partying going. After the party, a child was drifting in the break, the only screams left to hear.

> "i thank You God for most this amazing day:for the leaping greenly spirits of trees and a blue true dream sky;and for everything which is natural which is infinite which is yes"
>
> E. E. Cummings

HEALING

Years later, I am still drifting in between states, woods, water, and people. Most of them floating on the reality built in history before our time. But for the first time, alone in my tower at university, away from home, I looked inside. The girl in the castle wanted something different than these memories.

Prince Charming wasn't coming. Running from my father. Holding my mother. Looking for a lover. The trauma left me no other choice as I felt abandoned and turned to face myself. I knew how great my experience on Earth could be in an atmosphere that sprouted lilies and elephants. I felt awe in nature. But somehow, I felt abandoned by humans and their lack of divine gratitude.

In the university, where all the answers are found, I fell into myself. My dorm held sanctuary after class, away from my roommates, tucked away in the treetops. Walking the brick kingdom between classes, I allowed myself to think for as long as needed. How did I feel?

Overlooking a state forest, I headed into the trails to run and cry and be consumed in the living trees. My muscles screamed to be released, and my mind wanted to escape, so I kept pushing farther and faster. My dark mind painted the room and journals with my pain. My body stretched, ran, and swam into new form as I begged for change each morning.

I'd escape to the forest to heal. I fell in love with the birds sunbathing in the treetops with their wings spread wide draped across the moving creek. I hid like an eagle perched beneath a bush. I danced across the red iron bridges realizing what it meant to be alive again. I realized I was already a part of the ecosystem. I belonged.

The Stars in My Chest

Running in the thick heat. Swimming in the rivers. Listening to the water tremble.

I'd return to my room covered in sweat and smeared berries to read my environmental novels about Mother Nature, the fight to survive, and the atmosphere's chemistry. I was listening when the grass and trees called home to those who heeded the call, a call to your natural being. I'd write and read. I'd sit and be sad. I prayed to myself and my own dreams. Finally, I was able to find my light again.

It was a gentle but sudden divine to be touched, even startled, by my own love. The warm embrace of a god within. I sat alone on the bathroom floor for years. Only then could I listen to the stars in my chest. No one had ever told me that I was a miracle from plants and the planets. And this life is the one chance we get for ourselves.

I listened to my soul in silence and asked what the little girl inside me called for. Every day I checked in, did what I enjoyed, and wore what I wanted for my dedication.

I forgive my mother for trying her best. I forgive my father for battling his demons. I forgive those who have harmed me, not for them, but for me. Because I let them go, they no longer linger when I walk. Then, I can walk stronger alone. And I can walk beside others with love.

I return home to myself. I sit with her in the darkness. I have been running from her since childhood, when I watched TV, when I partied with friends, when I was constantly flooded with others' opinions, and when I did anything but spend time alone. I return home to myself and praise her for whatever she wants to be.

I now know the power in my mind. I see the strength in my body. I could find a path forward by finally listening to my heartbreak. I could drown out the other voices and listen to my own intuition. I am a divine being whose heart beats with the sun and the stars, and I will treat myself as greatness. I am a girl found in the hands of nature and reborn through glory within.

Magnificently MADE

A ME POEM
Never Ending Story

Beach waves &
high percentage ipas.
The sunburn glows
in cold night sheets.

Early mornings in
a garden of animal noses
and homegrown corn.
Ripe air dews
the sun rays
in the horizon break.

Hide and seek
behind pine trees
splashing ankles
in cedar creeks
frogs croak and dried flowers
sprinkle the fairies home.

Sangria fruits float
at a bar hanging over the bay
where Bruce Springsteen plays
shaded by tall greens and cat tails.
Long walks on the marsh trail.

The Stars in My Chest

Under the stars we dance
at a bonfire next to the brush
to praise the atmosphere and the sun

in a dreamy jungle
against a falling black sky
as our hearts pumps
on space dust.

Writing wound scripts
on the porch swing
grabbing into the night
with *the stars in my chest:*

the human's guide
toward earthly living.

ABOUT THE CONTRIBUTOR

Kayla Harris has always felt connected with the natural world. Growing up along the Jersey Shore, she was immersed in the Pinelands, marshlands, and sandy coasts. She eventually moved to Delaware, where she pursued her passion for English at the University of Delaware. Today, she resides once again in the Garden State, surrounded by her loving family.

Kayla is an artist, activist, and environmentalist. Her professional journey has led her to TerraCycle, a global recycling innovator in sustainable solutions. Simultaneously, she manages her small business, The Imperfect Eco, which promotes accessible, sustainable products to help individuals embark on eco-friendliness, zero-waste living, and improved well-being.

In her free time, Kayla loves to write poetry, go to the beach, and spend time outdoors. She serves as the Secretary for the Bordentown Township Environmental Commission and wields her editorial skills as the Poetry Editor for NJ Indy. Her unwavering passion fuels her efforts to communicate the urgency of environmental protection and the importance of fostering change for a sustainable future.

Stay connected with Kayla's inspiring journey by following her on Instagram @ecopoetkayla.

Bits of Her Heart...
Kayla Harris

"To fall in love with yourself is the first secret to happiness."
-Robert Morley

FUN FACT...
Kayla is an eco-poet. Her writings have a strong emphasis on the environment, the ecosystem, nature, culture, and ecology.

SECTION 10

WE ARE HEALERS AND HEALING

CARRYING THE WEIGHT OF MY WORLD
by Brianna McCabe

HEALING OLD WOUNDS OF WORTHINESS
by Patty Lennon

LOOKING THROUGH A DIFFERENT LENS
by Trisha Kilgour

COCOONING IS NECESSARY FOR GROWTH.

28

CARRYING THE WEIGHT OF MY WORLD

BY BRIANNA MCCABE

This chapter is dedicated to anyone who has ever struggled with their self-worth.

As a Libra woman, my scale is apparently meant to remain in a state of constant balance—yet for some reason, I seemed to maintain an unsteady relationship between myself and gravity whenever I would weigh myself.

I sometimes tend to blame my food addiction on my cultural upbringing with my Italian-American family who constantly served "mootzahdehl" (mozzarella) just because it was a Tuesday and that called for cheese chomping. That, or it could've been that I was genetically predisposed to bear a bit more "gabagool" (capicola, or an Italian meat) around the midsection. (All right, I think you probably have had enough of the *Soprano* slang by now.) Whatever the initial cause may have been, I myself continued to perpetuate the behavior and further satiate the appetite of this uncontrollable addiction.

When I was a child who didn't know any better, though, my family initially condoned my behavior—especially my Pop who loved to cook. In essence, he provided this never-ending supply of meals and, being that he lived next door, it was a quick sprint across the street for my next feeding. I didn't realize it at the time, but I was being force fed this food-centric lifestyle. Of course, food is critical to all existence... except in the case of my family and the way that they generationally have viewed chow time, I was routinely pouring the most greasy, artery-clogging oils into my engine. Like the Energizer Bunny, I was forever fueled—but a bit *too* much (and too lousily).

As you can presume, I quickly ballooned as a child. (All right, maybe not quite like Violet Beauregarde in *Willy Wonka,* but in comparison to kids my age I was definitely far outside of their size ranges.) In fact, I wasn't able to shop at the popular stores that my classmates constantly talked about because I couldn't squeeze my arms through any of the shirt holes or shove my legs into the jeans, let alone even attempt to button them. Instead, I was perusing the "junior girls" section of JC Penney while I was just entering the fourth grade. I didn't quite understand feelings of isolation at this point of my life, but this was the first taste.

The innate loneliness amplified as I grew in both age and circumference. Once I entered middle school I became an easy target for heckling. I had gum spit into my hair on numerous occasions, and boys would mockingly yell, "*Watch out for the big girl!*" as I walked down the hallway. After each hurtful encounter, I'd remind myself that once I got home I could shrug my shoulders and exhaustedly cuddle a bag of chips in bed. This was my first glimpse into turning to replacement behaviors to cope with my pain.

After repeatedly being told that there was something wrong with me physically for not fitting the mold, I started to inwardly feel as if I was worthless and deserving of these cruel comments and terrible taunts. Those words that the bullies would spew to me, well, after some time I would start to regurgitate to myself: I *am* ugly. I *am* fat. I *am* disgusting. I *am* nothing more than a slob who no one should or could respect. This corrupt societal standard fully funneled into depression, anxiety, low self-esteem, and poor body image—and yet, despite me hating food for turning me into this "monster," I used it to help me "get over it." It was this terribly toxic cycle of emotional overeating—and I was only an adolescent.

Noticing that I was tinkering toward being clinically diagnosed as obese, my mom encouraged me to play sports. This way, as she put it, I could increase my physical activity levels and also expose myself to other social circles. And so, I pursued softball. While I truly loved the intricacies of the sport, I wasn't a "peak performer" in terms of athleticism. However, when I did make contact with the ball up at bat, I sent it soaring given the momentum that backed my swing. (I attribute being the "powerhouse" who batted fourth in the lineup to the laws of physics.)

To ensure that I didn't pause the momentum of my physical exercise regimen in the off-season, my mom suggested that I perhaps try to give cheerleading a shot. "*It could be a nice balance,*" she advised.

"*Balance?*" I questioned. "*Mom, I can't even balance myself enough to do a cartwheel.*"

"*You never know!*" she supportively said.

I was probably the most lackluster leader of cheer that my school has ever seen. The sparkly bows, hideous white elongated shoes, and pretentiously swanky *"Let's go teams!"* made my stomach churn. On the flip side, though, I did get to spend some extra quality time with my one best friend, Lizzy.

Despite me having some of the worst pike jumps that my coach had to try and hide in the back of our formations, I stuck through cheerleading to surround myself in a group that was touted as popular. This shield didn't protect me from some of the attacks that worsened well into high school, though, especially by several of my fellow squad members.

My freshman year when I couldn't fit into any of the uniforms, the varsity cheer captain taunted, "*I guess she'll make for a sturdy pyramid base.*" Though consumed with rage, I was entirely too insecure in myself to have ever spoken up or defended my worth.

"*I'm more than just a fucking body!*" I'd envision yelling back—except I assumed that it would only further propel their laughter.

"*Screw 'em,*" Lizzy would say in the locker room. "*After practice, let's go grab a slice and laugh about them.*"

I'd regularly use my allowance money to splurge on food out of codependent needs. In fact, there would be days that I would self-impose serious stomach pains after having just inhaled an entire buffalo chicken pizza, side order of French fries, mozzarella sticks, and loaf of garlic bread for the sake of it being dinnertime. After about an hour, I would have to physically force myself to vomit to alleviate some of the pressure that now tormented my not-so-loving love handles. Sadistically, though, I knew that I was only making more room for dessert.

This toxic obsession impacted my life in more layers than the chocolate cake

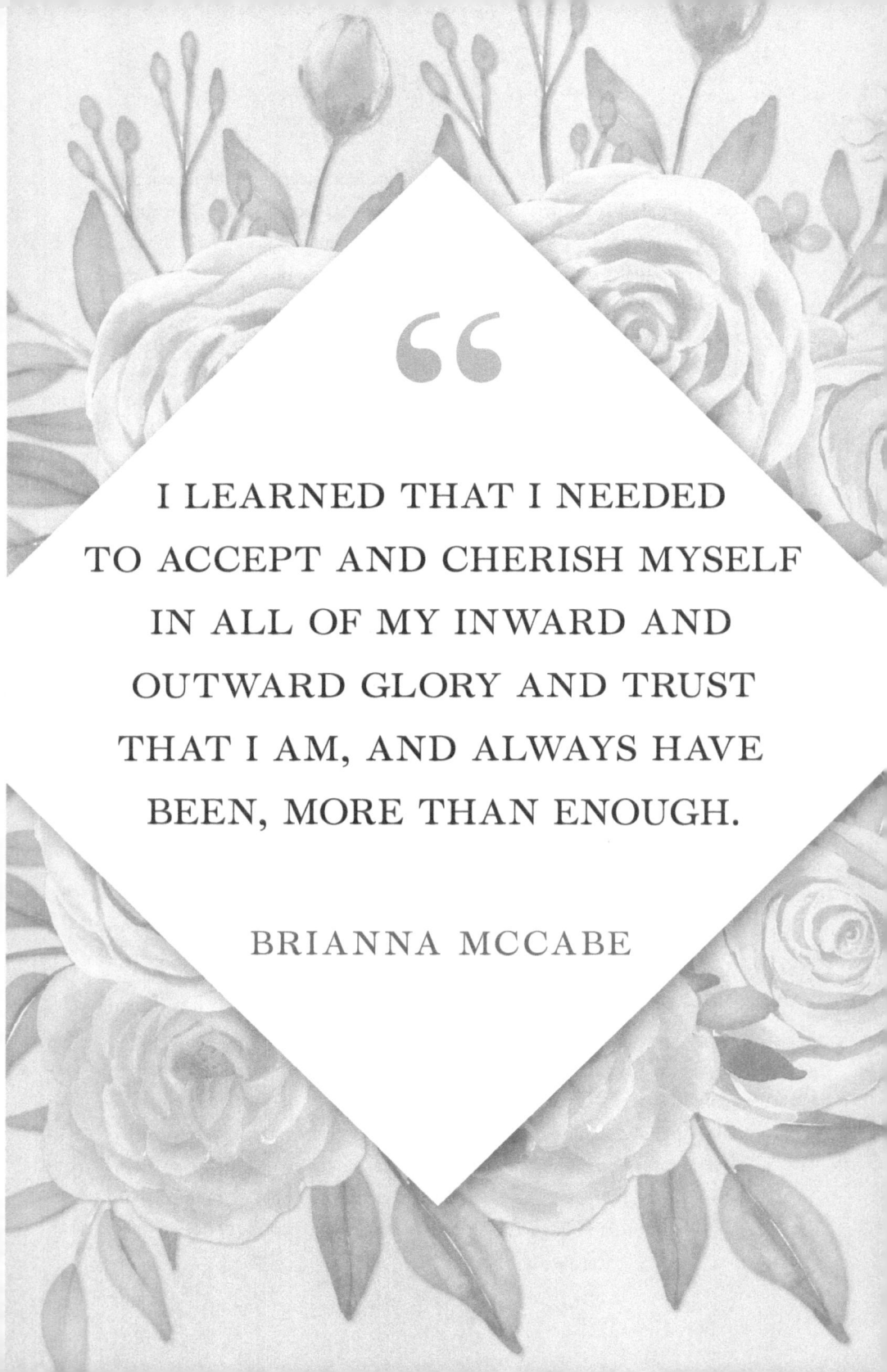

> "I learned that I needed to accept and cherish myself in all of my inward and outward glory and trust that I am, and always have been, more than enough.

— Brianna McCabe

that I constantly eyed at the bakery. I mean, sure, the feeling of food being crunched against my molars and grazing along my taste buds temporarily made me feel full—both physically and spiritually. However, as I'd look at myself in the mirror and notice the ways in which I was destroying my body, I looked to food to comfort me in this cyclical-like self-sabotage. As the grease continued to infiltrate my pores, the salt sucked the youth out of my skin, and the accumulated fat added extra love to the handles, I'd eat more to cope with my disgust. I was in a love-hate relationship with not just food, but my body.

Into my later high school years, as women around me would experience the pleasure of hooking up with men, the only thing my tongue swirled were the shafts of my popsicles sticks. Being gluttonous momentarily masked this frustration—but then my junior year when I was introduced to the mind-altering and numbing effects of drinking and smoking, I took to another vice (and replacement behavior): partying.

During periods of heavy intoxication, I felt free. Despite what people may have been saying or thinking, my spirit was in a daze so deep that I escaped not only reality but the barracks of bullies. I danced, I laughed, I smiled, and I ever-so-freely entertained the room. As people cheered for me to "*CHUG, CHUG, CHUG!*" while I sucked down room-temperature Natty Ices through the never-quite-cleaned-before beer funnel, I finally felt accepted... or maybe I was just so drunk that, for a brief blip in time, I dulled any internal and external heckles and paused any obsessive negative thoughts from further spiraling through this self-medication.

Being that I held myself in such little regard as a result of low self-esteem, alcohol helped me cement myself into this niche of being the "spunky party girl" where, for once, I didn't feel like an outlier in a given social circle. I was grateful, especially being that I now more than doubled my daily caloric intake whenever I'd drink (and eat for the sake of the munchies). My slippery slope's angle deepened and propelled me toward an even unhealthier state at a much faster pace as I rolled into college at nearly 260 pounds.

"*Brianna, you know that this really isn't a healthy weight,*" my OB/GYN warned during my annual exam right before the start of the semester. "*Can you also clarify when you had your last period? You left that field blank on the intake form.*"

When I responded that it's been quite a few months since my last cycle, the doctor then recommended that we do an in-office ultrasound to examine my insides "a bit more thoroughly." The imaging revealed what he described as a "string of pearls," or an arrangement of unreleased eggs, which then formed these tiny fluid-filled follicles within my ovaries. After a few moments of scrolling the transducer across the cooling jelly sprawled along my lower abdomen, my doctor placed the tool on the table, rolled back in his spinning chair, and said, "*Brianna, you have polycystic ovarian syndrome, or PCOS.*"

Essentially, the doctor explained the condition as a type of hormonal imbalance that can typically be related to obesity. Side effects or common symptoms can include excess hair growth, acne, infertility, and even more weight gain in addition to now having an increased risk of Type 2 diabetes, high blood pressure, cardiovascular issues, and even endometrial cancer. "*Brianna, if you start to lose some weight now you can curb some of these side effects,*" he advised. "*But this really needs to be made into a priority before your body starts to weaken and shut down.*"

Unamused, unconcerned, and unphased, I left the doctor's office and headed home to then get ready for my friend's final "banger" before he moved a few states away to college. In a confirmation bias–like manner, though, once I got home I scoured the internet for statistics on the prevalence of PCOS in women which, to my distorted liking, shared how it allegedly affects roughly one in ten women of childbearing age. In a sense, I thwarted the correlation from my weight and dismissed it as being an issue that "many others deal with." Intrinsically, I knew that my weight was spiraling out of control, yet I wasn't there mentally to put myself onto a path of overall betterment. In my typical diversionary tactic, I did a few extra *CHEERS!* that night to blur away my deprecating thoughts. Once again, I disguised my depression with the bubbly persona that accompanied whatever bottle of champagne I was to be popping that night.

I hoped that I could simply transition my late-high school persona into my freshman year's identity. It semi-worked—except that the men were much crueler, and the women were much pickier in terms of association. To many, the perception of who you allowed into your circle was reality—and my presence to some would apparently throw off the equilibrium. Luckily for me, though, my quirky and energetic party girl persona did attract several wholesome friends who welcomed me into their worlds.

While most of them would make-out with the hot upperclassmen during our outings, I found myself making small talk with whoever was manning the keg that night so that I could feel a more intimate connection with my buzz. I'd be lying to myself, though, if I didn't feel deprived of my womanhood—or envious of their hookups. After years of being verbally berated and made to feel physically unattractive, though, I was scared to even attempt to put myself out there.

"*But you know you're beautiful, right?*" my college best friend Luella questioned. She was this beautiful blonde with an hourglass waistline, captivating smile, and alluring sex appeal. "*You shouldn't be afraid to talk to anyone, especially guys. You have a stunning face, voluptuous body, and beautiful personality.*"

"*Just because you're my friend, you don't have to lie to me,*" I sadly responded after feeling that everyone shared the same low opinions of me.

"*I would never just say that, Bri,*" Luella said, as she tried to instill some confidence and self-esteem into me. "*I truly feel that way about you—and I hope one day you can feel it, too.*"

I had hoped that, too, except I was pushed down into such a hole in my mind that I forgot that I could redirect my thoughts and push upwards. Being that I still didn't have that mental strength to redirect the trajectory of my thoughts, Luella offered to guide me. Knowing that all I wanted was to feel accepted and equal in terms of where many other females were at this point in our college careers (sexually-speaking, of course), she sought to help me find my first college hook-up. And so, I was seeking another temporary fix of a replacement behavior: sexual validation.

As the two of us took some rather vile swigs of our cheap vodka and warm orange juice concoctions in preparation of the hook-up-oriented night ahead, I experienced the internal transition as my insecurities completed their shift as my puppeteer. Free from the constraints of my marionette's original manipulator, I now danced according to the sloppy string work of my inebriation.

As we drunkenly trucked across campus and maneuvered through the streets to the house party slightly outside of the school's perimeters, we danced to their DJ's bass that subtly filled the air. With each step toward the destination, the music became more affluent—that is, until we were fully engulfed in its seduction once we finally entered the premises. Immediately, we made our way toward the basement bar, filled up our iconic red Solo cups, and danced the night away.

I found myself standing in a circle amongst Luella, a few other football players, and several sorority girls as the night progressed. At one point, one of the football players briefly exited the group to retrieve an unopened bottle of Svedka.

"*All right, it's time to kick this party up a notch,*" he said. "*It's time for some Never Have I Ever.*"

As the game goes, you list a potential experience that you've never had and, if someone has done the act, they take a shot. If no one has done the act, then the person who initially posed the statement takes a shot. The game kicked off with an overly promiscuous sorority girl by stating something overtly sexual. A few of the girl's sisters took a shot and then giggled.

"*All right my turn,*" a football player interjected. "*Never have I ever had a foursome,*" he stated as he then looked over at his teammate and gave him a "bro" elbow.

"*That could be fun,*" I added despite me having zero experience whatsoever in that arena—but trying ever so desperately to fit in.

"*Yeah, with who?*" the player sarcastically asked. "*Because I don't know anyone who is into the Big Mac type of girls.*"

"*The what?*" Luella immediately barked.

"*I mean, no offense, but you look like eat more burgers than dick,*" he said as he peered over our group and invited them in to ridicule me. The sorority girls started cackling while several of the football players started letting out their respective *OOOOOH!s*. I felt like the universe was punishing me for trying to even attempt to gain some pseudo-sexual confidence.

"*Are you fucking serious?*" Luella yelled to the crowd. "*Why would anyone even say that?*"

My eyes now welling up after having just been stripped of my femininity, sex appeal, and overall dignity with those pungent words in front of a crowd, I cried, "*FUCK YOU!*" as I bolted out of the party.

"*That's probably the most exercise she's had in a while,*" I overheard the football player laugh in the distance which elicited a roar of amusement.

"*BRI WAIT!*" Luella shouted as she sprinted out from the front door of the party.

"*I'm a FUCKING JOKE!*" I drunkenly cried as I kept running full force toward the dorm building. "*I'm a fat fuck that no one finds attractive!*"

"*These people are superficial and don't appreciate the beauty that is you, so FUCK THEM!*" she yelled as she turned her head toward the direction of the party. "*He didn't deserve you anyway.*"

Carrying the Weight of My World

"*I just want to feel wanted for once,*" I bawled, except I wanted to be wanted for the wrong reasons.

I surrendered to these feelings of utter emptiness as I withered away into the blankets of my twin-sized dorm mattress that night. For the next two weeks, I stopped attending classes and barely left the confines of my white-washed cement walls. Essentially, I became a self-induced prisoner as I fell into a coma-like sleep. Though I tried to barricade these dark thoughts into the deepest layers of my mind to replicate what I was doing to myself physically, these horrors still managed to infiltrate my dreams. Regardless of my level of consciousness, my mind reminded me of just how much I didn't love or accept myself.

"*Bri, are you in there?*" I heard my other best friend, Kayleigh, say as she managed to crash into my dream state.

"*Huh?*" I wearily slurred while still semi-dozed off. "*I'm just... just not feeling good.*"

"*Can I please come in for a second?*" she sincerely questioned from the hallway.

After a few moments, I mustered up the energy and recalibrated from my disorientation to finally leave my bed, walk over to the door, and welcome her into my room. As she shuffled in, she warmly wrapped her arms around my upper body and gifted me with love—something that I have felt completely deprived of after that night.

"*I heard about what happened and I want you to know that we care about you so much,*" she said.

As I wept into the crevice of her neck, I told her that I couldn't keep bullying myself. "*It's bad enough that I have outsiders telling me how ugly I am,*" I explained.

"*You're so harsh on yourself and it breaks my heart,*" she sighed. After a long pause she added, "*Why don't you let me help you and show you how to practice better self-care?*"

Though she was going to school for exercise science while also studying for her yoga instructor certification, Kayleigh told me that she developed a healthy relationship with her body far before college. "*I just one day decided that I wanted to be kind to my physical self since it gifted me with so much in life,*" she said as she helped me get ready for our first gym session that next day in my room. "*But enough about me, let me show you the beauty of a good back day,*" she joked.

The sounds of barbells clanging and banging against the raggedy gym floor momentarily deterred me as we walked into the facility, but seeing the passion in Kayleigh's eyes motivated me enough to not turn around and dive back into my bed sheets. As she introduced me to the equipment and broke down the areas that each motion targeted, I started to feel this odd sense of excitement. With each follow-up question that I prodded her with, Kayleigh responded in a gleefully thorough way.

Despite feeling a bit of embarrassment that I couldn't keep up with her routine as I weakly pulled 20 pounds on the rowing machine, Kayleigh reassured me that "in due time" I would increase my strength, stamina, and endurance. And so, throughout that next sweat fest of an hour, Kayleigh helped me tap into a part of me that I didn't know existed. Like a sponge, I absorbed all of her knowledge over the course of a few weeks—and with each completed workout, the journey I now committed to was getting shredded.

Only it soon became a bit *too* much.

Once I felt that this was the path that I wanted to pursue, I completely immersed myself into it—except I tried to scuba dive into these physiology-filled waters while I was just merely a snorkeler. By that, I mean that instead of taking her wisdom and making small, incremental changes to slowly acclimate to different depths, in an almost addict-like fashion I channeled my extremist eating behavior into now plunging headfirst into an extremist gym behavior. Though the antithesis of "health," when I dropped nearly 30 pounds within the first full month, I couldn't help but feel like the most beautiful version of myself that I have ever seen. For once, I felt like I was tapping into this power of eroticism that I once envied so many others of hogging.

With a new air of confidence, I started to attract men into my life for the first time (but again for the wrong reasons). In a sense, though, I now craved the chase from a man to help me fill the emptiness that every other bully in my life had exacerbated. It seemed to replace the satisfaction that food had once given me—at least temporarily.

Inwardly, I still wasn't happy. It didn't matter how hard I worked out, how many pounds I lost, or how many men I may have entertained (which oddly felt like a "privilege" that I wasn't previously granted)—I was seeking these outlets to fill me with purpose. And because of my skewed motives, my diet and exercise never quite stuck. My weight would constantly fluctuate as fat attached and then detached from my bones. Round and round my off-balanced, chaotic "dieting" would go as I soon became a season pass holder to my own personal amusement park in *RollerCoaster Tycoon* and endlessly looped on the same sick ride ad nauseam.

This dysfunctional lifestyle and constant barrage of self-destructive statements was weighing me down—literally and figuratively—to the point where I felt as if I was being crushed by the greatest of all forces. I needed to break this perpetual compulsive cycle of relying on food, liquor, and men to feel alive and instead heal the deeper wounds so that I could actually live (because what I was doing was barely "getting by"). To do so, I desperately sought the help of a therapist.

Within the first handful of sessions, I was taught that I was essentially brainwashed into believing that beauty was solely physical based on years of bullies constantly reaffirming this (in addition to the proliferation of our culture as a whole). Instead, I was instructed to recalibrate my mind into believing that the goodness of one's character, the stillness of one's inner peace, and the radiance of one's inward happiness as it projected outwardly actually correlated to true, authentic attractiveness. As my therapist explained, there is no one ideal of physical beauty, but there is a warmth in being a good-hearted, genuine person toward whom others tend to want to gravitate. And while I may have had people in life try to tell me that they've admired the purity of my heart and comfort of my soul, I allowed other external noise to clog my eardrums and deafen this truth. Instead, all along I should've been tuning into the frequency of my own inner voice as I told myself: I *am* beautiful, I *am* strong, I *am* worthy of respect, and I *am* a being that is capable of love.

By allowing the perception of others to dictate my own self-worth, I neglected my own self-peace, self-respect, self-care, and self-love. Like a bandage for my wounded inner child's pain, I would pair my bottled-up intrusive thoughts with a physical bottle of liquor (and food). Those temporary crutches never helped to cure the root cause, though. In fact, they only deepened the hurt and further relinquished all control that I could've had over myself whenever I focused on those who didn't care about me as opposed to those who actually did. I dismissed the positive, healthy, and loving individuals in my life who tried to shower me in love and help uplift me instead of embracing them.

Naturally, when you don't love yourself at your core, you can't accept love from others. Instead, you will be loosely loving others from a place of void and scarcity, not abundance. I learned that I needed to accept and cherish myself in all of my inward and outward glory—which isn't always easy—and trust that I am, and always have been, more than enough.

While I should've initially engaged in a healthier lifestyle of nurturement and nourishment to thank my physical body for being here with me in the now (and try to combat my PCOS diagnosis), I tried to appease a vision of what others pushed forward as attractive. Through positive affirmations and the guidance of my therapist, I have freed myself of the shackles of those impure thoughts and warped standards, and I now firmly believe that I am beautiful. And though my lifelong goal is to seek improvements in my diet, exercise, and lifestyle choices when needed, I will ensure that I allow myself the liberty to, *well*, live—especially whenever the family brings out the dishes of fried "galamad" (calamari). (The Italian-American Libra in me should've recognized all along that life is about balance, not completely tipping the scale toward the one side of utter deprivation or the other of over-indulgence.)

After all of these years, though, the greatest weight that I've ever carried was not around my waist, or my thighs, or my arms: it was around the harsh judgements of others as I allowed their words to attach value to me as a person. By continually doing the work, practicing self-care, and facing the root causes of my low self-esteem, I've gained a deeper appreciation for just how much beauty I truly hold and seized a greater lightness in terms of my mental, emotional, physical, and spiritual freedom.

ABOUT THE CONTRIBUTOR

Brianna McCabe, MBA, is a marketing professional, professor, author, and podcast host with a quirky vibe, wholesome heart, electric personality, comforting smile, inquisitive mind, and old soul. She is a driven, well-rounded woman who is committed to maneuvering life with kindness, passion, and balance. She is oddly obsessed with binging Adam Sandler movies, immersing herself in cultures of the world, indulging in cheeses of all sorts, and smelling old books (and fresh cans of tennis balls...which is weird because she doesn't even play tennis).

Brianna McCabe debuted as an author in 2023 with her semi-autobiographical(ish) meets self-help book, *The Red Flags I've (Repeatedly) Ignored*. Within the chapters of her book, Brianna puts herself on the line in the hopes of cracking the code on sex, love, and relationships, but instead learns what it means to actually love herself. She navigates the dating scene—eliminating potential boyfriends one red flag at a time—and shares all of her funny, raw, and real details with readers along the way.

Bits of Her Heart...

Brianna McCabe

Be fearless in the pursuit of what sets your soul on fire.

FUN FACT...

Brianna's form of self-love is dressing like iconic costumes from Adam Sandler movies and catching one of his stand-up shows. You can find her cameo in his Netflix Special "100% Fresh" dressed as Billy Madison next to her friend—who was the penguin.

29

HEALING OLD WOUNDS OF WORTHINESS

BY PATTY LENNON

This is dedicated to any person who has ever wondered if they are enough.

Eight years ago, I was driving home from my favorite yoga class, feeling like I was on top of the world. We had just moved into a new home—our forever home. My speaking schedule was booked out a full year, and my business was thriving. Our kids were in a new school they loved, and everything felt right with the world.

I pulled into our driveway, ready to hop out, shower, and get my day started. But the Universe had other plans for me. The minute I moved my left foot out the door, a searing pain surged up my back. I slowly pulled my leg back in, inch by agonizing inch.

I sat there for hours and was eventually able to crawl inside. When my husband came home, he helped me into bed. I stayed there all weekend until my doctor could see me on Monday. He thought I had a herniated disc and sent me to a specialist.

After a week filled with doctor's appointments and X-rays, I learned the base of my spine was fractured—and it had been since I was seven.

You may be wondering (as I did) how someone can walk around for thirty-five years with a broken back and have no idea they were injured.

The doctors explained the technical reason is that the injury, which occurs in a small percentage of young girls between the age of seven and eight, is like a ticking time bomb. If you don't know that it's there you can live with it for years, but eventually, the crack will make itself known.

What I've since come to realize is that we all walk around this way on some level, with cracks in the foundation of who we are—wounds waiting like little ticking time bombs to reveal themselves when we are ready to heal.

HEALING CRACKS THE FOUNDATION AND FRACTURES

I engaged Western medicine's approach to healing my back—which included multiple forms of physical therapy—but I was more intrigued to understand what the injury meant on a spiritual level. For a few years, I had been playing with various types of self-healing through meditation and "listening" to my body, the theory being that all physical issues are symptoms of deeper emotional issues, and when the emotions are processed, the symptoms are released.

Each day I'd sit in meditation and ask my spine to tell me what it needed me to know. This process had helped me clear colds, sinus infections, and varying minor issues in the past. I was curious to see what would show up here. But each day my questioning was only met with a brick wall of silence.

Finally, one day I asked a different question: "What happened when I was seven to cause this fracture?"

Immediately I heard a voice answer, "You stopped flying."

Suddenly, I saw myself as a young girl of five, maybe six, standing at the edge of our staircase. I look down and see little toes—my toes—wrapped around the edge of the top step. I'm not nervous or scared at all. I'm poised, ready for flight.

It is so clear to me—as clear now as it was completely unclear moments ago.

This is my house. The house I grew up in. The dark wood railing, the white spindles, the wallpaper from my childhood.

The house is dark and quiet. It's the middle of the night. The moonlight pours in the window behind me. I'm standing on the landing and can almost feel the night air calling to me. I know this place. I've been here before.

> "WHEN WE START TO BELIEVE THAT WE ARE SAFE RIGHT NOW, WE CREATE SPACE FOR MAGIC.

PATTY LENNON

I can fly, and I'm getting ready to take off.

I do this at night because grown-ups can't see. It's not that they wouldn't understand or that they'd try to stop me; it's more that when I fly, I'm a part of another life altogether, one that does not involve them.

I already know what comes next. I want to brace for it, but I know I don't have to. So, I sit calmly and wait. I wait for this little girl version of me to be ready.

She is.

I bend my legs, push off, and—FLY!

I am literally freaking flying!

Down the stairs, out the front door, I swoop and soar.

Is this real?

I shared this story with a group of clients recently and their immediate question was, "Was that real? Could you really fly?"

The answer is I don't know. It certainly feels as real as any other memory I have ever experienced. I told them it wasn't that important whether it was real or not.

What matters is that as a small child, I felt like I could fly, and one day I just stopped. Everyone is born knowing how to fly. We are born believing in limitless possibilities—and then we are taught fear. We are taught that flying is dangerous. We are taught that the ground is safe. What we can touch and feel is what we should believe in.

These messages create real-life fractures inside us because they counter what we know is fundamentally true. They "break" our understanding of how powerful we are and how fully the Universe supports our path.

We are "broken" by the grown-ups in our lives who have nothing but our best interests at heart. They just want us to be safe, and they are simply passing on their own inherited and created fears. Our grown-ups were taught that the world is not safe and that if something is going to happen, they have to make it happen. They were taught there is no magic. There is no flying. And believing in it is unsafe.

We learn to shrink our hopes and dreams to fit within what we can control and create with our own human limitations. We keep the dreams we pursue small so that we can guarantee success for ourselves. We limit ourselves by what we know we can accomplish because we fear the judgment and rejection of others.

And all these fears stem from a belief that we are "not enough."

LEARNING NOT-ENOUGH-NESS

We are taught our "not-enough-ness" in a thousand different ways, spoken and unspoken. This not-enough-ness makes the world feel unsafe, and we are taught to focus on filling up the not-enough-ness—rather than reaching for the "everything" we were promised by our Divine parent at birth.

The slow steady beat of not-enough-ness motivated everything I did as a child. In fact, until that memory of flying spontaneously dropped in, I could not recall a single time as a child I had felt that free and limitless... and yet I must have. Looking back on it all, I can see it was simply that I felt how much not-enough-ness existed in my parents, and I wanted to fill it all up for them. Because I never could, I was always operating at not enough.

I was the perfect daughter—as much as I had the power to be.

I was great at school and helped around the house. I didn't talk back and tried to ask for as little as possible. Without knowing it, I understood that money had a lot to do with enough-ness and therefore its absence created not-enough-ness.

Now having worked with thousands of women to help them release their attachment to not-enough-ness and receive abundance on every level, I can tell you that the relationship between money and enough-ness is a strong one. It doesn't matter if there was a lot of money or a little money in your home growing up. It was the relationship to what money meant in your childhood home that often taught you about your own enough-ness.

THE WHISPER OF "NEVER ENOUGH"

In school, I remember working on the short story "The Rocking Horse Winner" by D.H. Lawrence. The story is about a family who lived beyond their means, and the feeling that there was never enough was felt to the point that the children said they heard the house whisper, "There must be more money."

The teacher asked us questions about the story, and I remember her being so thrilled with my answer. I had connected the dots—the house wasn't actually whispering, but the children could feel their parents' feelings and interpreted them as the house whispering.

That memory stands out to me because I was very young and none of the other students seemed to see what I saw in that story, so I felt special. And the teacher was clearly beside herself with joy that I had this insight, so I felt REALLY special.

At the time I would have told you that story had nothing to do with my family. My parents never lived beyond their means; in fact, as Depression-era kids, they were just the opposite—always conservative in their spending. But that whisper... my little self recognized that whisper.

I think ours sounded more like, "There isn't enough money," and my little self translated the feeling to mean, "There isn't enough me."

I have seen this same whisper play out in households of every economic persuasion. A few years ago, as part of an exercise to earn a Girl Scout badge, I asked each child in my daughter's Girl Scout troop who they wanted to *become* when they were older. (I very specifically did not ask them what they would *do* when they got older.) Even so, one girl—whose family seemed to make significant income—said, "I want to become someone who makes six million dollars." When I asked her why, she told me that "six million dollars is how much money we need before my mom can slow down. It is definitely not just a million."

I know her parents. They are good people. They love their kids and work hard to give them every opportunity in the world. Their daughter has a generous heart. She is always the first to volunteer her allowance to help others. They have a beautiful home and cars and go on wonderful vacations.

But even in the midst of so much abundance, somehow, she heard the whisper not enough. Although money is often the "thing" we attach the not enough to, it shows up in other ways. It can be in relationships—especially romantic relationships—or other forms of material wealth like homes, experiences, or professional success.

Underneath this drive to get more money, a romantic partner, a different home, or a particular type of job or career is really the drive to feel safe. It's a belief that something outside ourselves has the power to make us safe, when in reality, we are safe right now. And when we start to believe that, we create space for magic.

This feeling of not enough is what keeps most people from accessing the magic that is readily available to them. We believe some people are luckier, have more advantages, and are set up for success—when really what we are saying is that some people seem to be more enough than us.

Healing Old Wounds of Worthiness

RELEASING OLD PATTERNS

Releasing patterns of not-enough-ness isn't a straight line. Even when we understand at a conscious level that the Divine loves us completely and we are enough... in fact, we are perfect just as we are... it can be challenging to get the subconscious part of us to get it.

If you find yourself in overwhelm, exhausted, or not having enough of something you need like time, money, or love... it is quite likely that a subconscious belief that you are not enough is at play. Over the years I've learned to release this belief system of not-enough-ness. I haven't gotten to the point where I'm literally flying (yet), but life is exhilarating and exciting in ways I never thought possible. Learning to receive all the gifts of time, love, money, and support the Divine (and other humans) offer me is a lifelong process.

Receiving and deserving are tightly linked. In order to experience greater abundance, the first step is to believe you deserve more. Teaching others to open to all the Divine has in store for them has become my greatest love. (We teach what we need to learn!)

In 2019 I opened The Receiving School® to offer a system that has helped me navigate the world in a more open and loving way. That system, The Receiving Method™, can guide you to embrace your own worthiness and live a life grounded in a sense of your own greatness and light. Since then, I've made it my mission to share The Receiving Method™ with as many people as possible.

What I've discovered from my own journey and having the privilege of watching thousands of people incorporate The Receiving Method™ into their life is a profound truth. We all have the power to transform our lives in magnificent and magical ways. The journey is not always easy, but what really good story ever was?

When I stumble (and I do), there are two people who make me get up no matter what. They are my children, and here is why. When we heal any wound, especially the wound that we are not enough, we heal it for seven generations before us and seven generations ahead of us.

If you are in the process of healing wounds of worthiness you have my deep love and respect. It is not an easy journey, but it is a profound one. If at any time you struggle, I want you to remember what you are doing isn't just changing your life... you are transforming the world for generations to come. Thank you.

> **NOTE FROM CONTRIBUTOR:**
>
> As a reader of this beautiful collection of *Magnificently Made* stories, I'd love to gift you a simple way to access The Receiving Method™ now. I've created a special training and meditation just for you!
>
> Visit pattylennon.com/MagnificentlyMade to access your gifts.

ABOUT THE CONTRIBUTOR

Patty Lennon is a best-selling author, keynote speaker, and founder of The Receiving School®. She is a former Type A corporate banker that discovered there was more to living than making money. She left banking to help others do the same.

Patty is a certified coach with a master's in psychology and has been featured in *Forbes*, *Fast Company*, and *Daily Worth*. She blends brain science and metaphysics to help her fellow humans find clarity, focus, and inspiration so they can easily manifest their dreams into reality.

Patty hasn't found a crystal shop or bookstore she can't get lost in. She loathes shopping in all other forms. She loves chocolate, autumn in New England, and watching her two teen children discover what lights them up. She hosts the *Space for Magic podcast* and is the author of *Make Space for Magic*. Patty can be found on the web at www.pattylennon.com and at www.thereceivingschool.com.

Bits of Her Heart...
Patty Lennon

"Whether you think you can or think you can't, you are right." —Henry Ford

FUN FACT...
Patty once paraglided off Mount Chamonoix at ten-thousand feet when she was twenty. She'd love to share a meal with Jesus, and the book that changed everything for her was Outrageous Openness by Tosha Silver.

LOOKING THROUGH A DIFFERENT LENS

BY TRISHA KILGOUR

This chapter is dedicated to anyone who has ever accepted less than they deserve and who is ready to live a beautiful, honest life beyond their wildest dreams.

How many times in life have you dealt with something that you just accepted because you thought that was just the way it was? We hear phrases like, "It is what it is," and we feel guilty for wanting something else or wanting more. We buckle down, figure it out, and just accept whatever "it" is because powering through and dealing is highly valued.

I get it. I spent much of my life doing that, and I got by. Everything was fine, and I had a pretty good life. But something changed in me when I began to look at life through a different lens. The lens we choose to see things through is powerful. It can make all the difference. But before I tell you the big WHY behind my shift and how I learned to change my lens, I have to go back to a time in my life when I just accepted things as they were because I think many women can relate to my experiences.

I was ten years old when I got my first period, and I didn't want anyone to know. I had to tell my mom. She spoke to me about it, but I certainly did not want to talk about it. And I definitely didn't want to talk to my friends about my period. Times were so different then. It was 1987, I was in the fourth grade, and I would not even know how to start a conversation about periods.

Over the years, mine became heavily associated with painful cramps and killer headaches. Sometimes I felt so bad, I didn't even want to get out of bed. I just thought that's what a period was, so I accepted it and medicated myself with Advil to get some relief. I sometimes had to take 2 or 3 just to be able to get through the day. I eventually became allergic to Advil, I think, because I had to take it so much during "that time of month"! Eventually my eyes would get all swollen and itchy. It wasn't until one day when I was at work in pain with cramps, did I realized that my swollen, itchy eyes were probably due to me taking so much medication to ease the pain of my cramps and headache. So, I switched to taking three Tylenol, and for a while it worked.

As women, we talk about so many things. I've had conversations about relationships, weight, exercise, children, and careers. But for some reason, when it comes to certain things, like our reproductive system, we don't always open up the same way. I think I always had a lens of accepting that periods suck and it's not always easy to be a woman in that aspect. Marketing and commercials and movies and media validate that for us, and so other than complaining about the pain of periods, there isn't a much deeper conversation. I've realized though, over and over again in my life, the lens we choose to view things from can change our entire experience around it.

Throughout my life, my reproductive system has given me a run for my money. In my early thirties when trying to have kids, it was challenging. I couldn't get pregnant. I went to a specialist, and with the help of IUI (Intrauterine Insemination), which is where my doctor collected sperm from my then-husband and injected it directly into my uterine cavity near the time of ovulation, I got pregnant. It was a long process, with rounds of medication and being very aware of timing. Thankfully it worked! But all of this was due to me getting my period at such a young age making my reproductive system much older than average. Now, if I had known that, if we had conversations around it, if it had been common knowledge that someone who gets their period before age thirteen can be at risk for an aging reproductive system, maybe I would have felt more equipped. But again, I just accepted it all. I went on to have my second child, with infertility being an issue yet again. My doctor wanted to clear my tubes out, but by the grace of a higher power I didn't have to go through that, and I got pregnant on my own. Then thankfully, getting pregnant with my third was a breeze compared to my other two pregnancies, with the first one being the most challenging.

Throughout the years, even after having kids, my periods were still heavy with very painful cramps. They made products to deal with heavy periods, and so again I accepted this as normal. I mean, isn't this part of a woman's journey? I was in my early forties and still having heavy periods lasting up to ten days with lingering spotting and painful cramps. I knew something may be amiss, so in 2019 my doctor ran my bloodwork, and it seemed I was in the start of perimenopause. In case you don't know, perimenopause is the period of time surrounding the last years of a woman's reproductive life, a transition period a woman experiences before menopause enters her journey.

My doctor informed me it can last from a few years to ten years and can be accompanied by specific symptoms in hormonal changes. Since 2019 I have experienced these changes in my cycle —some months I would miss a period, other months they seemed to be heavier, and some months I would have longer periods of cramping, even to the point where I couldn't walk! I felt like I did when I was younger. Back in 2019 when I was told I was in the start of perimenopause at just forty-two years old, I really didn't think much about it and just accepted it with the thought of this is just part of what women go through.

Acceptance can be funny like that.

I mean, in 2019 when I was told my levels indicated perimenopause, I didn't question or dig any deeper than what the doctor told me. Sometimes, I would even experience night sweats, to the point where I would wake up drenched and have to change all my clothes. I assumed this was all part of being a woman in perimenopause and just dealt with it.

Accepting things as they are can be a wondrous, beautiful thing. But, it can also hinder us from going deeper into the source of issues. It can also block us from being the absolute best version of ourselves. Our lens makes all the difference. So let me tell you what happened between 2019 and now that helped me view life differently, and it has nothing to do with my period.

I got sober.

Yes, I drank a lot—probably the healthiest amongst my friends at the time

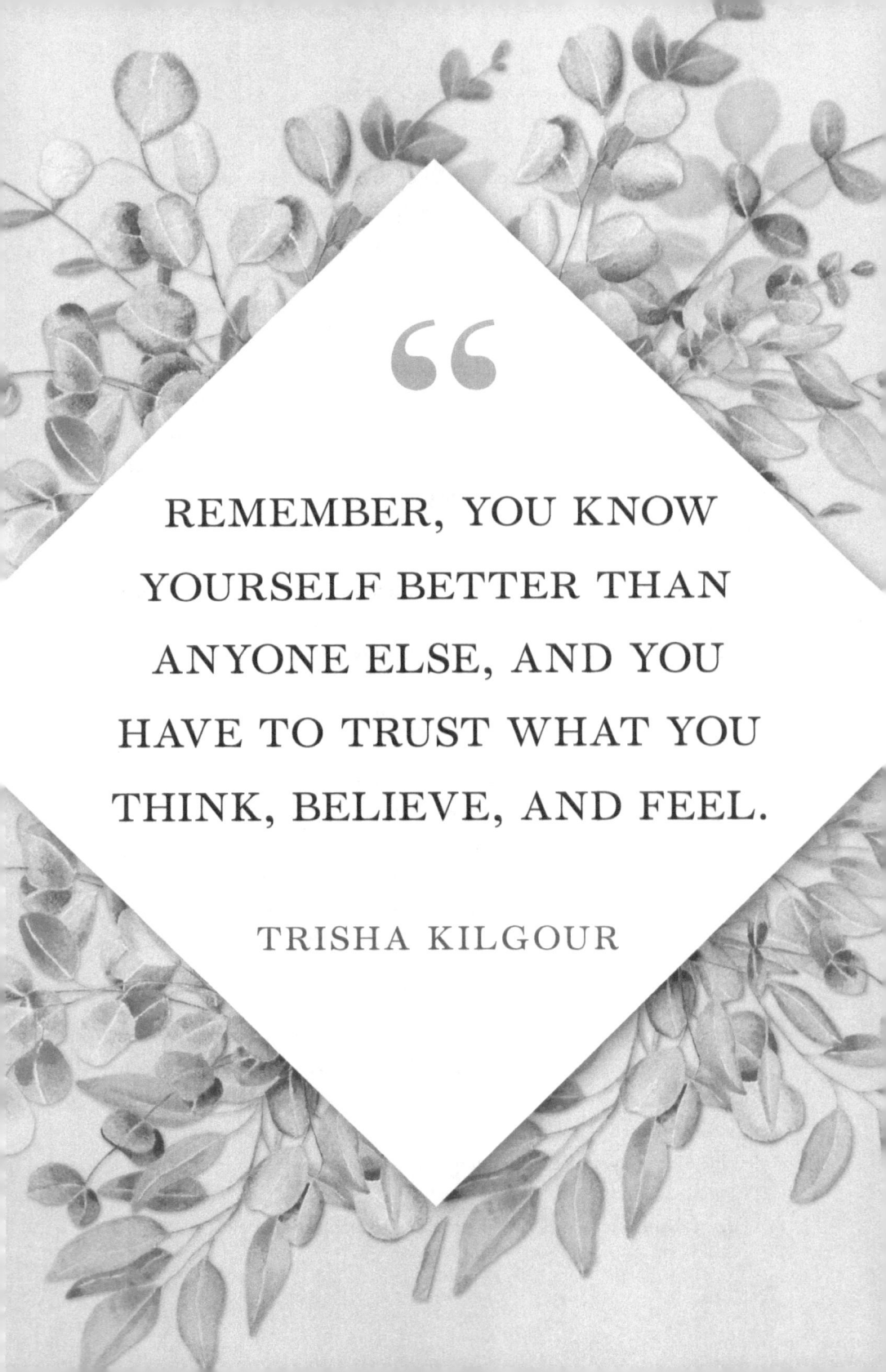

> REMEMBER, YOU KNOW YOURSELF BETTER THAN ANYONE ELSE, AND YOU HAVE TO TRUST WHAT YOU THINK, BELIEVE, AND FEEL.

TRISHA KILGOUR

because of my love for working out and eating healthy. I functioned well. I was career driven. I loved my children. I just liked to escape by drinking. And I didn't realize I had a drinking problem because partying and having fun was just what we did on weekends. I accepted that everyone drank wine to wind down. I accepted that good relationships were ones where couples partied with friends. I mean, that is how my ex-husband and I connected and had fun. Isn't this what everyone does? Isn't this just the way it is?

When I was twenty-four years old, I went to a New Year's Eve party in White Plains, New York with my (now) ex-husband. At the time, we weren't married yet. I was living at home with my dad and coming out of a five-year relationship. My ex-husband and I partied the night away drinking and celebrating in our black-tie attire. It was a fun, exhilarating, fast-paced relationship, and just six months later I moved in with him. We bought a house together in West Long Branch, New Jersey, in the same town we both grew up in. In 2007 we finally got married and had our first child in 2009, as you know, after a difficult time of conceiving. We then had our second child in 2011 and our third in 2012.

Even though we were our own little party of five, we still enjoyed partying, hanging out with our friends, and drinking. We were now the family with the big yard and pool. We would entertain a lot, and it always involved drinking. We did not balance each other out since we both like to drink a lot and so did our friends. We even walked around the neighborhood on Halloween with Solo cups and coolers. It was just the way it was. I didn't question it at all. Everything was usually surrounded by alcohol or planned with drinking in mind.

The crazy part is, I did not grow up like this. I barely remember my parents ever drinking at all. My husband and I lived like this for years. We moved a few times, growing into bigger homes, partying all the while. I even started a career in real estate. I loved every part of it. I worked long hours to be successful, and my ex-husband and I worked together to care for our children and the house. Work hard, play hard. I felt like a success!

When COVID came in March 2020, I was worried how it might affect my career that I worked so hard for. Thankfully, the real estate market was good, and I was thriving, as were many agents. What the pandemic did affect was our drinking and our marriage.

I actually think that COVID saved me.

I know so many people got sick, lost loved ones, and are angry with it all. And I don't minimize its effects on many. But for me, I am thankful for COVID because it helped me to want to find myself. It forced me on a path that I never thought I would be on. Sober and divorced. Yes, I am finally alcohol-free for three years, and I feel amazing. I never thought I could ever go without drinking. I feel so present for myself and my kids. I actually now realize that I can feel. Feel love, pain, happiness, sadness, and joy. I am not escaping or numbing myself anymore, and I am enjoying this beautiful life with my three amazing children.

I realized that when we just accept things without question, we can miss out on what is on the other side. Sure, I had fun with friends while I was drinking, but I never felt quite fulfilled. Something always felt off. I had the family I dreamt of, the career I yearned for, and yet something was missing, and alcohol filled the void. And I realized during COVID that what was missing was ME being honest with myself and then turning that honesty over to my children. I mean, I couldn't honestly look at my children and have them think that a healthy relationship and love was arguing, then drinking and partying, then arguing because one of us drank too much, then letting the cycle repeat. Divorce is tough. But even more than just my relationship with their dad, I wanted my children to have a mom they could be really proud of, not a mom they would worry about getting in the car with after a night with friends.

I remember one day sitting on our front porch by myself with a glass of wine in my hand while everyone was out back drinking and I thought, *this is not what I want. I don't want this life, I want more.* Other than the drinking, I was a healthy person. I was disciplined in other areas of my life, and so with my healthy way of eating, exercising, and being honest with myself about my desire for more, I quit drinking.

On August 19, 2020, I had my very last drink.

I wanted my kids to see that there is SO much more to life than what their father and I have been showing them for all these years. All the years I feel I missed out on their lives. And following this honesty and no longer accepting "what it is" just because "it is," in January of 2021—I made it official and told my ex I wanted a divorce. It was hard, but it felt good, and more than good, I knew it was right. It was super scary, but yet it felt like a weight was lifted off my shoulders.

By questioning this instead of just accepting it, life under a new lens emerged.

Looking Through a Different Lens

Of course, I continue to work on myself daily to be the best version of myself that I can be for myself, my kids, and for my relationships with people.

Living alcohol free... is not what I ever thought it would be. It is beyond what I thought. Who knew I could enjoy so many things with complete feeling? I am now present for myself, my kids, my family, my friends, and my clients. Even the sun beating down on me feels different. I am taking back my life!

Taking on the role of being a single mom and staying determined to be successful while getting used to a life of being sober can be challenging. Finally, I am in charge of my life and fully present. I am now living life my way with feeling, meaning, and purpose. To go from being married for almost fourteen years to now being on my own, I had to look fear in the face and take the leap of faith trusting that the universe had my back.

Since making the choice to listen to myself, no longer just accepting, and looking at life through a different lens, when something feels off, I take action to figure out what is right. I went into perimenopause at forty-two years old and had been dealing with it for years. But recently something in me was really off. I was bleeding for almost six weeks, tired, and depressed and so instead of just accepting it as I would have done in the past just treating the symptoms, I did everything I could to get to the root of it. My doctor did more bloodwork on me, sent me for an ultrasound, and did a biopsy. My bloodwork showed I will be in full blown menopause within two years, and I was highly anemic. Turned out, I needed iron infusions. This explained my exhaustion and shortness of breath. Working out for me was almost impossible. Working out and running was my outlet to relieve my stress, a form of therapy to clear my head and ground me. So, I went for five rounds of iron infusions at the hospital with the thought of *I will one day have energy again* as my doctor told me. He assured me I would feel incredible after because my body was so depleted from my iron level being so low.

And he was right! Recently on a crisp spring weather day, I was excited to get out for a run after having the infusions and not being so short of breath anymore. I figured it was time to get back at it. As I went on my six-mile run, though not nearly as fast as I used to be, but I was out there, and I was able to run up the hill and not stop from being out of breath. It was an amazing feeling to be able to do what I love. As I ran through town my thoughts were racing as per usual. But this time I couldn't help but think how I am forty-five and entering the next phase of womanhood, starting the journey of menopause. I wondered why do we as women accept so many things and deal with them alone?

Why is this not talked about more? Why don't I see anyone even post about it on social media? I mean I have almost two thousand friends on Facebook and not one post from any woman talking about any of this. Why? Why are we so quiet about it? So, that day, after coming back from my run, I decided to make a post about it. I'm so glad I did! It definitely opened up discussions, and women sent me messages that confirmed I'm not alone in this. And, it turns out that some have actually experienced the same things I am going through: the bleeding that won't stop, the uncontrollable weakness, the night sweats, being anemic, and getting iron infusions.

Whether menopause, alcoholism, or divorce, I know for sure we will all go through something on this journey, and everyone's experience will be different yet similar. I accept that I am in this phase of my life, but I won't accept suffering through it quietly. And I especially don't need to be a "trooper" and handle everything alone. Neither do YOU. We, as women, are warriors, and we all need to reach out to one another. We need to be vulnerable and speak up to be able to help each other on the things in a woman's journey that are often so unspoken of.

I want to encourage you so that you can live the exact life that you choose. I want to inspire my kids to do what it is that gives them the greatest joy in life and to question the status quo when something isn't feeling right deep down.

We all have done things in this life that we may feel bad about. I'm not proud of some of my choices, but I do know that by learning to choose again and knowing that I have the power to choose again, I am better for it. We may choose to stay silent and accept less than we deserve from ourselves, our bodies, or others. We go through things, we grow through them, and that can be hard. We have to heal and forgive ourselves for the role we may have played in our choices of the past in order to fully enjoy every present moment, to live this life with meaning and purpose. To love ourselves and our kids wholeheartedly.

The present moment allows us to listen to our inner being, so we can be who we truly are, not worrying about what others think. Remember, you know yourself better than anyone else, and you have to trust what you think, believe, and feel. You need to go deep inside yourself and go beyond all your fears. Fear is what

Looking Through a Different Lens

holds most of us back. What we have a hard time seeing is that there is always something amazing on the other side.

When you are in it and you feel like life is just depleting you, you forget that it won't always feel this way and that at there is a light the end of the tunnel. We forget that going through the tough stuff along our own journey is what helps us to grow, evolve, and become who we are meant to be. We all deserve to be happy, and it starts within ourselves and not from the outside. We all need to find our inner peace, inner joy, and love. You can and should love yourself, and that love sets the stage so that you can do anything in life. Mindset is everything.

You could feel stuck in your job, your relationship with your spouse or significant other, your relationship with friends, your relationship with alcohol, or your relationship with yourself, your relationship with your body and health, and you are not alone. So many people today feel stuck and struggle in their life in one or many areas. Many people just keep on staying on the hamster wheel because it's safe and because they can't see beyond the fear of change and how much good is on the other side. To get unstuck, you have to be open and at times that feels vulnerable. I have learned that it is okay to be vulnerable. It's real, and it's true. Whatever it is, it doesn't just have to be "what it is." There is always a way to improve; to take the leap; to trust the process; and to give yourself the power, courage, and strength to live your best life. It doesn't matter how old you are; if you are here on this earth living and breathing, you can do anything your heart desires. You create your own reality; you write the chapters of your life. And you have the power to choose the lens you look at life through.

ABOUT THE CONTRIBUTOR

Trisha Kilgour is a mom, healthy living advocate, and realtor. She combines her love of community with a passion for real estate to provide a dedicated and personal approach to assisting her clients. Her success in residential sales concretely reflects her tireless work on behalf of her clients. Trisha, an Accredited Buyer Representative (ABR) and a Sellers Representative Specialist (SRS), has lived in Monmouth County for over forty years. Her knowledge of the geography and social communities also adds to her qualifications to advise clients.

With a long-standing involvement in the community, she has been active in supporting charity events and volunteering at her children's schools. Having a personal health-focus, she participates in half-marathons and distributes pertinent and current articles regarding the maintenance of good health in her monthly journals.

Bits of Her Heart...

Trisha Kilgour

It's a good day to have a good day!

FUN FACT...

Trisha drinks her coffee black and she can drink it all day! She doesn't like water unless it has lemon it.

SECTION 11

WE ARE COMPASSIONATE, CARING, AND KIND

CALLED TO SERVE
by Veronica Yankowski

PREPARE AND PROVIDE
by Risa Baghdadi

I WISH HE WOULD HAVE KNOWN
by Kara Burke Manna

CALL FORTH THE TRUTH OF WHO YOU ARE–A LIMITLESS, EXPANSIVE, DIVINE, POWERFUL HUMAN BEING.

31

CALLED TO SERVE

BY VERONICA YANKOWSKI

Hello new friend, Thank you for taking the time to get to know me a little bit better. I must be honest. This isn't easy to write at all. Much of what I write about in this chapter I haven't even expressed aloud yet, so I haven't had time to even digest it. I know being honest and vulnerable will open myself up to being judged. There's nothing I hate worse than that. But I hope if you connect with anything I say, we're kindred spirits, and I know you'll instantly understand my fears. All I want in life is to make the world a better place in any small way that I can contribute. I want to be remembered as a passionate and empathetic person who would help anyone in need. I always say that I wish I could win the lottery and have millions of dollars so I could make more of a difference—the kind of difference only disposable income can make. In the meantime, I will strategize on how to make my millions and manage to be a good person helping those who call on me along the way. I leave you with this message: Smile and be kind. The world needs it right now.

Some people rescue animals. Others take care of plants and gardens. I tend to people.

"A lot has happened," he said. "You'll never guess where I spent my weekend."

"I have no idea, jail?" I asked somewhat jokingly.

"Nope, even worse," he said, with a sadness in his voice

I thought for a moment and exclaimed "rehab!" like I was answering a game show question. My answer, however, didn't come with a prize.

"Nope, the psych ward," he said, "and it was the worst 72 hours of my life."

I listened intently as Rich, my ex-fiancé (you read that right) told me about his recent breakup and how he was feeling depressed and lost. He explained that on that eventful evening he was out having drinks with a friend when he came across his ex-girlfriend's profile on a dating app and that he just lost his mind. She swore to him she wasn't going to date anyone "for a VERY long time, if ever" so seeing her profile was shocking and pushed him over the edge.

He left the bar abruptly to return home to call her and ask why she said those words if she didn't mean them. Was she just trying to spare his feelings? They argued, and Rich hung up the phone with the words, "I'm done, I'm just done."

He then took over a dozen sleeping pills.

He can't even explain how it happened, almost like he blacked out, but that it happened so fast. The next thing he remembered the police were banging on his door, and they hauled him to the hospital. His ex had called the police. Thank God she did.

Rich insisted he wasn't trying to take his life. He was pleading with me to believe him. I told him he needed help and that I would be there no matter what.

"You know Veronica," he said, "the best thing you did was get rid of me years ago. It seems like you attract damaged people, and I sure am damaged."

Wow, that struck a chord. I quickly thought back to all the serious relationships I've had in my life, and admittedly that statement hits close to home. In many of my relationships, whether platonic or intimate, I tend to attract folks who look to me for some type of guidance. For me, learning to discern between being called to serve and attracting people who need fixing is key, because they are two entirely different things.

Rich and I dated for eight and a half years while in college and into my twenties. We were engaged to be married, and we broke it off three months before the wedding. To me that felt very embarrassing, especially at an age when all my friends were also getting married.

But it was the right decision. We were so toxic together. We fought often, broke up seemingly every other month, and were the couple that made our friends uncomfortable because we were always bickering. At that time, I loathed him for what he put me and my family through. I didn't communicate with him for over a decade. I honestly had no interest in ever seeing him again. He eventually contacted me years later when he found out I was getting divorced from my first husband to express his condolences and to let me know he was finally marrying the girl he dated after me. He got divorced six years later. It turned out, marriage was not for him. I wasn't surprised. Marriage was for me, however, as I did get remarried, happily I might say, to a man who indulges my lost puppy syndrome and gives me space to tend people who call for guidance or a listening ear.

The one thing I have come to trust in my life is my intuition. It's never steered me wrong. I've been known to have a "sixth sense" reaction to people or events—almost like a premonition. I get a cold and eerie feeling in the pit of my stomach, and I immediately know that something bad is about to happen. And it always does. For as long as I can remember, my nightly dreams have been so vivid and real. Most days, my husband or my friends ask what crazy adventure I had in my dream the night before. Often loved ones who pass away visit me in my dreams because they know I'm the one open to relaying messages to family here on Earth. I also have dreams about people I haven't heard from in a while, like with Rich. And if I'm left with that uneasy feeling about that person, I reach out.

As usual, one night recently Rich was in my dream, and I woke up feeling cold and worried. I decided to text him to see how he was doing since I hadn't heard from him in over a year. We chatted on the phone for about an hour, and he sounded depressed and anxious, definitely disconnected and not himself. He asked if we could continue the conversation the next day. The next day never happened, nor did the day after that. That third night I had yet another dream about Rich that was nagging at me. I decided to text him to see what happened and why he never called me back. That's when he told me about his stay in the hospital psych ward and his overdose.

As a very spiritual person, I believe there is a reason he appeared in my dreams. During this difficult time in his life, I have become a friend, someone he can confide in and be vulnerable with. I take that role very seriously. In essence we have known each other for over thirty years, and I'm the only person he associates with who has known him since he was a teenager. Many of his demons stem from that far back. I believe in my heart we were meant to reconnect because I was called to be there for him and help him somehow. Our history no longer matters. The hurt and anguish he caused me so many years ago dissolved the second he mentioned an overdose. He is a human being in need, and I've been called to serve.

In my life, I have this innate desire to help everyone: friend, foe, stranger, or colleague and yes, even exes. If there is a person in need, I rise to the occasion. It gives me purpose and satisfaction. It brings me joy knowing I'm needed. But I honestly haven't decided if this is a positive or negative for me. It's so intrinsic to my personality, but it has also caused immense heartbreak and pain when the relationship can no longer be sustained or if my help isn't enough or is no longer needed.

The truth is I love helping people; it doesn't stop with just my loved ones. I'm often helping complete strangers. And yes, I'm certain being helped in some way feels like a blessing, but it's me who feels blessed to do it. I've been this way my entire adult life. I can reflect on so many special moments over the years. I once paid a grocery store bill for a frazzled mom because her wallet was left at home, and she had a screaming toddler in the shopping cart. I've been that mom in the supermarket, so I felt called to help her even though I hardly had any money of my own at the time because I was a single mother barely making ends meet. For several years during my single parent days, I would go to Kmart around Christmas time and anonymously pay off someone's layaway plan in the hopes of giving them some joy. I first heard about this on the radio, and I thought it was genius. During one of those trips a cashier pointed me out to the mom, and she tracked me down in the store crying. I refused to give her my name, trying to remain anonymous, but she hugged me and said she would never forget that gesture and how my generosity saved her Christmas.

I once gave a nun who was lost and wandering alone in a parking lot a ride to her doctor. She seemed confused, so I stopped to offer her assistance. She gave me rosary beads in return that I kept for years until a car accident totaled my car and they were ruined. I urge you, if you ever feel a tiny inkling to do something for someone, do it. You have no idea how it can change their life and yours. Helping others helps me feel good, too.

When I was in my early twenties, I helped an elderly woman I met make her dream come true. I was fresh out of college working for *The Trentonian* at the time as a photojournalist. My editor asked me to drive around and "find" something newsworthy, which was typical on a slow news weekend. I noticed this this elderly woman named Anna sitting on her front porch in downtown Trenton playing her

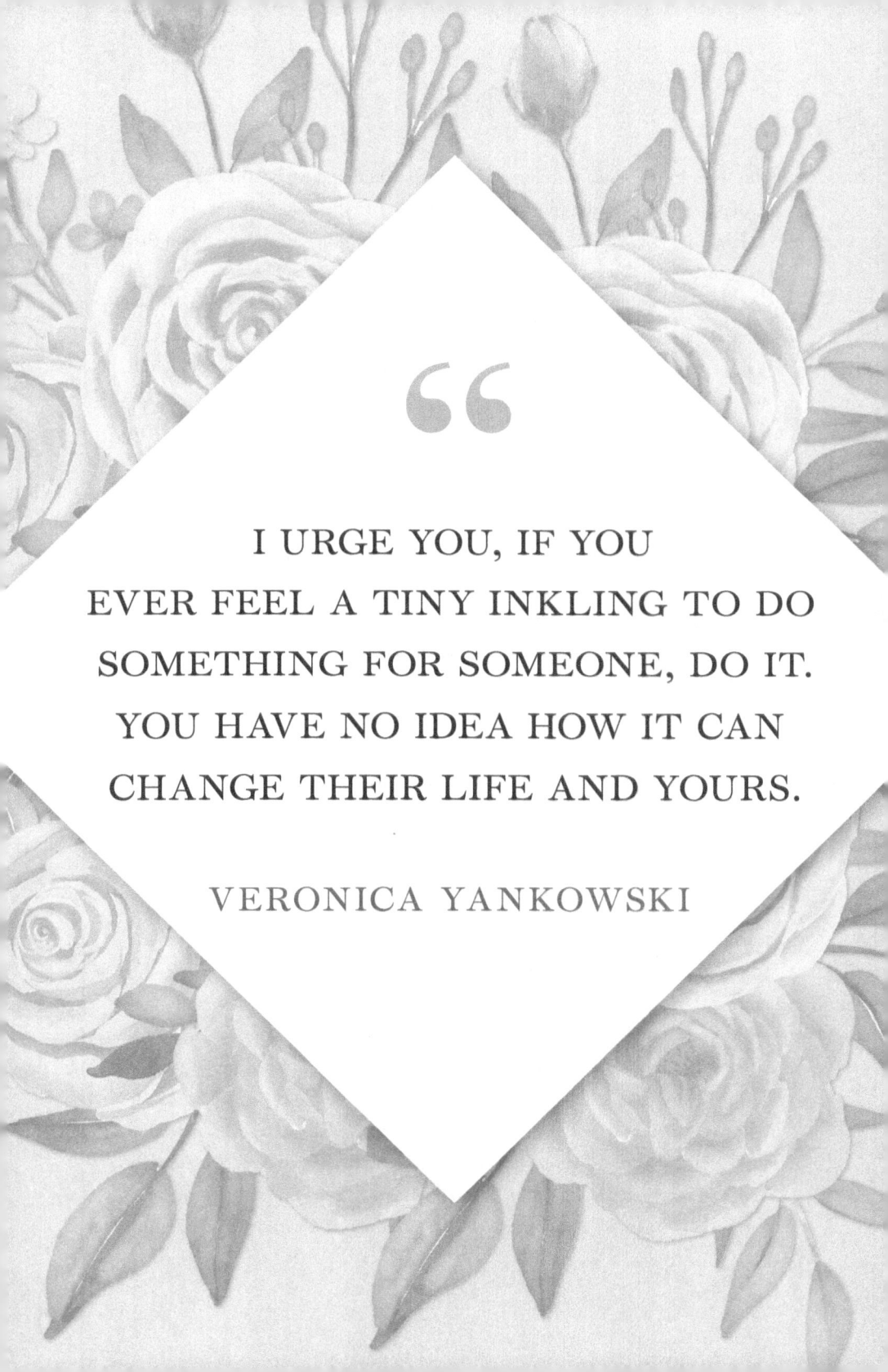

"

I URGE YOU, IF YOU EVER FEEL A TINY INKLING TO DO SOMETHING FOR SOMEONE, DO IT. YOU HAVE NO IDEA HOW IT CAN CHANGE THEIR LIFE AND YOURS.

VERONICA YANKOWSKI

violin. I stopped to chat with her and take a portrait, and we became fast friends as I told her about my adventures as a journalist and she shared stories about her life. Her porch overlooked the *Trenton Thunder* stadium, and she confessed that her dream was to play at that stadium for the crowd. Of course, I knew what I had to do. I contacted the PR team at the stadium and explained the story and they invited her to a game. She was beyond overjoyed as she played her heart out and the audience cheered for her. I remember looking up at her from the dugout where I was shooting and just seeing her beaming with joy sent a wave of happiness over me as I knew I did something special. Several months later I received a letter from her son thanking me for giving his mother such a special gift.

Most recently, I had a similar experience while in Puerto Rico on vacation.

Two of my girlfriends and I had planned a girl's trip to Puerto Rico for a few days. We were looking forward to the sunshine and bonding to help cure the winter doldrums. My girlfriend Karlene and I were flying into San Juan on a Thursday. We were spending the night waiting to pick up our other friend, Mary Grace, on the Friday evening. Unfortunately, a snowstorm was threatening the East Coast and Mary Grace's flight was canceled. We worked hard to try to get her booked on other flights, but it just didn't work out. So, the trip was now just me and Karlene. We made the quick decision to wing our trip and change some of our plans. We downgraded our suite we no longer needed and stayed an extra day instead. We changed our sightseeing tours and decided to just explore aimlessly.

The next morning Karlene woke me up early as she loves watching the sunrise. I'm not a morning person, but I got up and walked to our balcony. The hotel blocked our view of the sunrise, so she insisted we head down to the pool area to get a better view. I threw on some clothes and some sunglasses and pulled the curlers out of my hair and begrudgingly took the elevator downstairs. Upon our arrival at the door to the pool a security guard stopped us and explained that we were not permitted outside until 7am. Apparently, the Governor of Puerto Rico was coming to the hotel in a few hours, and security was ramped up in preparation for his visit. Karlene was not accepting that she would miss sunrise, so she spoke to a manager who escorted us to a side entrance facing the exact direction of the glorious sunrise. We were the only ones there to enjoy the spectacular view except one other security guard we learned was named Eric. Eric was a young man in his early twenties who was very sweet and friendly, and we ended up chatting with him over a half hour. He asked about our trip and where we were from. He showed general interest in chatting up two middle aged women. When we told him we were headed to Ponce, a resort town on the south coast of Puerto Rico, he was so excited because that was the town he was from. Eric offered to be our tour guide and show us around since it was going to be his day off. Because it was just the two of us in a place we hadn't been, and we canceled tours, we told him we'd love for him to show us around.

The next morning, we texted Eric and he met us at the resort, and we all hopped into our yellow Jeep Wrangler we nicknamed Big Bird and spent the day strolling the town listening as he shared fond memories of shopping with his family in the town square and showing us his high school and other places from his childhood. We loved every second of spending the day listening to him recall memories and getting to know Eric better. We decided to take him out for lunch, and it was there we learned that he hadn't eaten steak before, which was so shocking to us. And then reality began to set in. There were lots of things young Eric hadn't experienced, not just foods you and I take for granted. Eric had never left the island of Puerto Rico. He had never seen snow or voted in an election or taken a hot shower. (We learned that in Puerto Rico you choose air conditioning OR a hot water heater. Most folks choose air conditioning because at least the warm temperatures make the shower water tolerable and not too cold. Can you imagine?)

Over the next few days, we would have Eric join us at the resort where we would invite him for dinner and to swim or to join us sightseeing. We began developing such a fondness for each other and he would lovingly call us his "mommas." I was Momma Vero, and my girlfriend Karlene was Momma Karlene. He was teaching us some Spanish and taught us an endearing blessing he said that is spoken from a young person to a parent or elder. The young person would request a blessing. Eric would say "bendicion" and the response would be "dios te bendiga," which translates to God Bless You. (We still say that ending every phone conversation.) He even took us to his home that he built with his mother and grandfather, and we met his mother. Through her very little broken English she expressed how grateful she was that we were giving him such wonderful experiences. The tears in her eyes said it all.

On our last night Karlene and I were so saddened to leave Eric and the beautiful island of Puerto Rico. We had initially wanted to pay Eric for his time sightseeing, but we quickly realized he would be too proud to accept money from us. Eric wasn't able to finish college because he needed to work in order to help support himself and his family. He was working a security job that paid him $11 an hour, and just in the short time we were there he was carjacked and on another instance the property he was guarding was robbed—he had to detain the robber until police came by beating him with a stick. Hearing these horror stories was heartbreaking. To think this poor kid had to work hard for such little money and put his life on the line regularly was too much for me to bear. I called my husband and pleaded that we needed to help him get to the States and help him have a better life.

My husband agreed we would do whatever we could to find him a home to live in and a way to finish his education so he could fulfill his dream of becoming a mechanic. On our last night we invited Eric back to the resort to visit with us for the last time. I was prepared to tell him this good news and was so excited. Karlene and I made sure we treated him to meals and whatever we could as we knew he didn't have a lot of money. He was so appreciative and would try to treat me once in a while, but I told him that once he makes a decent living, he can take me to dinner. That evening he walked in with two huge gift baskets he and his mother spent the day shopping for. He explained that after our time together he considered us family and that he spent the day with his mother handpicking the gifts inside because they were sentimental. He chose a mug from Ponce, his hometown, a plate from San Juan where we met, cookies from Puerto Rico because we talked and tried so much new cuisine and a big teddy bear to remind us of him. I was speechless and cried. All week we were happily spoiling him, and this young man took the time to personally choose gifts to show his appreciation. It was a moment I'll never forget.

That night I told him that I would help him move if he wanted. I would assist him in finding a place to live and a college to finish his degree. He called me his angel. When I returned home, I began to ask around to find a place for him to stay, but I had no luck. So, my husband and I decided he could live with us until he was self-sufficient, however long that took. When I called him and told him he could come live with Momma Vero, he was in tears. I could hear his voice crack on the phone. I felt his gratitude, and it made me so happy. How could I not give back to help this loving and hardworking young man who just needs the opportunity to succeed? Every fiber of my soul told me that this was the right thing to do. Of course, some well-meaning folks thought I was crazy, but I knew I was called to help him.

I'm certain that my purpose in life is to help and serve. How those opportunities present themselves is always a mystery. Lately we've been so bombarded with negative talk and divisiveness, and we are so disconnected as human beings. To counter this, I make it part of my daily routine to treat people with kindness and offer them grace as often as I can. I really feel like God has blessed me in so many ways, and I await my next opportunity to serve His calling. You may not feel called in the same way I do, but I know you have a purpose in life too. We can all serve each other with the gifts we have been given. Listening to our intuition and using our gifts connects us more to one another, and maybe one day all of that negative news will just be a thing of the past.

ABOUT THE CONTRIBUTOR

With a dynamic personality that matches her trademark red hair and signature sunglass collection, Veronica L. Yankowski has made a name for herself behind the camera by inspiring and empowering clients through her creative approach to photography for almost three decades.

Veronica's career as an acclaimed photographer has evolved and grown over the years from photojournalist to portrait artist. Whether it be a portrait session, a commercial session, fashion and lifestyle, or event, Veronica handles each with calming ease and masterful posing and lighting. Over the years she has grown her business to include a team of creatives to document events like bar and bat mitzvahs and weddings impeccably. An avid traveler, Veronica continues to travel the globe for work and pleasure with a keen eye for new ideas to make every shot extraordinary. She recently opened her studio in downtown Montclair, NJ.

Bits of Her Heart...
Veronica Yankowski

Live. Laugh. Love.

FUN FACT...

Veronica has five cats and a bunny! She says no movie quite mirrors her life, but her favorite movie to watch is *The Wizard of Oz*. Her most cherished photograph is the one she took of Rosa Parks at the Million Man March in 1995.

32

PREPARE AND PROVIDE

BY RISA BAGHDADI

To all the Imperfect Perfectionists, who walk life's fine line between emulating Martha Stewart and Lucy Ricardo.

*To all the Type A control freaks who spin around efficiently, but sometimes still
get slammed by the unexpected, unimaginable, unforeseen, and unplanned.*

To all the planners and doers, who still manage to pull it off even when their detailed lists fly away.

To all the Guardians of the Home, who place security, harmony, and a good dose of fun at the top of their lists.

My chapter in this Magnificently Made adventure is dedicated with love and gratitude to my husband and daughter, who are my immediate cheerleaders and supporters, and to my parents and my father-in-law, the inspirations for my story.

Being prepared was an admirable trait and coveted skill when I was a Girl Scout for a few years in grade school. I had earned enough badges to fill half the material on the green sash. Being prepared usually starts with knowing what you are preparing for. Is it the term paper that determines your final grade for your last college course before graduation? Is it getting all the ingredients for the special dessert recipe your grandmother handed down to you? Is it packing your suitcase for your first trip to Italy?

I am a list-maker, and even though my desk is covered with messy piles of papers on the precipice of avalanche, my lists keep me grounded and feeling like I am in control. I like to check things off a "to-do" list, usually announcing to the empty room: "Done." Sometimes that control is a lie.

I was one of the lucky wives on 9/11 whose husband came home to Brooklyn after escaping to New Jersey via one of hundreds of rescue boats that showed up in lower Manhattan. The trip from Brooklyn to Wall Street to Weehawken and back to Brooklyn took sixteen hours on September 11, 2001. He was able to call me from the New Jersey Senior Citizen Center that welcomed the Manhattan refugees with coffee and pay phones, and we spoke for about a minute. He was okay and was with our nephew who worked in the same firm. They were together and were trying to find their way home, but the bridges and tunnels were closed, trains and subways were halted, and there were no rental cars to be found. He assured me they wouldn't give up, though, and told me to take care of the baby. I hung up and looked at our eight-month-old daughter. All I could think of was getting prepared and ready, but prepared and ready for what?

No one on CNN, CNBC, or any other cable news shows could answer that for me, but if New York City was a target, I had to prepare to leave quickly with the baby. All incoming and departing flights across the nation were cancelled, and flights that were already in the sky were directed to land at the closest airport. That edict silenced the skies over my house, located just a few miles equidistant between two international airports. About an hour later, when I heard a low-flying thunderous noise, the TV told me it was the U.S. fighter jets over Manhattan. The sirens in the streets opened the roads to NYPD, NYFD, and ambulances on missions of rescue and hope. It was time to kick "preparing mode" into high gear. The items on my mental list collided into the fears I couldn't speak out loud, inside my head, like a noisy pinball machine born of fear and uncertainty. As the list of frightening, unanswerable questions multiplied, so did the list of what to pack.

Will there be more attacks in New York or in the nation? Pack more diapers, wipes, and Desitin. Prepare enough sterilized water for the cans of formula. Pack

Prepare and Provide

enough clean clothes for a week, with her favorite blanket and stuffed animal for comfort. Get those books made of soft, puffy fabric that she loves, and the small photo album filled with family faces.

Will there be war? Gather clean underwear, socks, jeans, shirts, Advil, toothpaste, toothbrushes, and tissues.

Where will the war be? Find the passports and make a list of addresses and phone numbers of out-of-state family and friends who might shelter us. Get the credit cards and the emergency cash. Coincidentally and luckily, we had filled the car with gas the night before, and we could pack it and leave if we had to.

As the bag became fuller, my head space became roomier and quieter. I was still anxious and frightened and had no answer to "what next?" but I was accomplishing something I could control to prepare for something I couldn't imagine. It wasn't until I closed the last zipper that I realized my Jell-O legs had given way; I was on the floor, hugging the bag tightly and crying into the canvas and polyester pockets.

I placed my new "go-bag" in the corner of my dining room, daring anyone who entered my home to ask, "What's that?" The only person who asked me was my mother, who, with my father, stayed with me and the baby until my husband came home. She didn't press further when I replied "stuff." I think she suspected. I didn't want to give a name to my fears, and yet didn't need to explain them.

My husband (and our nephew) did come home to Brooklyn late that night, dirty and tired. His clothes were sweaty, wrinkled, and covered in a dust whose origins I didn't want to think about. (I'm not really sure, but I think that night I just threw those clothes out in the garbage.) My World War II veteran father cried when he hugged my husband, as my mother continued to feed the baby and look over in prayer and gratitude. The next few days were filled with television news, seeing the faces of friends and neighbors hanging or taped on church fences, with loved ones' phone numbers underneath. Holding hands five days later at Sunday mass, we cried when the organist played "God Bless America."

That bag stayed parked in the corner of my dining room for a year. It was moved to the baby's room only when we hosted a Sunday or holiday dinner. Every week, I changed the bottles of water. Every month or so, I changed the size of the diapers and seasonal clothes, and eventually Similac was replaced by powdered milk and toddler snacks. The Advil and toothpaste were replenished on their

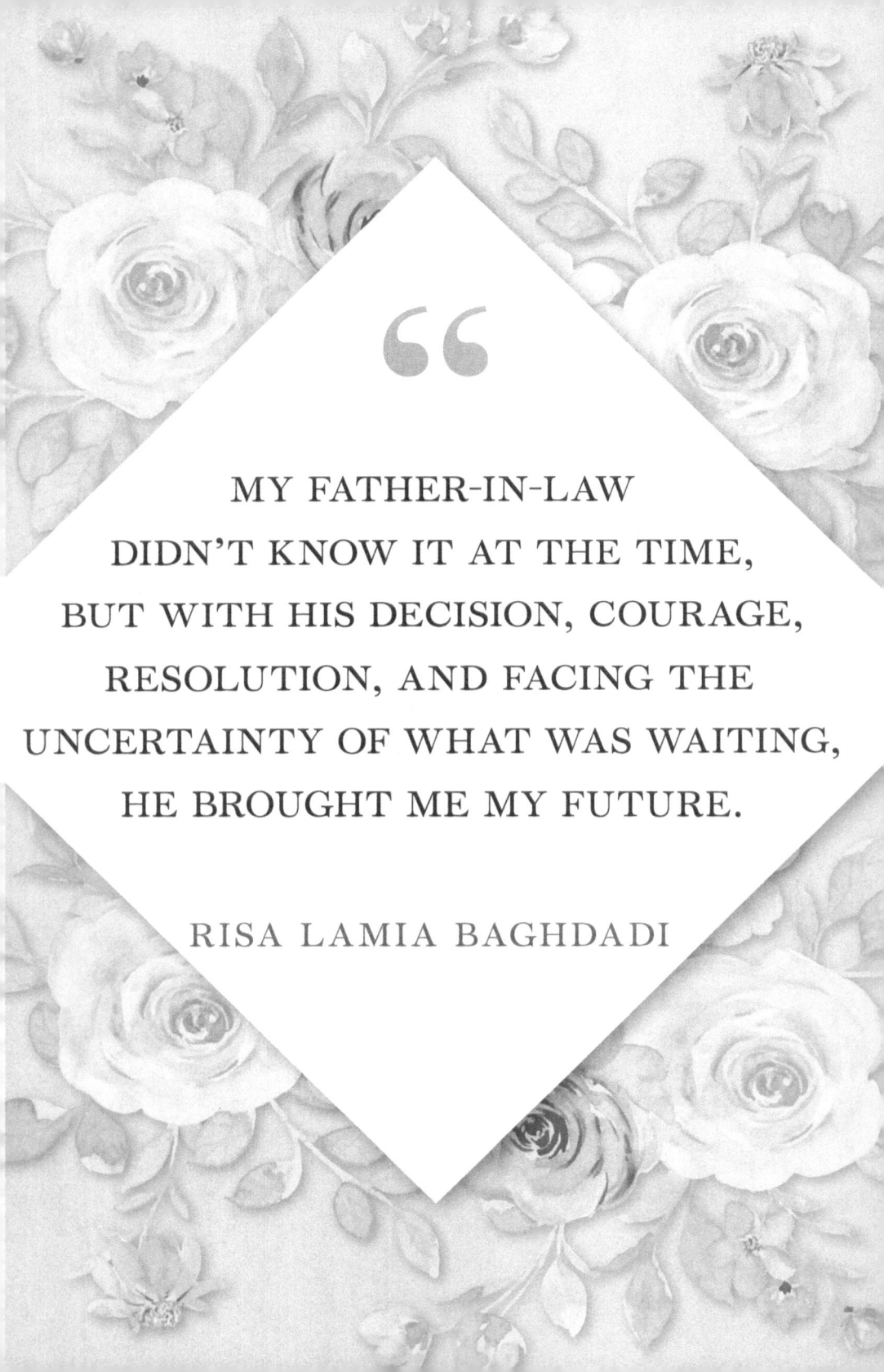

> "
>
> MY FATHER-IN-LAW DIDN'T KNOW IT AT THE TIME, BUT WITH HIS DECISION, COURAGE, RESOLUTION, AND FACING THE UNCERTAINTY OF WHAT WAS WAITING, HE BROUGHT ME MY FUTURE.
>
> RISA LAMIA BAGHDADI

Prepare and Provide

expiration dates. I still needed to be prepared to flee. I slept like a fireman, with my clothing and shoes laid out and ready for an alarm in the middle of the night. That bag mocked me at times: "You're paranoid. You haven't needed me in over a year, and I predict you never will." At other times, it comforted me with a whisper, "I'm here. Just in case. It will be all right."

When I eventually unpacked the bag for good in 2002, life in the house was different. After returning to the Wall Street office for about six months, my husband became one of the first managing directors allowed to work from home. The commute to his trading desk took one minute and about ten steps to the spare bedroom, which had become his home office. We had lost friends and neighbors, but we also lost two more pregnancies in that year. We became more self-focused as we tried to prepare for what was next in store for our family, while at the same time watching our city try to heal.

Fast forward nineteen years, when, in March of 2020, not just our city but also our nation and the world were told to lock down. We had been given about six days to prepare our homes, pantries, and medicine chests for the possibility of a two-week house arrest. At the beginning, I thought this couldn't be so bad. I mean, if they were giving us notice and time to prepare, danger was not imminent. And it wasn't so bad, as I checked my pantry and kitchen cabinets, made lists for the necessities, went to the supermarket, and returned home with the bounty. The eight-month-old baby from 9/11/01 was now nineteen and being sent home from college, with enough clothes and supplies for two weeks.

The first few days were pleasant, as everyone was getting ready to hunker down. I didn't get scared, that really "where are our wills?" scared, until my cousin paid me a visit on our front deck. She was making the rounds, visiting me, her elderly mother, and my elderly father. That seemed like a nice way to spend a morning, until she told me she was taking her four kids and renting a house in the Adirondacks for a few months, until this coronavirus thing was over. She was afraid that one of her asthmatic sons would become seriously ill if he caught it, and, according to the media, we'd all get it soon if we didn't distance ourselves. She advised me to take special care of my 98-year-old father, and 93-year-old father-in-law, and as she walked down my front steps to her car, she turned and did something completely uncharacteristic. She stopped halfway, turned to me, and said "I love you."

She is funny, smart, loyal, sarcastic, quick with a retort, challenges the status quo, and is a devoted wife, mom, daughter, sister, and friend. But she is not one to verbally pronounce those three words. That statement took my breath away and gave me goosebumps and a feeling of dread in my gut, worse than any news report could have done. If she is worried enough to take her kids and leave, if she is concerned enough to tell me she loves me, then this whole lockdown thing must be a lot more dire and serious than I realized. She wasn't coming over to say, "See you after all this blows over." She had come to say goodbye.

I went back in the house on a mission, and double-checked the cabinets and pantries, making a master list, color-coded for our home and my father's home. I would have to stock his freezer with enough dinners for two weeks, in the event that my family became sick and couldn't visit him. I packed his medicine kit with enough of his prescriptions and over-the-counter meds to last him. In contrast to my 9/11 "go-bag," I needed to build my "stay-shelter." This time, when I went to the supermarket, I could see and feel the difference from a week prior. Everyone was wearing makeshift masks, bandanas covering their faces like bank robbers from the wild, wild West. There were limits on how many packs of paper towels and toilet paper you could buy. The shelf that usually held Dad's favorite cookies was empty. Purell and Lysol were as valuable as gold. Supermarkets, pharmacies, and liquor stores were considered essential. Especially the last one.

Once I became accustomed to shopping for two weeks' worth of groceries for two households, we added a new activity that created a bit of tension, but also a good dose of humor to break it. Our family began the ritual of cleaning and wiping down every box, canister, and can that entered the house. We created a list and system, with everyone having their task and role. One of us would unpack one bag at a time and lay the parcels on a tablecloth. One of us would wipe down each item and place it on a different tablecloth on a different surface. One of us would place the cleaned items in the cabinet, fridge, or pantry. Of course, those tablecloths were then immediately tossed in the washer, to be cleaned with hot water. The comic relief came into play one afternoon after a large shopping trip, when one of us yelled at the others, "No! No! Not there!! That's the dirty pile!!" At that moment, I remember we laughed at the panic that invaded our kitchen, the system we had created and still messed up, and I thought we must have looked like Lucy and Ethel at the conveyor belt in the chocolate factory: grabbing at

Prepare and Provide

things, working fast, and still not getting anywhere. Needless to say, we abandoned cleaning our groceries.

A strange calm would come over me after I had stocked the house with our necessities for the coming two weeks. I was prepared. My "stay-shelter" was full. This time, I knew what I was preparing for: empty shelves and quarantining with my family.

But when my father-in-law died in April of 2020, there was very little we could prepare for. Our checklist was very short. COVID regulations prohibited us from conducting what we thought were necessities. No two-day wake with neighbors and friends comforting us at the funeral parlor. No funeral mass at the family church, with music, mourning, and memories. No large gathering at the cemetery for the final prayers and sendoff. And definitely no restaurant repast for a group of fifty. As we moved through those days, waiting for the cemetery to give us permission to have only four, then only ten, then finally all fifteen of the immediate family at his gravesite, we discussed that these traditions were important to us all, but in the end were not necessities. Overflowing flowers were not a necessity. Four limousines to get us to the cemetery were not a necessity. Deciding who should speak, where to have the luncheon, who to invite, who would be insulted if they were not included... all unnecessary. And on some level, having to obey the restrictions offered relief. We were able to mourn solemnly, intimately, and privately with the most important fifteen people in his life.

Restrictions intensified, and then eventually began to wane. Stocking my house with what I needed to survive for two weeks became habit, and store shelves were not as sparse. My cousin and her family returned to Brooklyn. My daughter and the college kids went back to their dorms, and having my family well was the only real necessity.

Looking back, I'm not surprised it was my father-in-law's passing, which came with so few frills, yet was still filled with so much love. My father-in-law taught his family how little was really needed to survive during the Civil War in Lebanon, in the mid-1970s. My husband talks about the electricity curfews, and how, for hours at a time, there would be no power. His mother, aunts, and the women of their small town would share resources and bake bread, and pickle and jar vegetables, and the door was always open to a neighbor in need. The frequent shelling in their town forced them to leave their one-story house and seek shelter together in a neighbor's house, which offered more protection. My husband was the youngest and fastest and was given the task of bringing his grandmother with him to safety during these attacks. It sounded like a movie scene as he described to me how he counted the seconds between hearing the bomb's whistle and the final explosion as a measure of how fast he had to run before the next bomb was launched. The town's baker would only open the security gate one foot off the sidewalk to hand bread to the hungry people waiting in a crushing line. He had a fondness for my then-eleven-year-old husband and allowed him to crawl through the opening, gather bags of bread, and run out the back door. My husband learned at a young age how to prepare and provide for his family.

Providing for his family meant something greater than bread to my father-in-law. He packed up whatever they needed, left the family factory and retail store, and brought his wife and two teenage sons to the United States. His was the classic American success story, born out of a desperation for safety, American citizenship, and working hard to have a better life. My "go-bag" was designed to provide for a couple of days, my "stay-shelter" pantry was designed to provide for a couple of weeks, but his decision would have to provide forever. My father-in-law didn't know it at the time, but with his decision, courage, resolution, and facing the uncertainty of what was waiting, he brought me my future.

That future was my husband, and it included our home, our marriage, our daughter, vacations spent together with my father-in-law and my parents, and Sunday and holiday dinners around the table. When we host something as important as a surprise engagement party, as traditional as Christmas dinner, or as simple as a meal for six, my husband invariably asks, "Do we have enough food? I don't think we have enough food." Back to that theme of preparing and providing, he makes me wonder for a brief moment if he's right. Then I look at the platters, trays, side dishes, wine bottles, and desserts in the fridge, and I know this is how an Italian girl and a Lebanese guy host, and I answer, "Yes, we have enough."

In each of our cultures, food equals love. As each platter overflows, so does the heart. The kitchen is a happy mess of leftovers (I told you we had enough food!) and dirty dishes, coffee perking, and fruit and desserts looking for a clean tray on which to land. There are always enough trays, platters, dishes, and glasses. The dishwasher cranks three times before I go to bed.

When I was young, my mother would give me the honor of setting our dining room table for holiday dinners, and she would bring out the good china, the crystal goblets, and the fancy silverware. The tablecloth had been ironed, and the special trays and platters were ready. She didn't believe in saving these pretty pieces in a box in the basement, and neither do I. Today, when someone asks me why I don't use paper goods for such a large crowd, the answer is simple. The most important things at my table are the people seated around it and at the Costco tables in the living room for all the nieces and nephews, not the things on those tables. But that said, I look at these utilitarian items on the table as pieces of art and pieces of my family history. Those colorful Murano wine goblets, my mother's china, and treasures I have collected are my way of saying to my guests, "YOU are my treasures," and I want to prepare and provide for those guests in a special way. Setting the table is the gathering equivalent of writing my to-do list and preparing my "go-bag" and "stay-shelter." It's about the love that goes into the preparations, in whatever way the preparing may present itself. Preparing gives me an illusion of control when deep down I know I simply cannot control this precious life; there will always be uncertainty, and I can rest in the knowing that we will always have exactly enough of what we truly need.

Through civil war, through 9/11, through COVID lockdowns, through the loss of loved ones, what does it really mean to us to have enough? How little or how much is enough? Is "enough" in times of uncertainty the same as "enough" in times of peace and plenty? Can we ever have enough?

When we feed our bodies, we are also feeding our souls in the simple act of gathering.

Hamburgers on paper plates feed as well as filet mignon on Limoges china.

Beer in Solo cups quenches as well as champagne in Waterford flutes.

The family stories behind the goblets are as colorful and valuable as the glasses themselves. The beauty of these possessions is undeniable. The beauty in the hearts of my guests is immeasurable.

And so, preparing and providing, having and holding our loved ones well and together: that is enough.

ABOUT THE CONTRIBUTOR

Risa Baghdadi is the wife and mom of two of the best people in the world. She is blessed with a large, incredible family from her cousins, who are more like sisters and brothers, to her in-laws, to her nieces and nephews... all of whom are the kindest and most loving people you would hope to meet.

In her professional life, Risa is a Speech-Language Pathologist who worked for thirty-four years in the NYC Department of Education, multiple group homes, and private practice, and she is currently an adjunct professor in a graduate-level SLP program.

Risa loves hosting big and small dinners and parties and was crowned "Favorite Italian Aunt" (only Italian aunt!) by her Lebanese nieces and nephews. She is a lifelong football fan, self-taught guitarist, music lover (every genre except opera), and the family historian, letter writer, and storyteller.

After years of caregiving, Risa and her husband are making a point of returning to traveling the world, adding to their already-visited destinations of Italy, Sicily, England, Ireland, Lebanon, Canada, the Caribbean, as well as many US cities. Her bucket list is long and varied, exotic and mundane.

Most importantly, Risa makes sure the people in her life know how much they are valued and loved. She believes we can agree to disagree, as long as we can laugh and love anyway.

Bits of Her Heart...

Risa Baghdadi

Have a great day.
On purpose.

FUN FACT...

Risa's family has been dubbed "The Laughing Family," and her house has been referred to as "The Fun House." She enjoys an occasional Scotch with her husband, and if you ever catch her doing karaoke you might hear her belt out "Hotel California."

I WISH HE WOULD HAVE KNOWN

BY KARA BURKE MANNA

*This chapter is dedicated to anyone who struggles with acceptance, purpose, love, and strength.
I am writing from the place of the little sister who needs to be heard. Please listen carefully!*

Have you ever seen greatness in someone who hasn't seen that greatness within themselves? Oh, how you wish you could just make them see themselves through your eyes, take their pain away, and let them know how important, how incredible, how worthy, and how amazing they are. I have been there. And maybe I couldn't get through to them in that way while the person was here with us in physical form, but now I finally feel I have the chance to express all the things I couldn't when I was younger about someone who had such a huge impact on my life and left us far too soon. It is my hope that if you are reading this and you haven't found the words to express these things to someone you love, please just open your heart and try. Don't wait another minute. And, if it is YOU who doesn't see how "magnificently made" you are, please know that nothing could be further from the truth.

My story starts as the youngest sibling of three. I am the little sister with two older brothers: two older brothers who couldn't be more different in heart, soul, personality, and biology. I was six years younger than my oldest brother and five years younger than my middle brother. I was the only girl, and, because of the age gap, I spent most of my time alone or with my grandparents. My parents thought they were done having children until, "uh oh!" Yep, the accident was me. Let's just say I was taught many lessons by my older brothers, and I am happy to say that I am the person I am today because of them.

They both loved me so much, each in their own way. My brother Patrick, although as he hit his teen years may have had a tougher exterior, was really a big ball of mush. He had a heart of pure gold. He treated me like the little princess of the family, always helping me in one way or another and never forgetting anything that was important to me even when he was just a young boy himself! I remember I was turning five years old, and Patrick was around eleven. We had this children's cookbook, and since it was my fifth birthday, he wanted to surprise me with something special from it. There was this recipe for a castle cake in it, and he followed it to a T! Yes, Patrick made a huge castle cake that had buttercream frosting and ice cream cones as turrets. I remember my eyes widened with excitement when I saw it. It was amazing, and to a five-year-old girl it doesn't get any better than a castle cake! I will never forget this beautiful and thoughtful surprise Patrick made for me.

And, as incredible as that story may sound, it was not out of the ordinary for Patrick to want to make me feel special on my birthday. It didn't matter what he had going on in his own world or what he was doing with friends, he would come out of the woodwork when it was my birthday to celebrate! As we got older, there were times I literally would not see him for months and then I would hear his white Isuzu Amigo (complete with running lights and pinstripes) pull up out of nowhere. He would hug me every time like we didn't miss a beat. These hugs made me understand our relationship meant as much to him as it did to me. But, wow, we could not be more different. He lived on the wild side, with his *Ice Ice Baby* shaved eyebrow, homemade tattoo, and need for speed. I was a little bit of a "goody-goody." I guess you could say I was a bit more naïve and stayed out of the fray.

The cake story was one of many memories I have of Patrick. Like I said, he always tried to take care of me. I remember when he was babysitting me one night—I wasn't feeling well so he wanted to take my temperature. He sat me on my parents' bed and pretended like he knew what he was doing. He was probably around twelve or thirteen. He took my mom's thermometers (she had two thermometers, one rectal and one oral) and stuck one random one in my mouth. I was hoping he used the oral one.

When I had nightmares, I knew I could always crawl into his bed, and he would protect me from the monsters in my sleep. I'm not sure I quite knew what a gift it was to have a brother who was so loving, kind, and protective. It was just what I knew as normal.

When I was threatened by a high school classmate, it was Patrick to the rescue again! I innocently commented on how proud I was of my classmate after she was bragging about not smoking for some time. I assured her how amazing that was, but she took my compliments the wrong way, and to my surprise she threatened to shove my glasses down my throat! I got off the bus and walked upstairs to the garage loft where Pat was with some friends. They seemed to know this girl pretty well and somehow had her wanting to be my best friend the next day. She obviously didn't know when she threatened me that I was Patrick's little sister. He teased me about my innocence, and this brought the need for him to break open my shell a little. He was a great friend and brother, but he was no stranger to partying and got me to experience some things I dare not mention here.

I never knew Patrick as being any different than my other brother, but he always felt he was different because of his biology. To me, it was just that—biology. Feeling-wise, he was 10,000% family, just like my other brother. But I know he felt different for reasons that to this day I still don't fully understand. You see, my parents struggled to have children for many years. They chose to adopt a baby, and little did they know how their lives would be changed forever. I use the word "chose" for a reason. Some babies happen unexpectedly, like me, but Patrick was chosen. He really was wanted. My parents were waiting for a baby through the agency when they received a call from their case worker. Their wait was over because there was a baby coming sooner than they thought. They had only a moment's notice but were thrilled with excitement. My grandmother and aunt quickly ran to the store to shop for the essentials that my mom would need. My parents received Patrick when he was two months old from the blessed nuns that took care of him in the nursery.

I am not sure my parents were prepared to understand the psychology and emotion that went into this journey. All they knew is how badly they wanted to

> "When you don't see the greatness in yourself, know it is there. You are born for greatness.
>
> KARA BURKE MANNA

I Wish He Would Have Known

start a family and how much they had to offer in doing so. After Patrick, they were blessed two more times to make us a family of five.

Once Patrick was out of high school and a bit older, he and I would have these talks where he would start to express his frustrations and emotions about being adopted. He struggled with the decision of seeking out his biological parents. I tried to encourage him to do so because I wanted nothing more than my incredible brother to be happy. I thought this would help him feel more whole and identify with himself. I knew he had issues happening—he was partying a lot more as he got older and running with a rougher crowd. He didn't grow out of it as most thought he would. He actually grew more into it. He struggled deeper with issues that I still cannot forget; issues that I feel sorry I wasn't able to help him with. Aside from our occasional talks, Patrick didn't really communicate with anyone. Instead of seeking help or expressing his feelings more, my brother chose the substance abuse cycle over resolving issues at the root of his struggles. From what I saw, he would temporarily feel better and that would numb the truth of how he actually felt—a temporary high to take away the deeper pain. Patrick was so brave for others and protected me any chance he could. If only he had been brave enough to protect himself, to embrace his difficulties deep down, and communicate through them, maybe he just might have been able to rise above and learn how to really enjoy life. Unfortunately, nothing can make you feel whole except for yourself. Protector that Patrick was, looking back, I think he might not have wanted to hurt any one of us by expressing his true feelings about his adoption. In place of communicating with us, he took on that burden alone with alcohol and drugs. He thought he would hurt us with his truth. Little did he understand that the substance abuse cycle we all rode with him hurt everyone so much more, because there were great days and many miserable days, and we never knew what we were going to get. No matter what I got from him I always showed him my love and support the way he always loved and supported me.

Patrick taught me unconditional love on a whole other level. He loved that way, and his differences taught me to love everyone for who and what they are no matter what, without judgment or expectations but just as they are. I wish Patrick could have loved himself unconditionally. If only he knew the true impact he had on me and how precious he was to us all.

Even with all of his roller coaster ups and downs, my parents would bring us to church on Sundays. I stood in between my brothers, and when it was time to hold hands to say the Lord's Prayer, they would squeeze my knuckles together until I wanted to scream. I always felt a connection at church with God and continued to go by myself as a young adult, sit front row center with my grandmother, and now attend with my husband and children. If I didn't have my foundation of faith in God, I could never have dealt with these difficult life events I am about to share with you. This faith always gave me comfort and the ability to try to reason with events that made no sense.

I knew Patrick was suffering, and I tried to warn my parents that the substance abuse cycle was an indicator of something more. I probably didn't have the language since I was young, but I knew I was trying to wave the red flag, and, as typical little siblings go, no one listens to them until it is too late. Inside, I was so worried about Patrick that I stayed home and started my college career locally, so I was close enough to him to continue listening to him. Until one horrible day, as I was studying in the hallway in school, when I saw a police officer pass by with our town's social director shouting to security, "Here she is! We found her!" as my dad trailed in the back. They brought me into an empty classroom where my dad put his arms around me and told me we had lost Pat.

Lost Pat? What does that mean? Did he run away? Did he get hurt? How could this have happened? Who was there for him? Thoughts were flooding my brain so fast, but just as quickly I came to find out he died in his sleep at his girlfriend's house. All we had left was an 8x10 manila envelope of his belongings that sat on the carpeted steps in my house for days until we had the courage to open it and see his beeper and wallet.

How could I go on without my protector? I felt completely lost.

But, thankfully, after jumping so many previous "grief hurtles" of losing loved ones in the past, my parents taught me the biggest lesson of resilience. They taught me, just by the way they lived, to get right back up and keep pushing through. So, I followed suit. That is what I did. I got right back up, helped my mother off the couch from crying her eyes out, and went full force ahead.

We mourned and moved forward. With my parents' support I was the first in our family to graduate from college and graduate school and get my real estate license. I love helping others, especially children, so I focused the beginning of my career on education.

But resilience is funny. It is a great power to be resilient, but sometimes it can fool you into thinking that you are totally okay. You bounce back quickly, but if you don't deal with the issues you are trying to bounce back from, they pop up again in some way. I like to believe they pop up when you are more equipped to deal with them. I was young when we lost Pat. I don't know if I was ready to actually take the time to grieve and acknowledge his life in a deep way. I was sad, of course, but I got back up and I worked myself so hard for years and years, until recently when something struck me like lighting. I never honored my brother's life in any way. I never stopped long enough to even think how to.

When I heard friends talking about this anthology and how we are all "magnificently made," and I felt this strong pull to share things I had never shared about my incredible brother. I owe it to him to write this story, and I hope that it touches someone somewhere to feel that even though you may not "fit," and you may struggle with life, you may have someone who loves you unconditionally and needs you whole. You are important, your life matters, and you are chosen to be here. Please know how fearfully and wonderfully made you are; it is everything. You are everything. Patrick was chosen, not only as a child of God but literally chosen by my parents. Even though to us, my brother had a world of opportunity in front of him, he did not feel worthy of it. He could not clear his mind enough to communicate the challenges and focus on all that was good in his life. I know Patrick is tugging on my heart to let me know he sees it now and to tell others just how worthy they are.

And I urge you, when you see the greatness in others around you, tell them. When you don't see the greatness in yourself, know it is there. You are born for greatness. We all are; there is greatness in all of us, no matter what.

NOTE FROM THE CONTRIBUTOR:

To my brother Patrick...

Thank you for teaching me the actual meaning of the quoted phrase "the blood of the covenant is thicker than the water of the womb." You opened my eyes and my heart for the short time we had you here on Earth. I am blessed that you continue to give me the strength, courage, and support to carry on, and now I am able to honor your life's struggles in a way I never thought possible. Thank you for always being true to yourself and humble. I do regret not being able to battle your demons better; I have no regrets knowing you left this Earth with a heart full of love from me. Continue to listen to my prayers and protect me until we meet again.

ABOUT THE CONTRIBUTOR

Kara Burke Manna was born and raised in Ocean Township, New Jersey, by two amazing parents, John and Patricia Burke, and blessed with two brothers, Patrick and Jason. She married her sweetheart Michael in 2008, and together in 2009 they opened Burke & Manna Real Estate Agency.

Kara has also found a new love for paddle tennis, and Pilates. She looks forward to always meeting new people and creating new friendships while loving and cherishing her lifelong friends. A dreamer and believer with lots of faith, Kara thanks God every day for all the blessings He has given her and the ability to continue to do what she loves!

Bits of Her Heart...

Kara Burke Manna

Life is short.
Don't take anything
for granted.

FUN FACT...

Kara has a sweet tooth. She could skip breakfast and just eat dessert. She could actually trade all food and just eat sweets, especially mint Oreo ice cream!

WE ARE

Magnificently
MADE

ABOUT OUR EDITORIAL

Jenn is a treasure-hunting, coffee-loving, stargazing journal-keeper since kindergarten who believes deeply in the power of the human connection, that sometimes 30-seconds of insane courage is all we need, and that we are magnificently made, born for a purpose, and capable of more than we know.

She is a proud wife of the yin to her yang and momma of her two most precious gifts from God, and the Founder & CEO of Inspired Girl Enterprises. The Inspired Girl Mission is to bring forth content that connects us to our personal power and to one another.

A published author herself, Jenn has penned four books with a fifth on the way! She founded her media company to create and publish content that highlights human potential, as she is so inspired when witnessing someone reach a personal goal, overcome incredible odds, create something purely out of their imagination. From artists to bakers to song writers to entrepreneurs to parents to teachers—there is no one who does not amaze her with their unique gifts.

Bits of Her Heart...

Jenn Tuma-Young

Time is a gift; how we choose to spend it is our love letter back to it.

FUN FACT...

Jenn loves love and lives for her kiddos. You may often see her with some shade of red in her hair as inspired by her favorite characters Strawberry Shortcake, Annie, and Red Fraggle.

PHOTOGRAPHY CREDITS

Chapter 1, Susan Giacchi: Vincent Ioia - Total Exposure Photography

Chapter 2, Jenn Garcia Mawson: Jessica Morrisy Photography

Chapter 4, Denise Cesare: Joanne Moorhouse Photography

Chapter 8, Danni Heuer: Bobby Bates Photography

Chapter 9, Reilly Carroll: Jessica Morrisy Photography

Chapter 10, Unwavering Faith: Jessica Morrisy Photography

Chapter 11, The Walk Home: Jessica Morrisy Photography

Chapter 13, Wendy Laffey: Dav Giuliano

Chapter 15, Jazimin Garrett: Matt Dayka & Iris Moore

Chapter 18, Nichole M. Palmer: Marizen Sawyer

Chapter 19, Alicia Marie Geczi: Elle Studios

Chapter 21, Tracey Hall: Jessica Morrisy Photography

Chapter 22, Emily Yablonski: Lori E. Chapin

Chapter 24, Dr. Veera Gupta: Jessica Morrisy Photography

Chapter 27, Kayla Harris: Molly Sorensen

Chapter 28, Brianna McCabe: Jessica Morrisy Photography

Chapter 29, Patty Lennon: Dyan Baptista of DBPress

Chapter 31, Veronica Yankowski: Sabrina Palko (headshot), Boris Kraizman (waterfall)

Chapter 33, Kara Burke Manna: Michael Burke

A HEART FULL OF THANKS

A huge thank you to everyone who had anything to do with the making of this book…

To the contributors, to the editors, to the designers, to the consultants, to the entire Inspired Girl team and advisory board.

To the printer, to the papery, to the delivery driver who will be dropping off thousands of copies for us to sort through and deliver.

To coffee that kept me going and to iced tea on those hot summer days.

To Jess for cheerleading, event planning, following up, trying to keep time and stick with schedules but being flexible and trusting me always.

To my LuLu and Little Man and Hubby for spending countless hours ideating with me, lending your creativity, listening, sharing ideas, managing operations, helping with logistics, and assisting in every aspect of the word.

I could go on and on; I have so much gratitude in my heart for every single person involved. YOU ALL ROCK!!!!

All the glory to God for bringing this book together in the most amazing of ways.

A HEART FULL OF THANKS

A huge thank you to everyone who had anything to do with the making of this book…

To the contributors, to the editors, to the designers, to the consultants, to the entire Inspired Girl team and advisory board.

To the printer, to the papery, to the delivery driver who will be dropping off thousands of copies for us to sort through and deliver.

To coffee that kept me going and to iced tea on those hot summer days.

To Jess for cheerleading, event planning, following up, trying to keep time and stick with schedules but being flexible and trusting me always.

To my LuLu and Little Man and Hubby for spending countless hours ideating with me, lending your creativity, listening, sharing ideas, managing operations, helping with logistics, and assisting in every aspect of the word.

I could go on and on; I have so much gratitude in my heart for every single person involved. YOU ALL ROCK!!!!

All the glory to God for bringing this book together in the most amazing of ways.

www.ingramcontent.com/pod-product-compliance
Lightning Source LLC
Chambersburg PA
CBHW020047170426
43199CB00009B/194